Emirates Diaries

From Sheikhs to Shakespeare

Emirates Diaries
From Sheikhs to Shakespeare

Published by
Medina Publishing Ltd
310 Ewell Road
Surbiton
Surrey KT6 7AL
medinapublishing.com

Design: Ian Denby-Jones

ISBN 978-1-911487-09-8

Printed and bound by
Interak Printing House, Poland

CIP Data: A catalogue record for this book is available at the British Library.

Emirates Diaries

From Sheikhs to Shakespeare

Peter Clark

To Paul, Katie, Gabriel and Nathaniel

The Cultural Ambassador's children,
from the age of about three,
have had nothing but celebrities
for breakfast, lunch and tea.

from Gavin Ewart, *The Cultural Ambassador*

INTRODUCTION

Apart from a few years in the 1970s, I have kept a diary for all my adult life. When I was overseas I knew I was having a full life and meeting interesting people. I would write 300–400 words a day, every day. Just as some people are compulsive photographers, I have been a compulsive diarist. For the four years I spent in the United Arab Emirates I must have written more than half a million words. Nobody would be interested in some of the preoccupations of my diary – malicious gossip, personal trivia and narcissism – and the published diaries have been edited to bring out my growing affection for the Emirates and its people, and to celebrate the importance of international cultural relations.

It is 25 years since I was working in the Emirates. I am not the person I was, and I have written the linking passages in the third person and past tense. I do not wish to deny that the Peter Clark of 1988 to 1992 could be smug, snobbish, cocky, irritating and wrong-headed.

I am grateful to people who have commented on the previous edition of my diaries, *Damascus Diaries: Life under the Assads.* I have benefited from reviewers – Diana Darke, Roger Hardy, Ian Simm and Paul Starkey. I am most grateful to Penny Young, who has meticulously read every word and made helpful observations, to colleagues and friends in the Frome Writers' Collective, and to Theresa, who shared the life and commented constructively on the text.

FOREWORD

My friend Peter Clark's diary entry for 5 October 1988 records the words of the British ambassador who told Peter that he is making an impact in the United Arab Emirates and people say that "he's interested in Arabic." Those people were unquestionably right, but they would have been fully accurate had they said this: 'He's interested in everything and has, by the way, mastered Arabic.' His diary confirms his interest in everything and discloses wonderful insights resulting from his linguistic facility. His impact has extended itself beyond his time in the UAE and beyond the UAE itself because of his splendid translation of Muhammed al-Murr's short stories into English. And now, to ensure his place in the history of our country, Peter has published Emirates Diaries, the entrancing record of his days in Abu Dhabi and throughout the Emirates.

His very precise and straightforward account reminds those of us who shared those days with him of the excitement we enjoyed. Everything in our old culture was new. The UAE was becoming a global crossroads and, as Peter describes it, 'a linguistic museum'. He daily enhanced that museum. He led the British Council in schooling thousands of people in English while at the same time honoring our cultural history and our beloved Arabic.

Peter's diary demonstrates his innate curiosity and respect. He learned everyone's story. He valued people and took the time to record their details. His dated entries abound with names, places, vivid descriptions, and carefully recalled events. Peter followed a distinctly Arabic form related to the practices of hadith scholars and originating sometime before the eleventh century in Baghdad. The ta'rikh-diary in Islam was a dated record of notes kept by the author for personal use in writing other historical compositions. Some scholars believe that such diaries, exemplified by the autograph diary of Ibn Banna' (1005–1079), were the world's first diaries of the sort we know today, the kind of diary that Peter Clark maintained while he lived and worked in the UAE.

Just as Peter once reunited Wilfred Thesiger with our country, so his diary connects us again with an important period in the history of the United Arab Emirates. A stranger to those days will surely note that talented people from all over the world were contributing significantly to the development of the UAE.

Citizens of the UK were eminent among our international colleagues, few more prominent and none so observant than our friend Peter Clark. In presenting his personal diary to the public, he has enriched the historical archive and provided readers an endearing glimpse of a remarkable human being.

I am confident that this book will be received with great interest by readers everywhere. Readers will enjoy this opportunity to observe, through Peter Clark's diary, the various aspects of an international relationship that continues to grow and prosper to the mutual benefit of both the United Kingdom and the United Arab Emirates.

Nahayan Mabarak Al-Nahayan
Minster of Culture, and Knowledge Development United Arab Emirates

CONTENTS

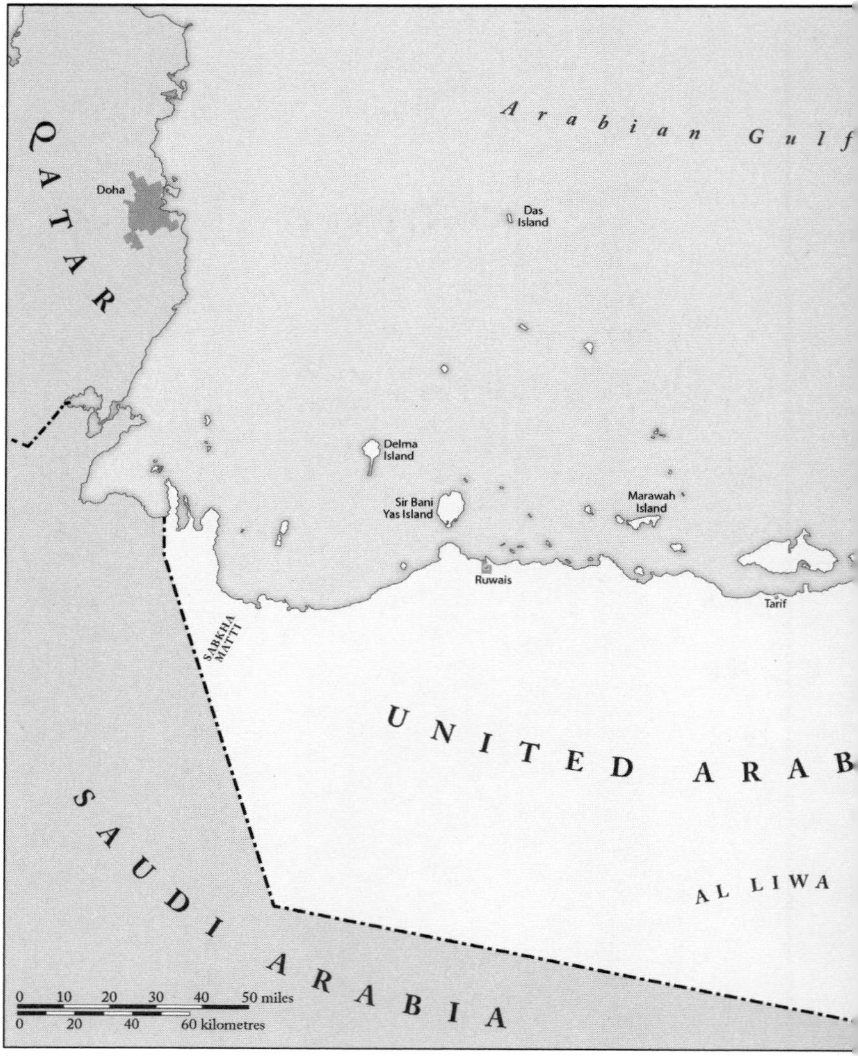

Arabian Gulf

QATAR

Doha

Das Island

Delma Island

Sir Bani Yas Island

Marawah Island

Ruwais

Tarif

SABKHA MATTI

UNITED ARAB

AL LIWA

SAUDI ARABIA

0 10 20 30 40 50 miles

0 20 40 60 kilometres

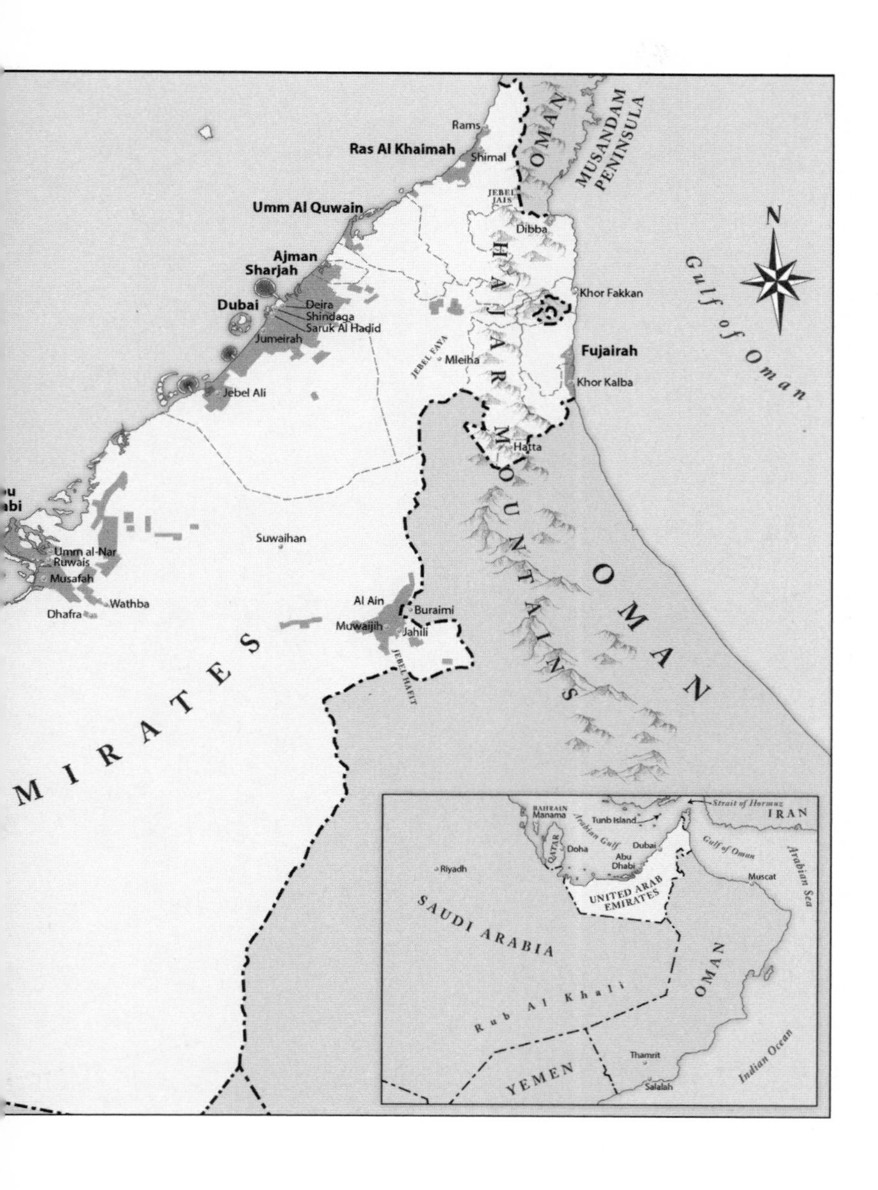

Rams
Ras Al Khaimah
Shimal
OMAN
MUSANDAM PENINSULA
JEBEL JAIS
Umm Al Quwain
Dibba
N
Gulf of Oman
Ajman
Sharjah
Khor Fakkan
Dubai
Deira
Shindaga
Saruk Al Hadid
Jumeirah
HAJAR MOUNTAINS
JEBEL FAYA
Mleiha
Fujairah
Khor Kalba
Jebel Ali
Hatta
Suwaihan
Umm al-Nar
Ruwais
Musafah
Wathba
Dhafra
OMAN
Al Ain
Buraimi
Muwaijih
Jahili
JEBEL HAFIT
MIRATES
BAHRAIN
Manama
Tunb Island
Strait of Hormuz
IRAN
Arabian Gulf
QATAR
Doha
Dubai
Abu Dhabi
Gulf of Oman
Arabian Sea
Muscat
Riyadh
UNITED ARAB EMIRATES
SAUDI ARABIA
OMAN
Rub Al Khali
Thamrit
Salalah
YEMEN
Indian Ocean

1988

Peter did not want to go to Abu Dhabi and resisted being posted there. He had been working in fascinating countries with ancient histories and cultures – Jordan, Lebanon, Sudan, Yemen and Tunisia. The United Arab Emirates was, he thought, brash and modern, with no culture or ancient monuments – an artificial creation grafted on to the Arabian Peninsula.

Peter had been working for the British Council since 1967. He had been recruited into the overseas career service and preferred to work overseas than in the London headquarters. The British Council was the British government's agency for cultural relations. It operated (in 1988) in nearly 100 countries of the world, always at the invitation of the host government. It promoted English-language teaching and exchanges of professionals and academics, and managed overseas tours of musicians and actors. In many countries its British staff had diplomatic status because this made it easier in those countries to get things done and have access to government officials.

Peter was 49 in 1988. He and his wife, Theresa, had met in 1959 and married in the 1960s: but not each other. Their first marriages had each produced a child. Theresa had a daughter, Kate, who was 20 in 1988; Peter had a son, Paul, 16. The first marriages of Peter and Theresa broke down in the 1970s and they married each other in 1980. They had two boys, Gabriel, born in 1981, and Nathaniel, born in 1983. The older children were receiving education in Britain while the youngest shared their lives in the Emirates.

As head of British Council operations in the United Arab Emirates, Peter's official designation was 'Representative'; this was changed to 'Director' in 1990. The post had diplomatic status, and, from the Emiratis' point of view, Peter was 'British Cultural Attaché'. The diplomatic status made no significant changes to the work he did or how he did it. He was part of the Ambassador's staff and was sure to respect his wishes, and maintained a cordial, even affable, relationship with the Ambassador and Embassy colleagues. But Peter's line manager was in London and he managed a budget that was quite separate from that of the Embassy.

The British Council had been working in the Emirates for about 20 years. Its main activities were English-language teaching and some exchange of professionals. From the early 1970s the British Council had been under budgetary constraints and discovered 'paid educational services'. This meant that the British government did not have to fund or subsidise British Council activities if other people could be found to pay for them. Saudi Arabia needed universities and English teaching programmes. OK, then the British Council could manage these at cost. Or it might be that an International Lending Agency (ILA, to use the acrostic jargon of the day), like the World Bank or the European Development Fund, would pay for an educational project in a developing country that could be managed by the British Council. It was thought and hoped that there might be some pickings in the Emirates.

British Council policy in a particular country was determined in those days by a 'Controller's Letter'. The senior management in the British Council were – following the BBC analogy – called 'controllers'. A Controller who had no direct management responsibility for a particular country would visit the country, meet British Council contacts and lay down what should and should not be done in that country for the next three or four years.

The policy within which Peter had to work was defined by a controller who had toured the Gulf in 1987. It stated categorically that there should be no British Council cultural activity in the United Arab Emirates. The argument was that 80% of the population was expatriate – Arab, South Asian, European and American. They were the main beneficiaries of cultural activity, but they were not part of the British Council's 'target groups' (another self-explanatory cliché).

The United Arab Emirates was a federation of seven separate Emirates, established in 1971. Previously called the Trucial States, they had been under British protection. These seven Emirates – Abu Dhabi, Ajman, Dubai, Fujairah, Ras Al Khaimah, Sharjah and Umm Al Quwain – were all headed by families: 'the ruling families'. Male members were referred to as sheikhs, female as sheikhas. Although the Arabic word sheikh means old man, in the Emirates a small boy could be sheikh if he was from a ruling family.

The seven states were distinct in size, population, wealth and character. Abu Dhabi was the largest and, thanks to oil, the wealthiest, and provided the Head of State for the country. From 1971 to his death in 2004, this was Sheikh Zayed bin Sultan Al Nahyan. (Zayed was his given name, Sultan was the name of his father. In this context, 'Al' introduced the family name, which in Sheikh Zayed's case was Nahyan. 'Al', with a long 'a', is not to be confused with 'al', the Arabic definite article.) Abu Dhabi's oil resources were vast, of good quality and easy to extract and export. Dubai had been a considerably larger city than Abu Dhabi in the 1940s and had always been a trading city, an international gold market, with close commercial and social links with Bombay/Mumbai and the rest of south Asia, and also Iran. Sharjah saw itself as a cultural centre. Ajman, Umm Al Quwain and Ras Al Khaimah dotted the Gulf coast as you travelled north. Fujairah was the only Emirate not on the Gulf coast, being on the Gulf of Oman to the west.

Peter and his family left his previous posting in Tunisia on Saturday 9 July. Peter arrived in Abu Dhabi on Thursday 21 July. Theresa and their sons spent the rest of the summer at their house in Brighton. For Peter, the 12 days between the two countries were spent being briefed at his headquarters, checking on the house in Brighton, and seeing old friends and his ailing, 90-year-old mother in Suffolk.

Tuesday 12 July

I call on colleagues at my headquarters. It is not inspiring. It is also boring and I fight to keep awake.

Thursday 14 July

I have asked to be briefed by the Department of Trade and Industry, and see the man who keeps an eye on British exports to the Emirates. It is the best briefing I have had so far. We talk about the economic situation. British exports to Turkey are now more than those to the UAE, which stand only at £450 million. We talk about all sorts of things: from the role of the English language to the overlap of interests between the British Council and exporters.

I go on to the Foreign Office. The desk officer for the UAE tells me that in the next year there are likely to be visits from the Prime Minister, Margaret Thatcher, the Prince and Princess of Wales, and the Secretary of State for Foreign and Commonwealth Affairs, Sir Geoffrey Howe – whom, as I leave, I see arriving in the inner courtyard, a small grey man in a small grey suit.

Friday 15 July

Theresa, our sons and I go for a walk on the Sussex Downs above Ditchling. I soak in the green, the lovely views over the Weald, little churches tucked into woods, fields neatly laid out in different shades of yellow and green. I look at it all, thinking I shall not see the likes again for 12 months.

Monday 18 July

I go to a headquarters training session on the New Financial System. I keep myself awake by making anagrams of the names of my colleagues. Controller Finance is Piers Pendred, which is an anagram of Spender Pride. My own name comes out as Leper Track. I have a drink with Richard Hale. He would like to be posted to Zimbabwe. This would be appropriate, as his name is an anagram of Harare Child.

Wednesday 20 July

I do not sleep well. I am anxious and nervous about going to Abu Dhabi.

It is a new world and I am initially going alone. I am apprehensive about the 20,000-plus British expatriates. I fear being patronised for knowing Arabic. How can I establish myself? In the month before Theresa arrives, can I build up a circle of Arab or non-Arab friends who are sympathetic? I dread the lack of exercise, the institutionalised leisure, the architecture, the materialism.

Thursday 21 July

I arrive at Abu Dhabi, where the temperature is 94° Fahrenheit. I am met at the airport by Bryson, whom I am replacing. He talks non-stop about the iniquities of his predecessor, Geoff, who knew nobody and was disliked by everybody.

I am taken to the Holiday Inn, run by smooth Asians. I have a room on the 14th floor. I go onto the balcony and my glasses immediately steam up.

Friday 22 July

My body clock is all awry. I come down to breakfast at half past ten. The waitresses are Filipina and Thai, in smart suits, smiling and distant.

Late in the afternoon I go for a walk along the Corniche. It is still warm. I have great difficulty accepting the sunset. It sets over the Gulf, which should be in the east, for we are on the eastern side of Arabia and the western shores of the Gulf. And Al Ain, inland, is in the east. No doubt in time I will get used to it. I pass a rough piece of land where football is being played. All the people I see are Indian, speaking Indian languages or English. Some shop signs are in Urdu; others in Persian. Shops are full and there is a general air of contentment and well-being. The town planning has been excellent: wide streets, plenty of space. The Corniche is dominated by a fountain built on an artificial hill. It is big enough for all those who mill around it – Indian families, mostly. I walk into the new souk. Shops are managed by Palestinians, Yemenis and Indians. There are Sudanese around. It really is a bizarre place.

Saturday 23 July

Bryson collects me and takes me to the office. I am still jet-lagged and cannot concentrate. But Bryson talks most of – indeed all – the time. It is clear that there is not a lot of work to be done. Can the Representation be jazzed up? At present there seems to be no direction, no vision.

We go on to his flat on the 17th floor. It has a piano, well-tuned, and, yes, fantastic views. Bryson's wife, Alma, does not work. She never has. She is quiet and deferential, overwhelmed by her husband's ego.

Sunday 24 July

Bryson collects me and takes me to Al Ain, 100 miles away. The road is dual carriageway all the way, with flowers and greenery between the two highways, and street lamps every 30 or 40 yards. There is a speed limit, enforced by sleeping policemen every few miles. It is quite extraordinary. Bryson talks, talks, talks. His taste for malice and gossip is extensive and his list of hates long.

There are two hotels in Al Ain, and we book into the InterContinental. I have what seems to be a triple bed in a well-carpeted room, with a bowl of fruit and chocolates waiting for me. There is the indication of the *qibla,* the direction of prayer for Muslims, and views over a well-tended garden with swings. You can have riding lessons, and a health centre includes video games. All is comfortable and opulent.

Monday 25 July

Bryson and Alma collect me and take me to the Ambassador's Residence. The Ambassador, Michael Tait, is 52, affable and professionally smooth. One of the guests is David Heard, who was a student with me at Keele University. I have not seen him since 1962. He came to Abu Dhabi in 1963 as a young geologist with the Iraq Petroleum Company (IPC) and has been here ever since. The IPC consortium held the concession for oil exploration, operated locally by Petroleum Development (Trucial Coast) Ltd. This latter became the Abu Dhabi Petroleum Company (ADPC) in the 1960s. David represented the interests of the non-UAE shareholders. Kirsteen, the Ambassador's wife, has been working in the Abu Dhabi archives, and has got interested in the poetry of an early 19th-century ruler of Abu Dhabi, Khalifa bin Shakhbut, which throws a lot of light on local life.

David tells me he called on Sheikh Shakhbut, the older brother of Sheikh Zayed, who was Ruler of Abu Dhabi from the 1920s to 1966, at

Al Ain: 'a marvellous old man of eighty-four'. He was replaced in 1966 by his younger brother, Zayed. He also tells me that Wilfred Thesiger's *Arabian Sands*[1] was banned here by cautious Palestinian censors in the Ministry of Information. When Sheikh Zayed heard about it, he ordered that it should be unbanned, but the latest edition has a new Introduction by Thesiger referring to Abu Dhabi as 'an Arabian nightmare'.

Tuesday 26 July

Bryson takes me to Dubai. There is a British Council office there, run by Allen Swales, who is on leave. The office was opened by the Ruler of Dubai, Sheikh Rashid, in 1972; it is spacious and well sited, but there is nobody there. We go to the house of Linda, the officer-in-charge, but she is not there either. So we have coffee at the palatial Ramada Hotel, which has, it is said, the loftiest stained-glass window in the world.

Wednesday 27 July

I walk the mile or so to the office, which has a prayer room. I meet Carl, the Director of Studies, and throw out the idea of getting commercial firms to sponsor a classroom for, say, £1,000 a year. They can advertise to a target audience.

Most of the locally engaged staff are from Kerala – no UAE nationals. The accountant, Jamal, is the 'foreman'. When Bryson asks a junior staff member to do something, that colleague looks to Jamal, who nods, rather like the bandleader in the film Casablanca turning to Rick when Victor asks the band to play the 'Marseillaise'. The staff all speak Malayalam to each other and call me 'Sir'.

Bryson leaves.

Thursday 28 July

At the hotel, I help a helpless Yemeni from Sa'da settle his bill. He speaks no English and the Indian receptionist speaks no Arabic.

I have lunch with David Heard. 'What should I do?' I ask. He talks about my predecessors. Bryson was the best. He dismisses Geoff with

---

1 Wilfred Thesiger, *Arabian Sands* (Collins, London, 1983).

something between a snort and a snigger, as if to say, 'I could tell you a tale or two'. David's German wife, Frauke, has written the standard history of the Emirates.[2] They have both been close to the ruling family. I point out that all my local staff are foreigners. He suggests I should recruit a young Britisher whose family has been here for 20 years. He need only work for a couple of years before he goes off to pursue his own career. But he could provide the hinge between the British Council and local life. In the Emirates there are sheikhs, nationals and the rest. Most of us here are hirelings, dispensable, and could be swept away like autumn leaves.

I walk the three miles back. I am soaked to the skin with sweat.

Friday 29 July

I do some laundry and put the washed clothes on the balcony, expecting them to be dry soon. But not so: the atmosphere is too damp.

I write to Theresa and tell her how nice it is here – though I blush to acknowledge it.

I am reading Frauke's book, about how the federation was put together and how it works. She has an Abu Dhabi perspective and is full of appreciation for Zayed, who really made the federation and was very generous.

Sunday 31 July

I put on my jacket and go to the Embassy to attend the weekly meeting of senior staff, known as 'prayers'. The Ambassador talks of Margaret Thatcher's brief stopover in Dubai next week. The Consul-General in Dubai, Jolyon Kay, is concerned that she should wear a trouser suit when boarding a helicopter. It is my first prayer meeting and I announce that I come with three preconceptions. First, the British Council operation in the UAE is worth £1.3 million, of which we earn 90% – so we are a significant invisible-export earner. Second, my basic objective is to make friends for Britain. Third, the target is the 600 captive nationals who attend our English classes. I would like to have cultural activities that embrace them.

---

2 Frauke Heard-Bey, *From Trucial States to United Arab Emirates: A Society in Transition* (Longman, London and New York, 1982).

Tuesday 2 August

Carl and I interview three people for the post of receptionist. One is an undynamic Copt. The second is an underwhelming South Yemeni, brought up in Mombasa: her family comes from the Hadramaut but she has been neither there nor to Aden. We decide on the third, a Palestinian who was in Bourj el-Barajneh in Lebanon during the Israeli massacres there. Two hours later, another candidate turns up, a bouncy Egyptian woman dressed like a nun.

At 5 pm I drive to Dubai. Traffic is very well under control. Speed limits are generally observed. The road is boringly straight, with nothing to relieve the eye. Carl has warned me about burst tyres when cars travel at speed. You have to be on your guard against your own tyres bursting but also those of others, with cars going out of control. Camels are another hazard, potentially lethal at night when they are attracted by the lights.

I meet Linda and Paul, who are looking after the Dubai office. After drinking the bottle of wine that has been provided gratis in my hotel room, we cross the Dubai Creek on an abra, a long, open passenger ferry boat. We are conspicuously the only non-Indians. The cost of the ferry is a quarter of a dirham – about 8p.

Wednesday 3 August

The hotel is anxious to please, but does not. I have a sleep in the afternoon and put a 'Do Not Disturb' sign on the door, but I am disturbed by a phone call from the Guest Relations Officer who asks if everything is all right.

Thursday 4 August

Linda takes me to call on some Dubai officials. We also go on to Sharjah, dry and ugly – lofty monochrome buildings of little architectural distinction.

We drive on through Ajman, a sprawl of buildings with neither core nor centre. We move on through marshland, sabkha. The road is dual carriageway to Ras Al Khaimah. We go on to Sha'm, in the mountains. Here are villages with small houses that seem to be more in harmony with the environment. We double back. I drop Linda off in Dubai and return to Abu Dhabi. I note there is still, albeit disused, a customs post on the Dubai–Abu Dhabi border.

Friday 5 August

I have now been here a fortnight and have hardly met anyone. I have built no circle of friends, and few acquaintances. There is an active social whirl here, but I am not part of it.

I read some of Clive Holes's book on colloquial Gulf Arabic.[3] It is quite intensive but I learn words that are Persian or Turkish, like *jam* for glass and *darisha* for window. Others are Persianised English, like *kandishan*, for air conditioning.

Sunday 7 August

I attend the Embassy meeting. The Ambassador is away and the Chargé is in charge. He called on Sheikh Zayed yesterday, the 22nd anniversary of his accession. Sheikh Zayed had put his hand on the Chargé's arm and said, *'Shukran'* ('Thank you'). What was the meaning of that?

I have lunch with my American opposite number. He was in Karachi and reckons that the Emirates English-language press tells you far more about Pakistani politics than the Pakistani newspapers.

Tuesday 9 August

I have been told that my target constituency is UAE nationals. But I reflect that Indians, Sudanese and Jordanians should be just as much part of that constituency. They already have a bias towards the English language and British education. The individuals here would be a 'target' in Kerala, Khartoum or Amman. When they are here they can afford to send their children to study in Britain.

I go to Al Ain and call at the museum, meeting Dr Walid Yasin, an Iraqi from Tikrit, who has a PhD from Cambridge. He shows me round the museum. With tears of nostalgia in my eyes, I see the copy of a mosaic from the Bardo Museum in Tunis, presented by Habib Bourguiba Junior. I have lunch with Walid at an excellent Lebanese restaurant called Al Kharuf Al Dhahabi ('The Golden Sheep').

---

3 Clive Holes, *Colloquial Arabic of the Gulf* (Routledge, London, 1984).

I drive on to Dubai along a boring dual carriageway with other dual carriageways branching off to places that consist of a palm tree and a hut.

At Dubai I meet up with Linda and Paul at The George and Dragon. During the evening the (British) management provides us with champagne to celebrate the birth of a daughter to the Duchess of York. An Indian is at the doorway ready to refuse admittance to those wearing the Arabian white smock-like garment, the *dishdasha*.

Thursday 11 August

I call on Muhammad Morsy Abdullah at the Documentation Centre. This is in the old fort, the oldest building in Abu Dhabi, dating from the turn of the century. Structurally it is still the same but there have been a million and one refinements. The gardens are full of flowers and fountains. There are marble staircases and air conditioning. The centre is collecting all documents and copies of documents relating to the Emirates in all languages. Dr Morsy is Egyptian in origin, but wears a dishdasha like a national. He did a PhD at Cambridge, supervised by Professor R B Serjeant, on the history of the Emirates.

Friday 12 August

I am reading a volume of the stories by a Dubai writer, Muhammad al-Murr.

Sunday 14 August

I call on Jum'a al-Salami, Deputy Director General of the Abu Dhabi Chamber of Commerce; 28 years old, a very impressive young man, more *noblesse oblige* than *nouveau riche*. We go to a reception room on the top floor and talk. A photographer comes in to immortalise the occasion.

I read more stories of Muhammad al-Murr, and have started reading Wilfred Thesiger's autobiography.[4]

Monday 15 August

I have a visit from Faruq Ohan, an Iraqi, who is involved in the

---

4 Wilfred Thesiger, *The Life of My Choice* (Collins, London, 1987).

development of the theatre in the Emirates. He is actually an Armenian from Mosul. His grandparents migrated from Samsun, but he feels culturally Arab.

The Emirates is really a very easy place to live in. It is cheap and manageable. I am feeling quite content here.

Wednesday 17 August

I have a police guard outside my office. This morning he addresses me in French and I reply likewise, and then realise we are in Abu Dhabi and not North Africa. He is Moroccan, but, as in Tunisia, French is the language for addressing non-Muslims.

I have a lift in a taxi. The taxi driver is a bearded Pathan who has been here for 21 years and speaks a little English, and a little more Arabic. But I throw a few words of Urdu and Persian. The Gulf is a linguistic museum.

Monday 22 August

I drive to Dubai and meet Muhammad al-Murr. We have lunch at the Metropolitan Hotel, well out of town. He is in his thirties and has had nine collections of short stories published. His grandfather's sister married Sa'id, the father of Sheikh Rashid, the Ruler of Dubai. He comments on the lack of proofreading in the publication of books in the Arab world. A text goes straight from the writer to the printer. His books are banned in Saudi Arabia for allegedly being pornographic. Saudi writers are unable to write about whisky or prostitution. He has no high opinion of other younger writers.

After lunch we walk round old Dubai – Shindagha, where he was brought up, and the fort of Sheikh Sa'id, father of the present Ruler of Dubai. Muhammad points out the bench where Sheikh Sa'id used to sit and watch what was going on. In 1938 there was a major internal crisis in Dubai, about the Ruler's authority and the role of the *majlis*. Families were divided, including Muhammad's. His father's father was with the Ruler, while his mother's family were majlisites and were exiled to Ajman. Muhammad shows me the building that housed the first garage. Cars did not have numbers in those early days, but they did have names. One was yellow and called '*Samn*' ('Fat'). He observes that, because of tension a generation or so ago, the main barracks were located on the road to Abu Dhabi. In the old days, he says, 'you knew if a cat died. Now people can disappear without trace.'

We part and I cross the Creek by an abra. I love them. There is just a touch of Istanbul about these boats on the water.

Tuesday 23 August

I go with Linda to Fujairah. We call on Samih Qabbani, a Lebanese businessman who used to have a pharmacy in the centre of Beirut for ten years of the civil war. Today he does jobs for the ruling family. We discuss possible English-language classes. We are joined by others and I ask about the origin of the name Fujairah. One man says that a *fujaira* is a small well that flashes out of the mountain. Another says that the name is really 'al- Fujairah' and was originally *alfu jariya,* meaning a thousand concubines, referring to the days when Fujairah was a port bringing in slaves from Africa. This produces laughter but also denial. Samih takes us to Khor Kalba, a delightful spot, and to the Fujairah airport which, he says, has the best-quality runway in the Emirates. This may be because there are so few planes to damage it.

We drive along the coast of the Gulf of Oman via Khor Fakkan, seeing a long line of tankers and other cargo ships waiting to enter the Gulf through the Straits of Hormuz.

Wednesday 24 August

I call on Brigadier Michael Barclay, who has been military adviser to Sheikh Rashid for decades.

He is a big man with a demob haircut, and welcomes me saying he dislikes 'self-styled Arabists. Anyone who calls himself an Arabist is a fool.'

I ask him what advice he would give me.

'Have one big do, rather than lots of small ones. Pipe bands, model railways, something to do with camels. Have your promotional material in Arabic. Serve coffee or lemonade. Arabise the outfit. They love British humour too. *Fawlty Towers.* I've heard people refer in the middle of a conversation in Arabic to a black man as "a chocolate biscuit".'

I drive to Al Ain. It is part of several villages, some of which are in the United Arab Emirates, some in Oman. Collectively they used to be known as the Buraimi Oasis. There are no border restrictions among the villages. I drive into Oman for dinner. The Omani villages are scruffier. There are no marked lanes and you cannot make out the edge of the road. Drivers hoot – they do not do that in the Emirates.

Thursday 25 August

I call on the bank manager in Al Ain, a Bangladeshi. He tells me that Sheikh Shakhbut keeps up to date with the news of the world and you have to be well-informed when you call on him. The brigadier told me yesterday that the gardens and parks of Abu Dhabi were originally the idea of Sheikh Shakhbut: he wanted the city to be like Hyde Park!

I also call at the municipality and meet a Sudanese. We talk Sudan. He tells me that before the Emirates became independent 17 years ago, the British brought in several Sudanese to assist in the development of local municipalities.

Friday 26 August

The guard outside my office is, I guess, Sudanese. He comes from Darfur and from the town of Kutum, where Wilfred Thesiger served as District Commissioner in the 1930s. He talks of Darfur history, mentioning only two names. One is Ali Dinar, who was Ruler of Darfur before the British annexed it in 1916. The other is 'Mr Moore', Guy Moore, who was Thesiger's much-respected boss. On impulse I write to Wilfred Thesiger, saying with what pleasure I have read his book, and telling him of this Kutum–Abu Dhabi link.

Saturday 27 August

I bring in Wilfred Thesiger's book and show the guard pictures of Kutum.

Sunday 28 August

I go into a class this morning: Emirati women taught by women teachers. The students are well connected, and fiddle with their headdresses as I enter. But photographs are taken, sweets are chewed and I say a few words to them in Arabic. 'Are you Lebanese?' asks one girl.

Monday 29 August
I have a call from Mike Hall, the Shell representative. He is giving us £5,000 to support the Al Ain teaching operation. I say I will convert it into the sponsorship of a classroom. Mike started life as a teacher in Omdurman and is married to a Khartoum Armenian.

Wednesday 31 August
I am invited to a party of British expatriates. It is luxurious and very agreeable; the company less so. There is nostalgic talk of the old days of wife-swapping parties. 'That was the only party I've been to when both my wife and I were propositioned by the same person.'

Afterwards I go to the airport to meet Theresa and our sons. The plane is two hours late. One item of luggage is missing. We report it, and dawn is breaking by the time we get to the flat.

Saturday 3 September
I have to meet a senior official of the Ministry of Foreign Affairs, Abdullah Husain Dawud. He is an Omani, born in Mombasa, and brought up in Bombay. He speaks perfect English thanks to a Scottish nanny. As well as his home here, he has one house in Chelsea and another Mombasa.

Monday 5 September
We go to the Cultural Centre. This is a superbly equipped hall in lovely grounds, with an open-access library. It is the first meeting of the new season of the Emirates Natural History Group and we listen to a talk on falcons. We are not sure where it will be but we follow a man with a hooded falcon on his arm. He is the speaker, an American who works in a falcon hospital that must be as well equipped as any British hospital. Sheikh Zayed has funded it all. He likes to go hunting. He goes to Mali, with two planes packed with sheikhs and falcons. They camp, with electricity generators and the best food flown in. People come to see them from all over the country.

Wednesday 7 September
I go to a reception hosted by the Dubai Chamber of Commerce for Sheikh Nahyan bin Mubarak, Chancellor of United Arab Emirates

University. He is keen to found colleges of technology, for men and women, and has recruited a Canadian team of consultants. Sheikh Nahyan was head boy at Millfield School, spent one year at Oxford and then got a degree from the University of Buckingham.

Thursday 8 September

Back in Abu Dhabi, Carl, Director of Studies, and I call on Eid Bakhit Musallim al-Mazrui. He has taught himself English, and wishes to improve it and to get a PhD. He was living in Qatar and was called back to the Emirates by Sheikh Zayed. He has many interests and is the country's Chief Scout. In Qatar he had an educational job in which he was responsible for developing what he calls the coracle-um.

I also call on the Sudanese Ambassador, Hamad al-Nil, a grandson of the sufi buried just outside Omdurman, where there is 'dervish dancing' every Friday. We talk of mutual friends and of sufism. He is affable and tells me there are 80,000 Sudanese in the UAE.

Friday 9 September

I dream of a pack of wolves and foxes that are well organised and march along the road in step. I am driving a car and stop to let them cross the road, which they do in an orderly manner – left, right, left, right. Then I am aware of two of them at my feet in the car. I then wake up.

At dusk Theresa and I walk along the Corniche to the 'Coffee Pot Fountain', an amazing structure where a giant coffee pot – *dalla* – revolves pouring water into (proportionately) small cups. The air is humid but the gardens are full of people sauntering. There is no threat, no tension. By contrast, it is not possible to walk comfortably around Central Park in New York or any public park in London after dark. Here families sit around on the grass.

Saturday 10 September

I go to Dubai and spend the evening with Muhammad al-Murr. We go to Sharjah for a Lebanese meal. We talk books. He likes the short stories of Somerset Maugham; there is no moral lesson, no conclusion. Muhammad spent five years in the US. After dinner, we walk by the Khalid Lagoon and at about 11.00 pm take a boat ride round the lagoon.

He tells me a story of some women from a prominent family returning to Dubai from Europe. The customs officer asked to see the contents of their cases. They refused, saying they were from an important local family. The officer insisted and the cases were opened up to reveal a whole lot of sex aids. 'They are not for us,' they pleaded, 'but are presents for friends.'

Sunday 11 September

The Filipina waitress who regularly serves me at the hotel is called Victoria and comes from Manila. She was directly recruited by the hotel two months ago.

In the evening I go to the Creek, the *khur,* and take an abra. It is choppy and water splashes us. The Indian passengers giggle. I walk to the Ghurair Centre – bright and full of shoppers – and find the bookshop. It has a copy of my edition of Pickthall's novel *Saīd the Fisherman.* They did stock copies of my book on Marmaduke Pickthall but they have all sold out.[5] I walk along the edge of the khur, looking at the moored dhows, registered in Mukalla and Aden. I wonder how long they take to get there.

Monday 12 September

I have dinner with the Consul-General, Jolyon Kay, and his wife, Shirley. She writes books and I am a little shy of her, unwilling to talk as another writer. But I would love to talk about the techniques of writing.

Wednesday 14 September

Allen Swales, who is in charge of the Dubai office, and I go to Fujairah, to see if there is the possibility of any English-language teaching. I am shown an aerial photograph of a farm in England. It is near Lewes and belongs to the Ruler of Fujairah.

We call at the port and meet an Englishman, Captain Saunders, who has been here for six years. He used to work at the Port of Felixstowe, which has close links with Fujairah.

---

5 Peter Clark, *Marmaduke Pickthall: British Muslim* (Quartet Books, London, 1986). At the same time, Quartet Books also brought out a new edition of *Saīd the Fisherman,* with an introduction by Peter Clark. The novel was first published in 1903.

Thursday 15 September

We have lunch with Frauke and David Heard. They live in a lovely house, mature with a fine garden. They have pet gazelles and ducks, and a small swimming pool. They employ two tie-wearing male cooks and a nanny from Eritrea.

Saturday 17 September

I take a visitor, a specialist in fish farms, to the university at Al Ain. I go to see the Dean of Science at the Girls' College, a barrack-like building surrounded by walls topped with barbed wire. The facilities inside are excellent and the girls glide around in veils, *burqa,* swishing black chiffon gowns, with high heels and carefully applied make-up. They are collected by chauffeur-driven cars with darkened windows.

I have lunch with some academics, including the quietly-spoken Acting Vice-Chancellor, Dr Abdul Hafiz al-Kurdi. We talk in Arabic and then he says, in English, 'I'm sure your English will improve while you are in the UAE'.

Another Dean, Dr al-Amiri, did a PhD at University College London. He comes from Dubai and originally graduated from Shiraz. When he was in London some friends from Dubai came to see him. By accident he put salt, instead of sugar, in their tea. They did not object and he realised his mistake when he drank his own tea.

'Why did you not object?' he asked.

'We thought this was the custom in England.'

Tuesday 20 September

Jolyon Kay and I call on the Ruler of Sharjah. Jolyon and I meet beforehand at the extraordinary Continental Hotel in Sharjah, which at first I think is still being constructed. The Ruler, Sheikh Dr Sultan bin Muhammad Al Qasimi, looks older than his years and is suffering from backache. He receives us in the 'Lesser Divan'. It is all very informal and he is easy to talk with. We spend nearly an hour in a room furnished only with old-fashioned armchairs and settees. He is a little distraught, slightly scatty but most amiable.

'I miss you,' he says, almost pathetically, to Jolyon.

He talks about a book he has written in Arabic about the break-up of the Omani Empire, and another he wants to write on the influence of the British in the Red Sea in the 19th century. I give him a copy of my book on Pickthall, about whom he speaks highly, and says there is an Egyptian who is trying to discredit him – 'but he wants to promote his own translation'.

The Ruler recalls, as a boy, crossing the Gulf to Iran in a dhow ('You know dhow?'). The pilot fell asleep on the wheel and the boat swerved gently and nearly charged into a tanker. The captain suddenly became aware of the situation, seized the controls and drove the dhow hard to avoid hitting the tanker.

He is having a dispute with the British Bank of the Middle East 'about 55 million dollars' and is threatening to sever his connection with them. (In effect, says Jolyon afterwards, what he means is 'I'll take my overdraft elsewhere'.)

Wednesday 21 September

I have lunch with David Heard, who is very helpful. In any activity, I should aim at the top. He speaks very highly of Sheikh Nahyan; he is bright, close to Sheikh Zayed and pro-British. I should also get close to the oil companies.

I have now been here for two months. It is a fascinating posting and I am going to enjoy myself.

Saturday 24 September

I call on Najmuddin al-Hamouda, an Iraqi who has been here for over 20 years and has helped to build up the Ministry of Foreign Affairs. The former Iraqi prime minister, Dr Muhammad al-Fadl al-Jamali, whom I knew well in Tunis, recommended that I call on him. Some of his protégés call – the Ambassador-designate to Yemen, a Bahraini intellectual – as we talk about mutual acquaintances. He is passionately fond of Verdi's *Requiem*, which he plays to guests at home.

Tuesday 27 September

The Ambassador takes me to call on the majlis of Sheikh Mubarak bin Muhammad, the Minister of the Interior. Sheikh Mubarak was injured in a road accident in London and, as a result, has a speech impediment.

He is a cousin of Sheikh Zayed and was one of four brothers (Tahnoun, Saif and Surur being the others) who have powerfully supported Sheikh Zayed over the years. At the residence, we take off our shoes and I walk behind the Ambassador into the long first-floor room lined by comfortable armchairs. Near the door are AK-47-bearing bodyguards, plus servants and coffee-bearers. People stand up as we walk this gauntlet to be greeted by Sheikh Mubarak and his brother, Sheikh Tahnoun (who is the Ruler's representative in Al Ain), on his right. I take a seat next to Sheikh Mubarak's dutiful son, Sheikh Nahyan. Coffee is brought in to us. We talk or are silent. Other guests arrive. The servants by the door stand up. Sheikh Mubarak stands up. Other guests stand up as the visitor walks the gauntlet. Almost all present are nationals, but one man in a western-style suit is a Lebanese contractor.

We take our leave after 20 minutes and drive on the west of Abu Dhabi island to the huge palace of Sheikh Surur bin Muhammad, another of those brothers. We drive through one automatic barrier and, after 200 yards, a second barrier manned by a Gurkha. We go into a small majlis and join some young men playing cards and watching American television, transmitted through an enormous private satellite dish. After a while Sheikh Surur joins us and takes us off, driving us around the estate in a golf buggy. The Ambassador sits in front with the sheikh. I sit behind with a retainer and the sheikh's two-year-old son (also a sheikh). We tour the grounds – palm trees, chickens, a private beach, a herd of gazelle in an enclosure – and then back to the larger majlis, a cylindrical building with a long, curved window overlooking the setting sun. The whole estate is superbly landscaped. You go into the majlis building through a foyer with a huge chandelier – 15 feet of draping bulbs. In the majlis room are fitted carpets, and coffee tables made of solid glass in the form of inverted pyramids. We stay for 20 minutes.

Wednesday 28 September

I call on Dr Morsy at the Documentation Centre at the fort.

'You must meet Mr Henderson,' he says, and calls for this gentleman to join us for coffee.

Edward Henderson is 70, a slight man, gentle and bald, and carries a straw hat in his hand. He has just had his memoirs published.[6] A review in *The Independent* described him as 'a Victorian oil man'. He first came to Abu Dhabi in 1948.

'Did you like Abu Dhabi then?' I ask.

'Yes,' he says.

'What is it about Abu Dhabi then and Abu Dhabi now that has not changed?'

'A special tang,' he answers, 'which will last as long as Shakhbut and Zayed are around.'

Sheikh Shakhbut, he tells us, is a great walker. He was in London this year, and walked from Cromwell Road, where he stayed, to Hyde Park and beyond.

Edward Henderson shows me round the fort, pointing out an error in the Arabic on the lintel, and saying that the core of the fort goes back a long time and that Sheikh Shakhbut added some of the buildings after the Second World War. Edward is a delightful man, frail, charming, modest and amusing. He lives in a grace and favour home near the Ruler's Stables.

Friday 30 September

We go for a family stroll along the Corniche. All sorts of people from the city are out. I address a group of men sitting on the grass.

'*Al-salam alaikum*,' I say. 'Where are you from? Pakistan?'

'We are from the borders of Pakistan and Iran. We are Baluchis.'

It is all very friendly and relaxed.

Saturday 1 October

I have a call from a British consultant on sports education. He knows Saudi Arabia well, and tells me that sport is being encouraged from the highest level to divert Saudi (male) youths from drugs, homosexuality and a rising crime rate.

I call on an Under-Secretary in the Prime Minister's office who wants advice in setting up a primary school on British lines. The

---

6 Edward Henderson, *This Strange Eventful History: Memoirs of Earlier Days in the UAE and Oman* (Quartet Books, London, 1988).

Palestinian secretary – from Nablus – and I chat in Arabic. He talks of the sufferings of the Palestinians and I point out that tomorrow is Palestinian Historians Day, so dated because it is the anniversary of Saladin's liberation of Jerusalem after 80 years of occupation: so we must be patient.

My work is really quite fun. Time passes quickly as a result. I am totally and happily cut off from my headquarters.

Sunday 2 October

I have a letter from Wilfred Thesiger, in reply to mine of 26 August. He is delighted to hear of my encounter with the guard and to learn of the esteem in which the memory of Guy Moore is held. He wants me to find out more about Idris Daud, who was his companion on travels in Darfur and Libya in the late 1930s.

Monday 3 October

We go to a meeting of the Emirates Natural History Group to see the film *The Empty Quarter*, about Wilfred Thesiger's travels in southern Arabia in the 1940s. I saw the film exactly 20 years ago and could make nothing of the Arabic. I can make little more of it now. The chairman quotes from Thesiger's *Arabian Sands* about how he reached Dubai to stay with Edward Henderson, 'who is with us this evening'. Edward stands up, makes a bow and acknowledges a round of applause with a great grin.

Tuesday 4 October

We seem to be heading for getting our own house. We learn that it belonged to the widow of one Abdullah al-Malik, an Englishman who became a Muslim and worked in the Abu Dhabi army. He was given nationality and so was able to own land.

We are invited to a reception to say goodbye to a Total oil company executive and to welcome his successor. As I have had nothing to do with either of them, it is a mystery why we have been invited. But I meet some interesting people. Muhammad al-Dabali's grandfather was chauffeur to the father of Sheikh Rashid of Dubai. The local word for a four-wheel-drive vehicle was *dabal*, which became the source of the family name. He once drove Sheikh Shakhbut to Qatar. When he asked for wages, Sheikh Shakhbut said, 'Why? I am not asking for the payment of the food and lodging I have given you.'

Wednesday 5 October

The Ambassador tells me I am making an impact. A lot of people talk about me: 'He's interested in Arabic'. Good. That is what I aim at.

We have dinner with the Ambassador. One of the guests is Zaki Nusseibeh, the Palestinian interpreter of Sheikh Zayed, who was educated at Rugby and Oxford. He is the patron of the Alliance Française. He is a great admirer of the work of Muhammad al-Murr.

Thursday 6 October

We have dinner at the flat of Najmuddin al-Hamouda, a former Iraqi diplomat. He has a splendid picture of himself with Sheikh Zayed. Both are sitting on the floor, chatting. Zayed looks comfortable, Najmuddin stout and awkward. On the floor is a packet of cigarettes, a box of tissues and a transistor radio. He knew Wilfred Thesiger when he was travelling in Iraqi Kurdistan. 'What were the Kurds like?' he was asked. 'Disgusting,' replied Wilfred, who went on to spend happier times with the Marsh Arabs. Another old Baghdadi is present and observes about the Marsh Arabs, 'You hear about them, but you don't go to see them'.

Saturday 8 October

David Heard phones. Sheikh Zayed heard about the showing of the Thesiger film and would like to see it. He would also like to invite Wilfred Thesiger to Abu Dhabi and to have *Arabian Sands* translated into Arabic.

I telephone my headquarters and leave an urgent message. Could Films Department acquire the film, make a video, and send it out so the British Council can present it to Sheikh Zayed?

I am reading more of Muhammad al-Murr's stories. They are all so good. I would not mind translating them if I could find a publisher.

Sunday 9 October

At the weekly Embassy staff meeting ('prayers'), most of the discussion is about the annual 'Challenge', a regular sports competition between the British staffs of the Embassy and the Consulate-General in Dubai. The Deputy Head of Mission is keen on this and complains that last year one of the Dubai staff introduced their athletic teenage sons. Then it is suggested that Abu Dhabi's deputy accountant (an Indian) should be drafted. He used to be the UAE badminton champion.

Theresa and I go to a reception in Dubai. I talk to people in Arabic. The people of the Emirates are not so restrained as Tunisians in speaking Arabic with me. A lot of people in Dubai also speak Farsi.

Tuesday 11 October

I call at the Ajman University College and meet the principal, Said Salman, a former Minister of Agriculture and Ambassador to France. He gives me a lecture on the philosophy of the college, interspersed with trendy ideas like 'technosphere' and Gallicisms like *changement*. I am not terribly impressed.

In the evening we have dinner at the Emirates Golf Club, south of Dubai, with a senior official from the Ministry of Education. The venue is his choice, as it is a discreet place for him to drink Italian wine. He comes from Sharjah and used to enjoy British pubs in his student days. He cut down as a student to just two pub visits a week, drinking four pints on Wednesday nights and eight on Saturday nights. He talks nostalgically about a pub he knew in Ealing – the Dog and Partridge, he calls it. (Actually it is the Shepherd and Dog.)

Friday 14 October

Naguib Mahfouz has been awarded the Nobel Prize for Literature. He is 77 and is very surprised. He acknowledges his masters, Taha Husain, Mahmud Abbas al-Aqqad and Tawfiq al-Hakim. This is wonderful news. It ought to provide a fillip for all Arab literature, including translations.

Saturday 15 October

I call on Muhammad Ahmad al-Suwaidi, the Secretary-General of the Cultural Foundation. He is tall, in his mid-twenties, charming with the airs of an aristocrat. We talk for half an hour about contemporary Arabic literature and the stories of Muhammad al-Murr, and how pleased we are at the award of the Nobel Prize to Naguib Mahfouz.

In addition to being Chancellor of the Emirates University, Sheikh Nahyan is also chairman of a bank.

Sunday 16 October

The Director of Studies, Carl, and I go to the Dhafra Air Base in search of a contract to teach English to the Abu Dhabi Air Force. The base is not signposted and is off the road to Tarif, in a wild and lonely spot. In the reception room are other Europeans and foreigners. I feel like one of a mutually suspicious group of travelling salesmen, with encyclopaedias, vacuum cleaners or hairbrushes.

In the evening I take a taxi, the driver being a Pathan from Peshawar. I ask him about the current elections in Pakistan. He is all for Zia ul-Haq. All Punjabis are for Benazir Bhutto, all Pathans against. 'Why do you not split up the country, like Bangladesh?' I suggest. He roars with laughter.

Monday 17 October

I attend a meeting of British businessmen, called the 'Monday Club'. The Ambassador talks about the political situation. One man observes that the Iranians are well accepted in the UAE, much better than the Iraqis.

At the Emirates Natural History Group, Peter Hellyer[7] talks about the rise of the ruling family, the Nahyans. He has cleared what he has to say with the family; it is illuminating. Sheikh Surur is married to a daughter of Sheikh Zayed. Sheikh Nahyan's mother is a daughter of Sheikh Shakhbut, and his wife a granddaughter of Sheikh Shakhbut. But there must be an alternative view of history, to which it would be impolitic even to refer. Why are all the senior jobs cornered by three or four families – Qubaisi, Buti, Dhahiri and the ruling family?

Tuesday 18 October

I am invited to lunch with Eid Bakhit Musallim al-Mazrui. He collects me in his car and we stop at a flower shop (which he owns) to collect two of his friends. At his house we go into his majlis, where there is a Sudanese and a couple of tribesmen who look as if they have walked out

---

7 British-born (1948) journalist, historian and author; resident in Abu Dhabi from the 1970s and now a UAE national.

of the Thesiger film. We go into the dining room where, on a large table, we encounter a huge (cooked) sheep piled high with rice, together with some tabbouleh, salad and buttermilk. We gorge ourselves and then slip off to another room around a fountain with pictures on the walls of romanticised Emirates scenes.

Wednesday 19 October

David Heard invites me to be a member of the board of Al Khubairat School, the English-medium primary school attended by our boys.

'How many women are on the board?'

'Four. The Ambassador's wife, and three others who are useless.'

'I suggest Theresa. She has been a teacher, a school governor and a chairman of governors. She also has more available time than me.'

Thursday 20 October

I call on Suhail Mazrui, the General Manager of ADNOC, the Abu Dhabi National Oil Company. The décor is lavish. In the waiting room there is nothing to distract the visitor but the magnificent view through ogive windows over reclaimed land and the Gulf beyond. He offers the British Council the use of the company's theatre free of charge.

Sunday 23 October

We are getting some new premises at Al Ain. The Prince of Wales is due out next year and I suggest to the Embassy that he open the new centre there.

I have a visit from Yusuf Husain Yahya, the Sudanese guard who was outside my office. I had passed on to Wilfred Thesiger his praise of Guy Moore. I ask him, as Wilfred had asked me to do, about Idris Daud. By extraordinary coincidence, the guard is a nephew of Idris, who is alive and well, though with failing eyesight. He will be going on leave to Darfur in December, and offers to take a message from Wilfred and bring back news of Idris.

Tuesday 25 October

We go to a posh do hosted by the Italian Ambassador. I greet the Turkish

Ambassador in Turkish. We then switch to English. He was at Ankara College, a school I taught at in the early 1960s. There are five graduates of that college in the Emirates. Perhaps we should form a club! We have music around a pool. The fountains are turned off and we have live music from violin, viola and guitar. I am placed at dinner between an Italian lady from Camogli and a Lebanese lady. The latter thinks the civil war is all the fault of foreigners, by whom she means Palestinians. She is a beautician and believes in the significance of the signs of the zodiac. In spite of this we get on very well, chatting away in French and Arabic.

Wednesday 26 October

I have asked Robyn Davidson, the Australian travel writer[8] whom I met a year or two ago in London, to come to the Emirates and talk about camels. She writes back, a warm and friendly letter; she would love to come.

The Number Two in the Embassy pulls me aside and talks about the proposed visit of the Prince and Princess of Wales.

'They will go to the Dubai British Council office, because it is more attractive than the Abu Dhabi one.'

'Will they be going to Al Ain?'

'Yes, to have dinner in a tent in the desert.'

'As you know, the Prince does not like purely ceremonial tasks. It would be most valuable for us if he could open our new centre in Al Ain.'

Later I phone my headquarters. My line manager is on leave. His deputy is not in yet. A third senior colleague is at the dentist. I leave a message with another colleague asking the British Council (of which the Prince of Wales is Vice-Patron) to get in touch with his office and lobby for the Prince to open our Al Ain centre.

Thursday 27 October

The Ambassador and I call on Sheikh Nahyan. I have heard that my predecessor but one, Geoff, irritated the sheikh, more or less telling him how to run a university. He receives us in a brown *bisht,* a garment

---

8 Author of *Tracks* (Vintage, London, 1980), which won the first Thomas Cook Travel Book Prize, and tells the story of crossing Australia with camels.

that goes over his dishdasha. I present him with a copy of my book, *Marmaduke Pickthall: British Muslim*. He seems to be fascinated by it, and reads it, ignoring the Ambassador as he chats along. We get his consent to organising an exhibition of books on Islam at the university.

Friday 28 October

In Fujairah for the weekend, we meet people from the office of the Ruler of Fujairah. One is a Palestinian who has been here since 1961. It was first Coastal Oman, then the Trucial States, and now the United Arab Emirates. Fujairah has much potential for tourism – a superb coastline, mountains, and interesting and friendly people. On a rough patch of ground we see a bullfight, two bulls bent down wrestling with their horns.

Sunday 30 October

Outside a restaurant I see an announcement about 'Full Goat'. I make enquiries and learn that it is a translation of *kharuf mashi,* stuffed lamb.

Monday 31 October

We have dinner with the Heards. The other guests include Najmuddin al-Hamouda and Muhammad Rubaya, who, according to Frauke, is one of the most successful businessmen in Abu Dhabi. He recently bought Coppins from the Duke of Kent.

Wednesday 2 November

Our Education Adviser, Karen, is married to a Sudanese, Abu Bakr. They have a cottage in a rural corner of the island of Abu Dhabi. The parkland is home to Sheikh Zayed's stud: 300 horses, one of whom was born last night. Karen and Abu Bakr have a swimming pool and a garden.

The British Council driver takes Karen and me to the opening of the Sharjah Book Fair. This is held in ExpoCentre, a vast tent lacking air conditioning. There are heaps of stalls and the British Council one is centrally sited, with the exhibition of British books on Islam. The books had to go through the local censors: only six (out of 150) books were disallowed, including Frauke's history of the country!

Sheikh Dr Sultan and his party arrive late. He moves slowly round the stalls and stays awhile at ours. We have displayed his book[9] prominently, together with some of Shirley Kay's books, a volume of essays by Mana Oteiba, my book on Marmaduke Pickthall and the latter's novel, *Saīd the Fisherman*.

Monday 14 November

As usual I have a lift in a taxi with a Pathan driver. He is very critical of Benazir Bhutto.

'Women,' he says, 'should not rule. Maybe it's all right outside Islam.'

'Regardless of your own views,' I ask, 'who do you think will win the Pakistani elections?'

'Maybe she will. But maybe she will get shot.'

Peter and Theresa took a week off and went for a holiday in India.

Wednesday 23 November

I tease a Pathan taxi driver, congratulating him on Benazir Bhutto becoming Prime Minister. 'All women prime ministers are strong,' I tell him. 'Golda Meir, Indira Gandhi, Margaret Thatcher.'

Sunday 27 November

My line manager, Frank, has arrived for a few days from London. I take him to Al Ain to meet people there and from the university. I host a dinner party at the hotel. A visiting Professor of Engineering is pompous and self-important, but eases up as the evening progresses.

Monday 28 November

I take Frank to call by appointment on the office – the *diwan* – of Sheikh Saeed bin Tahnoun. Al Ain is a maddening place to drive round. The roads have speed restrictions of 45 km/h. All roads are dual carriageways and if you miss a turning, you have to go a mile or more before you can double back. There are hardly any pedestrians and when you find one

---

9 Sultan Muhammad Al Qassimi, *The Myth of Arab Piracy in the Gulf* (Vintage, London, 1986).

to ask directions, they may be Bangladeshi workers who have neither Arabic nor English.

We wait 20 minutes at the *diwan* before the young sheikh turns up, having expected us in another place. We start in Arabic, then switch to English, but it is clear he is happier and more fluent in the former. I talk about our needs, the proposed new premises and the invitation to Robyn Davidson to come and talk about camels. He is very affable and invites us to come and spend time with his camels.

Tuesday 29 November

I have been invited to the opening ceremony of an Arab Scouts event at the Cultural Foundation. It starts late: people have not been prepared! My friend Eid Bakhit Musallim al-Mazrui presides. He looks strange in trousers, shirt, scouts' neck-gear and Arab headdress. He gives a stirring speech. Women are in the gallery upstairs.

Wednesday 30 November

I call on the landlord of the premises we hope to take on for the British Council centre in Al Ain. We need to take over the premises for the royal visit in March or, as I put it, before Ramadan. I tell him if we can get the Prince of Wales to open the office he will be part of the receiving line and meet the Prince.

I take my line manager to Dubai, and we walk along the Creek. I talk to some of the dhowmen. It takes two days to sail to Bahrain, four to get to Abadan. It would be fun to go to one of these places, or to Karachi, by dhow.

We have dinner with Muhammad al-Murr, who tells me his books are also banned in Kuwait. Saudis come to Dubai for what he calls the three Ks – *kas* (a glass of wine), *kus* (women) and kebab. 'The Left criticise my writings because I do not talk of the workers' struggle. And religious people criticise my work for being immoral.'

Friday 2 December

I am due to give a lecture at the university in ten days' time on British contributions to Arab studies. I am reading essays by Taha Husain in order to make his beautiful and stylish Arabic part of me.

Saturday 3 December

The Director of Studies, Carl, is off to London to have an interview for the British Council overseas career service. I wish him good luck. Most of the tasks for recruitment are devised by people who are based in Britain. I consider a test: The candidate is injected with a 12-hour flu bug. He has to go to Paddington station to meet someone there. When there, he is told, No, you should be at Waterloo. He goes there, meets the person and has to talk intelligently about potted plants or Sri Lankan elections for 20 minutes. That would be a good test for someone embarking on an overseas career.

Monday 5 December

I drive to Al Ain. The main road is only for cars and is consequently fast. A mile to the north is a parallel road for lorries. There are connecting roads and, out of curiosity, I go onto the lorry road. Sleeping policemen every 200–300 yards oblige all the traffic to go slowly. I give up after a mile or two and return to the fast road.

For the next eight hours I spend time setting up the exhibition of British books on the Islamic World, and taking part in a conference on plant protection. The function is inaugurated by Sheikh Nahyan, who invites me to the front row (where I sit with the US Ambassador and the French Cultural Attaché) and then to a majlis close by. Sheikh Nahyan is courteous to everyone and then slips off so the rest of us can interact more informally.

In the library I see a poster, in beautiful Arab calligraphy, announcing my lecture.

Assured that all is well with the books for the exhibition, I leave Al Ain and drive to the British Council office in Dubai, where Allen Swales has organised an exhibition to mark the centenary of the birth of the precious and syphilitic Katherine Mansfield. A few of the Dubai New Zealanders, including the artist Margaret Henderson, have been invited.

Tuesday 6 December

Theresa has joined me and we drive from Dubai to Hatta Fort, where I add the final touches to a lecture I am to give. We drive on to the university at Al Ain.

My chairman is Dr Abdullah Abdul Wahhab, a Sudanese whom I knew a dozen years ago in Khartoum. He wrote a book about the Battle of Toski, between the Sudanese Mahdists and the British-led Egyptian army. His PhD was on the 1936 Revolt in Palestine. The hall is vast and I have an audience of 20 or so – Egyptians, Sudanese and a few nationals. I meet Dr Riad of the English Department, who did a PhD at Cambridge on Wilfrid Scawen Blunt, and Dr Fuad Sha'ban, a Syrian, who has done a lot of work on 19th-century Americans who interested themselves in Islam, one of whom was called George Bush.

I start by quoting what the Lebanese-American writer Amin al-Rihani wrote in 1924, that nobody had a comprehensive view of the Arab world except the British Colonial Office. I then talk about Edward Lane, Richard Burton, Charles Doughty and Marmaduke Pickthall. I touch on orientalism and talk about the relevance of their work and insights. I talk about the situation at present in Britain and the work of British Muslims, teachers of Arabic, journalists and writers. A lively discussion follows.

Wednesday 7 December

I have a visit from Faisal Siddiq to talk about the proposed contract with the Abu Dhabi Air Force. In earlier negotiations I have been puzzled by the deference shown towards Captain Suhail, a man of lower rank. I learn that Suhail is a Dhahiri, one of the leading families of Abu Dhabi, members of which have married into the ruling family. Faisal owns the Swedish Dental Clinic and tells me that Sheikh Shakhbut has recently had his teeth sorted out there. When he calls, he hands out 500-dirham notes to everyone except one black girl, to whom he gives 200 dirhams. Faisal disapproves but understands the old man, brought up at a time when black people were slaves.

Thursday 8 December

We are recruiting a maid, and become aware of the vast army of working-class people who help Abu Dhabi to function, from domestic staff to the Sri Lankan planters of coconut trees for the municipality.

Sunday 11 December

In the last few days I have been translating and polishing my Arabic translation of the talk I gave at the university. One of my colleagues, Munira, has corrected it and suggested improvements in style. I am writing it all out, one paragraph to a page, so I can easily read it. Tomorrow I will be fulfilling a 20-year-old ambition – to give a public lecture in Arabic. It is a challenge. Not only must the content be sound, but the style must be appropriate too. I take care over the vowelling, and have a selection of pretty phrases.

Monday 12 December

I see the Ambassador. He tells me there are apparently some problems about the Prince of Wales flying to Al Ain. It concerns the size of the aeroplane and the length of the runway. 'If we lost the Heir Apparent,' I tell the Ambassador, 'it wouldn't be very good for your career, would it?'

There are about 50 or 60 in the hall for my lecture. All are Arab except some technicians and television cameramen. I am televised when I speak the first few words. I stumble occasionally but all has been prepared, over-prepared, and I provide much food for thought in the next half-hour. There is a discussion and I am more fluent for that. I am drained at the end, and Theresa and I go off afterwards to the Holiday Inn for a meal and two bottles of (bad) wine.

Tuesday 13 December

The local papers report my talk generously, giving prominence to the importance of Arabic studies in Britain. There are also pictures and a longish piece in *Al Ittihad*. It is gratifying and convinces me of the importance of using the Cultural Foundation for our activities; it is where expatriates are the extras. I glow all day.

Carl tells me that his mother has been married six times, his father three. He is the only child of these nine marriages. His mother's third husband was a brother of Alan Paton, the South African writer.

Thursday 15 December

I write up some of my Turkey diaries of 1962 – about 4,000 words. Frank Richards[10] wrote 72 million published words in his life, which I

10 Author of the 'Billy Bunter' books (1876–1961).

calculate to be about 4,000 a day every day over 50 years. Hemingway recommended 1,000 words a day. Trollope used to write 1,000 words an hour. John Braine recommends no more than 350 a day.

Sunday 18 December

I attend a 'prayer meeting' at the Embassy. There is discussion about the forthcoming royal visit. The Prince of Wales is Vice-Patron of the British Council and I tease my Embassy colleagues by referring to him as 'my colleague'. Someone comments on the more relaxed security arrangements for the Princess Royal. 'She's dispensable,' says someone. The Ambassador finds recent remarks she is reported to have said about her dislike of children strange, coming from the Patron of the Save the Children Fund.

'She's like her father and his position with the World Wildlife Fund.'

'At least she doesn't shoot children,' observes the Commercial Attaché.

Thursday 22 December

I go with Eid Bakhit Musallim al-Mazrui to the airport to meet Avi Shivtiel of Leeds University. Eid is a potential external PhD candidate there. He swaggers into the airport in the nicest possible way, straight into the VIP lounge, where tea, coffee, fruit and succulent drinks are available for the Very Important. Avi arrives, and he and I are ushered through immigration and customs, then Eid drives us to his house, pointing things out on the way: how soil has been planted on the salt flats; the automatic sprinklers; how there are no guards outside the Ruler's house.

Saturday 24 December

Eid Bakhit takes Avi and me to Al Ain. As we drive along at 160 km/h he talks more about himself. He is about 40 but is already a grandfather. He is from a large clan in the Liwa oasis. His father died when Eid was about two and his mother married a Qatari. That is where he was brought up, until Sheikh Zayed personally asked him to return to Abu Dhabi.

We call on people at the university. In one meeting, a fly settles on my arm. I am about to swat it with my hand but the academic and Eid both say simultaneously, 'Don't kill it. Let it live.' Such is the tolerance and gentleness of people here.

After calling on people in the university we return to Abu Dhabi. Eid drives at 160–180 km/h, and simultaneously talks on his carphone and makes notes. Avi sees him as hard working and well organised. They chat in Arabic, swapping lines of poetry and discussing strange Arabic words. We branch off to Eid's farm. He has an aviary where 3,000 quails are being bred. The farm also has chickens, goats and a camel with a young foal. Eid hands us some aubergines to take back to the house.

Sunday 25 December

We take Avi and our boys to the beach and set up a barbecue. The place is fairly deserted but a young man drives up to us. He is already half-drunk on gin and Pepsi, but he sits down with us, and has a pork sausage and a glass of wine.

Tuesday 27 December

Avi and I go to the opening of the Federal National Council at the Cultural Foundation. We are greeted as we arrive by the Speaker, Hasan al-Lutfi.

We take our places half an hour before the scheduled start. The place gradually fills up. The 60 members of the Federal National Council sit like prefects. At the front of the stage are grey chairs and one brown. The grey chairs are occupied by the Rulers of the seven sheikhdoms; Dubai is represented by Sheikh Ahmad, brother of Sheikh Rashid, who is chronically indisposed. After ten minutes Sheikh Zayed comes in. He gives a wave and a big grin. He takes his place on the brown chair. Speeches are brief (and repetitive). The Minister of Works reads Sheikh Zayed's speech and Zayed chats to the Ruler of Sharjah and Sheikh Ahmad of Dubai. Sheikh Zayed then opens the Council with a few words.

Friday 30 December

The Embassy has a bungalow at Al Ain that can be rented by Embassy staff, including me. We spend much of the day there. It was once a rural retreat but the town is steadily encroaching on it. The visitors' book is interesting.

One day's entry includes Wilfred Thesiger, Dame Violet Dickson,[11] who used to be Grand English Lady of Kuwait, and Sir Hugh Boustead,[12] who ended up looking after Sheikh Zayed's horses.

Our children join a sponsored climb of Jebel Hafit, the mountain overlooking Al Ain. They end up at the bungalow. Five of the walkers strayed into a picnic hosted by Sheikh Zayed for the Deputy Ruler of Bahrain, the food being provided by the Al Ain Hilton Hotel.

Saturday 31 December

I have now completed half my first year here. Abu Dhabi is proving to be more exhilarating than anticipated.

---

11 Author and environmentalist (1896–1991), wife of H P R Dickson, British colonial official. Her memoirs, *Forty Years in Kuwait*, were published in 1971 (George Allen & Unwin, London).

12 Soldier, mountaineer and British colonial official (1895–1980). His memoirs, *The Wind of Morning*, were also published in 1971 (Chatto and Windus, London).

1989

Thursday 5 January

There is a letter in *The Gulf News* about Dubai taxis overcharging. It is signed 'P Istoff' – someone, I guess, taken for a ride.

I drive to Dubai and get lost around Jumeirah. I come upon a splendid Chinese house on the Iranian Hospital road. It has upturned tiled roofs and storeys tiered like a wedding cake. The oriental effect is spoiled by the fountain in the garden with six-foot-long marble effigies of fish dancing out of the water.

I attend a dinner of the Dubai Businessmen's Group in honour of the Foreign Secretary, Sir Geoffrey Howe. The Second Secretary at the British Embassy seems surprised to see me there. The food is boring and expensive. Sir Geoffrey's speech is not inspiring. It is largely off the cuff and is as much on the economy as on foreign affairs. He talks about the British Council, and Shell's sponsorship of our activities. Good. I meet him briefly afterwards. He has a son – as I have a stepdaughter – at the University of York.

Friday 6 January

I join Theresa, our sons, and about a thousand others at the Jebel Ali Hotel for a 'wadi-bashing' excursion. We set off in convoy onto a desert track. We are among the last of about three hundred vehicles. We get stuck in the sand and have to be dug out. We carry on and get stuck again, as do others. Our wheels are not spinning and there is a smell of burning. It appears we have a burnt-out clutch. There is, fortunately, a vast support staff with us all – marshals, sweeps, breakdown vehicles and even a helicopter. So we feel personally secure. But I am in a world I abominate. Somebody criticises me for the tyre pressure. We had taken someone else's advice on this before we set out. I do not understand these things. Everybody is an instant expert. A breakdown vehicle turns up to try to get us out. A German nearby comments loudly on the driver – 'He couldn't drive out of a paper bag'. I am mortified by the whole business. I hate putting myself in a position when I can rapidly be totally out of control. The hassles and aggravation, the tension and worry far outweigh any pleasure that may be derived from a trip into the desert. We abandon the vehicle and are given a lift in a pick-up truck back to the Jebel Ali Hotel. The boys are unaware of any crisis. At the bar they will not serve me because I am wearing shorts. They will not serve children. Anyway, they do not have any cider.

We find a quiet spot in the grounds of the hotel. I am depressed by the whole business. I prefer a cycle ride in France or a walk in the hills to 'wadi-bashing'. I console myself with reading some Taha Husain.

Saturday 7 January

I start doing some of the administration for recovering the car from the desert. It will all be possible but I have to get the clutch repaired – in a new car which we have not paid off yet.

In the evening I go to an exhibition at the Cultural Foundation about Mameluke Jerusalem. Muhammad al-Suwaidi and the Under-Secretary in charge of the foundation are there and we greet the sixth son of Sheikh Zayed, Sheikh Saeed, a graduate of the university and formerly one of our students of English. The Ambassador turns up and we are ushered to a room with the sheikh, AK-47-toting guards hovering in the background. I chat to Sheikh Saeed in Arabic about the exhibition as we sip coffee.

Sunday 8 January

We are up at 5.30 am and are soon on the road in a rented car. There is a particular pleasure in setting off before dawn, watching the sky become lighter and then seeing the great orb of the sun bursting over the horizon, illustrating the idea of the root of the word in Arabic, 'dawn' being also the root for the word for 'explosion'.

We drive on to Ras Al Khaimah, to the fort, and meet Mr Laxman, the Indian who is Director of Antiquities for that emirate. We also meet Geoffrey King, in charge of the archaeological dig at Julfar. Geoffrey is in his late thirties, a protégé of George Scanlon,[13] and taught in Saudi Arabia for seven years. He takes us to the site.

Julfar was a port and important city from the early days of Islam until about 1630, when it was washed away. It was the major city of the emirates in the classical age of Islam. Geoffrey King and Beatrice de

---

13 American archaeologist, for many years at the American University in Cairo; authority on Mameluke Cairo.

Cardi[14] have gathered together some finds for this year. But to do the job properly next season they need £25,000.

The extensive site today is a series of tells and mounds. Japanese, French and German teams have worked here. Some trenches have been left open. Strings mark sites of buildings, one of which has been identified as a mosque. You can pick up bits of pottery that came from China. We spend an hour on the site before returning to the fort to inspect the museum. In front is a cannon with 'GR' on it. It was one of the guns that pulverised the fort's predecessor in 1819.

We go on to Sharjah airport to meet the pianist John Clegg. The airport has a distinctive but slightly run-down architecture. It specialises in flights to countries with 'radical' regimes like Iran and Ethiopia.

Monday 9 January

I have a phone call from Stephen Day, who was my Ambassador in Tunis. He wrote a report for the Prince of Wales about objectives for the latter's tours. Stephen is still seen as his adviser on matters Arabian. The Prince dislikes a tour that is purely ceremonial. He wishes, five years after a tour, to be able to look back and say that such-and-such has been a consequence of that tour. He is deeply committed to the work of the British Council. Stephen is due to have lunch with the Prince next month.

Saturday 14 January

I am up soon after 4.00 am and drive before dawn to Dubai. There is a constant stream of traffic heading for Abu Dhabi – the weekly commuters from Dubai and Sharjah swarming to the federal capital for the week's work. It is tiring to drive into so many undipped lights.

I attend a conference on the teaching of English. The Acting Minister of Education speaks, and so do I. I speak in Arabic, having composed it in my head on the way. I say in Arabic that our objective is to encourage the English language, and then switch to English. (Appreciative laughter.)

14 British archaeologist (1914–2016).

Sunday 15 January

The British Council UAE failed to win the contract to take over all the English-language teaching for the Abu Dhabi Air Force, worth more than £1m; it would have been the largest British Council English-language teaching contract anywhere. One British company, who had also made a bid, complained to the British Council in London about Peter, saying they had an unfair advantage over the private sector. His headquarters passed on the complaint to Peter.

I write back to my masters in London about their questioning my bidding for the Air Force contract. We are urged to be competitive, but with whom do we compete if not with our competitors?

At 8.00 pm, Theresa and I go to the Marine Club for the monthly quiz evening. We join a team and win easily, the prize being a bottle of champagne and some unpopularity.

Monday 16 January

I attend the British businessmen's meeting. The Ambassador talks about the succession after Sheikh Zayed passes away.[15] Sheikh Khalifa is most likely to succeed and there is unlikely to be any challenge from his 18 brothers. Sheikh Muhammad is the eldest of five brothers from the same mother and is likely to keep them all loyal.

Tuesday 17 January

I call on Easa Salih al-Gurg, a businessman in Dubai. He tells me his life story. He is 61 and used to work for the British Bank of the Middle East. In about 1957 he was sent on a scholarship to London organised by the British Council, to which he has been grateful ever since. He stayed in digs in Tooting and, following guidance in a booklet for overseas students produced by the British Council, tried to help his landlady with the washing up. But he kept breaking things and was dissuaded from helping her. Today he sees her when he goes to London and gives her financial advice. His family is Sunni Arab, originally from Linga, on the Gulf coast of Iran. When the Tehran government strengthened its control – or, as Easa puts it, 'the Persians invaded' – his family were dispersed. Some went

15 He lived another 15 years.

to Bombay, some to Dubai. He has married twice; his second wife, who was his first love, was brought up in Bombay. He acted as interpreter for Sheikh Rashid of Dubai when he went to London and met the Queen and the then prime minister, Harold Macmillan. After that his business interests took over. He also met Abdul Nasser with Sheikh Rashid and seems to be one of the last of the Nasserites.[16]

Wednesday 18 January

The Director of Studies, Carl, tells me of problems with the British Council teachers. One is fed up with teaching and with Abu Dhabi, and wants to go to his mother in Australia. Another is involved with the local Lebanese gay community.

Friday 20 January

We are invited to join some ambassadors on a dhow trip from the InterContinental Hotel to one of the islands in the Gulf. We have a picnic and spend several hours on the uninhabited island. The Soviet Ambassador has a range of interests, including literature. 'Without Gogol,' he observes, 'there would have been no Proust, no early Graham Greene.' The wife of the Japanese Ambassador is a cultural anthropologist who has written books on the tribes of Saudi Arabia.

We sit around in the sun, chatting and drinking lots of wine. Our boys amuse themselves building sandcastles and smashing them down. A high-speed launch is at our disposal to take us back to the hotel if we want to dash back to go to the loo.

Saturday 21 January

I hear indirectly that the Prince of Wales finds the programme prepared for him by the Embassy is 'one of stunning boredom'. He likes to meet people.

Sunday 22 January

I suspect I am not the Embassy's favourite person in my agitation to

---

16 Easa Salih al-Gurg KCVO CBE served as UAE Ambassador in London between 1991 and 2009.

get the Prince of Wales involved with the British Council. But I see the Ambassador and ask, 'Why is the Prince going to go to the university?' There is no clear answer: it is just to fill in time. I am shown a draft programme and add to my unpopularity by pointing out some mistakes. I must keep the Ambassador on my side. He invites me to write notes on what the British Council wants out of the visit.

Monday 23 January

I call on Said Salman at the Documentation Centre. He is an expert on camels. In 1970, he arrived in Abu Dhabi having travelled from southern Jordan by camel. His father is a Bedu from Beersheba, his maternal grandfather Auda Abu Tayyi, the Howeitat tribal leader who featured in T E Lawrence's *Seven Pillars of Wisdom.*

I drive to Dubai and have dinner with Jolyon and Shirley Kay. The principal guests are Sir John Riddell and Dickie Arbiter, two courtiers on a recce for the Prince of Wales's visit. Sir John is the Prince's secretary and Dickie his press officer. I make the points I want to Sir John (who had a cousin in the British Council). Dick used to be with Radio Rhodesia for 14 years.

The British Council building in Dubai was put up in 1971 and, more or less, counts as an ancient monument. We need new premises, and I suspect the present building may have been constructed on the cheap, is unsafe and ought to be pulled down.

Wednesday 25 January

I am hoping to get BP to sponsor a classroom at Al Ain. I talk to the BP representative here and argue that we have overlapping interests: we are investing in influence.

Thursday 26 January

We have dinner with the family of the artist Reem Metwalli. Her father was once Iraqi Foreign Minister and there are several Iraqis present, including Qais al-Askari. His father was Ja'far al-Askari, his uncle Nuri es-Said. Both these men dominated Iraqi politics from the end of the First World War until the fall of the monarchy in 1958.[17] Qais studied at Victoria College, Alexandria; Dartmouth Naval Academy; and King's College, Cambridge. He has a fine aristocratic moustache and is charming with a command of slightly archaic gentlemanly slang. Another guest is the Tunisian calligrapher Nja Mahdaoui, who greets me with a kiss and a bear hug.

Friday 27 January

Theresa and I go to the Corniche Hospital to call on Marie-Reine, my Lebanese PA, who has just had a baby, Christina. The maternity ward is full of lavish bouquets. I dislike this auction of consumerism and am happy to offer a bowl of tabbouleh that I have made myself, a card and a small doll. The baby is big and has lots of dark hair. Her father, Nasrallah, coos joyfully to his daughter.

Saturday 28 January

I read more of Muhammad al-Murr's stories.

In the evening I go to the Cultural Foundation for an exhibition of paintings. Nja Mahdoui is there, as is Reem, in her finery; she has some of her own paintings exhibited. Some are of female nudes but they are hardly identifiable as such. I talk to a bearded artist who has done a picture of a camel with its head concealed.

'Why?' I ask the artist.

'The depiction of heads and faces is forbidden in our religion,' he says.

Even so, the painting, within the restraints he has set himself, is great.

Wednesday 1 February

I do not sleep well, and have all sorts of grim fantasies – suicide, becoming an outcast, dropping out of the middle class with no return, saddled with debts. It is all horrible.

---

17 Both Ja'far al-Askari and Nuri es-Said were frequently Prime Ministers of Iraq between 1921 and 1958.

Thursday 2 February
I translate one of Muhammad al-Murr's stories, about a young Emirates man whose ambition is to be a cook and open a restaurant. I read it to Theresa, who likes it. She observes that Muhammad may not wish to have his work translated. In Arabic, it is Emirates people talking to Emirates people. Translating his stories is like eavesdropping on private conversations. I will talk to Muhammad about it.

Sunday 5 February
I have a meeting with the Ambassador and his deputy about the royal visit. They do not have much idea about what to do with the Prince of Wales's visit to the university. As I am the only one with clear ideas, my ideas prevail. Sixteen students from the Faculty of Engineering went to Britain last year. What about him meeting them?

Monday 6 February
Outside the Oasis Cinema in Al Ain are some film posters advertising forthcoming films. Titles include *Carry On Behind,* with a picture of a girl's overexposed bottom, blacked out, adding to the titillation; *Group Marriage; Gift from the Red Cabaret,* with a tall seductive-looking girl; *The World is Full of Married Men;* and *Anita,* with a picture of two scantily dressed girls, looking as if they are about to make love. It is as near a public display of pornography as is possible in the country.

I have a visit from Muhammad al-Murr. I ask if I may translate some of his work. He has no objection. He tells me about Jack Briggs, who was for 20 years or so the security adviser to Sheikh Rashid. He is an old colonial policeman who learned Arabic in Palestine before 1948 and in Doha, which he loved. He is a working-class or lower-middle class man without broad culture – says Muhammad without a hint of patronage or snobbery – and retired to England. There nobody knew him and he felt miserable. But he did do a BA in Arabic at the School of Oriental and African Studies. In one class students 40 years his junior scorned him because he had not heard of Nietzsche, but he wrote far better Arabic essays than they did. He now wishes to do an MA on the short story in the Gulf.

Tuesday 7 February
I take Jim, an archaeological consultant, to Ras Al Khaimah. We meet Jay Laxman at the museum, which is impressively organised. The building was the Ruler's residence until 1964, after which it was a prison for 20 years. Jay was employed to clear it up for the museum. He is from Kerala and has been in Ras Al Khaimah for 15 years, doing odd jobs for the Ruler, Sheikh Saqr. He takes us to the Shimal site, where some German archaeologist shows us the sites of second millennium BC graves with artefacts from the Indus Valley.

Thursday 9 February
I go with the Embassy Number Two to Al Ain. We call on the Secretary-General of the university, Shabib Marzuqi, who prefers not to use his English. So Number Two has to struggle with his Arabic, which is atrocious. He uses English words when he is stumped for a word in Arabic, words that he should know like 'faculty', 'engineering' and so on. I sit by and occasionally explain things in better Arabic. But Shabib is polite and undemanding. The purpose of our call is to check over the Prince of Wales's visit to the university in five weeks' time. The Prince and Princess will meet the 16 engineering students who went on attachments to Britain. All is agreed and Number Two almost seems to think that this was his idea.

There are new film posters up outside the Oasis Cinema. One is for *Gimme an F*, another for *Sin*.

Sunday 12 February
News comes through of the death of Sheikh Shakhbut, the elder brother of Sheikh Zayed. He was Ruler of Abu Dhabi from the 1920s to 1966. I feel a sense of loss. I never met him, but would very much like to have done so. David Heard always spoke reverentially of him. Others have spoken of him with affection. There are to be three days' mourning.

Monday 13 February
I attend a meeting at the Embassy to decide on who from the British community can be invited to meet the Prince and Princess of Wales

next month. There is a community of 6,000 in Abu Dhabi but only 300 can be invited. That means one in 20. There is a discussion of people's merits. All the administrative and clerical staff at the Embassy are on the list – but not their equivalents at the British Council. I protest, and also recommend three long-serving teachers of English.

Tuesday 14 February

I go to the Gulf Training and Education Exhibition at Dubai. It swarms with people, including a junior Foreign Office Minister, David Mellor – young, energetic and relaxed. He dashes around the stalls and is photographed at many. 'These photographs will go back to boardrooms as evidence to justify my trip to Dubai,' explains one stall-holder.

I talk to an academic from the University of Kent at Canterbury, who tells me of Leofric, a classicist polyglot who wrote a book on Aelius Gallus, a Roman explorer of Arabia. In his Oxford finals he was instructed to translate some Homer. He did, into Serbo-Croat. Since then the examiners have specified that translations should be into English.

Wednesday 15 February

I am arranging for some musicians to perform at the Al Ain Hotel, a very friendly place in contrast to the big hotels. It is the oldest in Abu Dhabi – 22 years old – and I suggest they should trade on this. I learn later that it belongs to Sheikh Nahyan; that makes me warm to it even more.

Friday 17 February

Some telexes come in about a new book by Salman Rushdie, *The Satanic Verses*. It has been condemned in the eastern Muslim world and Ayatollah Khomeini has sentenced the author to death. It is all horrible.

Saturday 18 February

I call on the Dean of the Faculty of Engineering, Awad Sultan al-Hakim, to discuss the students meeting the Prince and Princess of Wales next month. I get the names of ten who went to Scotland and am ready to see if there are British firms who can take on ten more.

I also call on the Al Ain Women's Higher College of Technology. They started in October with 63 students, and now have 42. There are heaps of cultural obstacles to their function. The national policy is to train nationals to do jobs being held by foreigners. National policy is also to promote gender equality of employment opportunity. But the difficulty is with nationals' reluctance to accept the discipline of work and regular hours, and resistance against women doing work that is normally done by hired foreigners. The Princess of Wales is due to visit the college. Will she understand these subtleties?

Monday 20 February

I go to the Air Force, see the colonel in charge and arrange for cadets to see *Romeo and Juliet*, which the London Shakespeare Group are performing shortly. I am surprised how easy it is to work in this country. The colonel agrees at once. The Emirates is a new and innovative society, and ideas and new routines are rapidly absorbed.

I seem to be achieving things here. I am still making mistakes out of exhaustion, but I do not mind busting my gut for five days and collapsing for two.

Tuesday 21 February

Sheikha Fatima, the (principal) wife of Sheikh Zayed, has given approval to the Women's Association in Al Ain taking English classes at the British Council.

Wednesday 22 February

I spend half an hour with the students of engineering, talking to them about the royal visit and matters of protocol. They understand, as much of it applies to the ruling family here. One student is able very convincingly to put on a broad Glasgow accent.

Friday 24 February

We go for a walk along the Corniche. A national is pushing a pram with a baby, his fully veiled wife following behind. We go on to the Dhow Restaurant and as we linger there we see what looks like a frogman in blue tights and an enormous jockstrap emerging from the waters of the Gulf. It is the Ambassador. He has been, not very successfully, surfing. He has fallen over two or three times and is feeling a bit sorry for himself. He was ill last week and has thrown himself into this daft activity. I commiserate and we talk about less strenuous physical activities, such as cycling in France (which Paul and I did last year) and youth hostelling in Scotland (which we plan to do this summer).

Wednesday 1 March

We have a visitor from the Central Management for Direct Teaching from the British Council in London. I show him the new premises we have acquired in Al Ain. They are clean and bright. He is duly impressed, especially as I show him the location of the former premises. (*Wedding Night* is advertised at the Oasis Cinema next door.) The plaque for the Prince of Wales is ready for him to unveil. We have the Shell room, with the Shell logo and some Shell information packs. The Shell representative, Mike Hall, takes us to lunch with Julian Paxton, a big Shell man from London. His father taught English in Egypt for many years and translated a book by Taha Husain. Julian has bought my book on Marmaduke Pickthall. They are full of bright ideas. What about bringing out a music group during Ramadan to play at the Al Ain centre in the middle of the night? What about getting Harrods to sponsor a room that will be reserved for women's classes?

Saturday 4 March

We have Linda and Chris Simpson with us. They have become good friends. Chris is the leader of the Yorkshire-based folk-rock group Magna Carta. We are all invited for a day out on a boat belonging to friends of Chris called Elaine and Chris. Their vessel is a former lifeboat and is registered in Panama. It is very compact. Their children and the nanny sleep below at one end, the grown-ups at the other. The cabin above serves as living room, piloting cabin and kitchen. There is really no space for rubbish. Or for guests. But we join other boats and go to a deserted island near Umm Al Nar, where we spend several hours.

The company is new to us – 'hard men' and their wives. They do not mix with 'Arabs' or 'locals'. It is enjoyable to spend a day in their company. They are spontaneous and enjoy life.

The boat has a fishing line attached, and as we enter the long stretch returning to Abu Dhabi, there is a tug on the line and we land a barracuda, three feet long, baring fierce teeth. Our son, Nat, demands/screams to see it as it is battered to death, its blood dropping all over the deck.

In the evening Theresa and I go to dinner at the flat of the Japanese Ambassador. This is on the 19th floor of a block overlooking the Gulf. A Japanese diplomat who has been in Tehran tells us that Ayatollah Khomeini has been given a new lease of life with the Rushdie affair.

Sunday 5 March

At the Embassy prayer meeting we learn of a proposed State Visit to Britain by Sheikh Zayed in the summer. There are problems. He likes to spend the Eid in Abu Dhabi, to be greeted by all his family. But he has to arrive in London by 11.30 am, and this means catching a plane from here at 7.30. Nobody is empowered to wake him up at six, to get him dressed and packed and onto the plane in time.

The London Shakespeare Group has arrived in Dubai. Carl meets them and tells me they are very tense. They explode into a rage at each other every now and then. Oscar Quitak tries to help with the electrical installations at the theatre and is told, 'Piss off, Oscar, leave the fucking wires alone'. The leader, Delena, seems a nervous wreck. One actor is not talking to anyone else. Romeo and Juliet are sharing a room, and in the morning Juliet/Rachel comes down and announces that Romeo is not feeling very well. This is greeted with groans of irritation and disbelief – 'Christ, No!' Another actor is walking through the lobby after breakfast, and suddenly stops and shouts, 'Fuck!' He has left his room key on his breakfast table.

Monday 6 March

Standard Chartered Bank wants to give us £3,000 to sponsor classrooms in each of our three teaching centres – Dubai, Abu Dhabi and Al Ain.

Tuesday 7 March

The technician with the London Shakespeare Group has been to the Cultural Foundation, where we are planning for them to put on

Romeo and Juliet. He saw the facilities for lighting and so on. His first reaction was, 'Shit!'

The company all come to lunch, and are much nicer than reported. Delena Kidd is small and hyperactive. I have a long talk with her about target audiences. They played to two full houses in Dubai.

They perform at the Cultural Foundation in the evening. Superb. The Air Force cadets come in half an hour late, 110 of them, all in uniform, filing in. The audience is enthusiastic and appreciative. There are about 1,200 present.

Wednesday 8 March

We have a meeting at the Embassy about the programme of the Prince and Princess of Wales. She will be leaving before the Prince, on a commercial flight from Dubai, under the name of Mrs Wharfe. There will be a small dinner party for the Prince. I am to be one of the guests, with Number Two and the Defence Attaché. I feel enormously privileged. I wonder whether one should stand on his right or on his left.

'I don't think it matters,' says the Ambassador. 'Do not be too obsequious, though I do not think that is in your nature.'

The Shakespeare Group plays at the InterContinental Hotel, to a largely expatriate audience – the international bourgeoisie, as I call them. I see Zaki Nusseibeh there and buy him a drink.

'You were at Rugby, weren't you?' I say.

'Yes.'

'You must have been a contemporary of a celebrated novelist?'

'Yes, and also at Cambridge.'

Some boring woman butts in and monopolises him for a while.

'We were talking of Salman Rushdie,' he resumes. 'I have read *The Satanic Verses*. It is offensive to Muslims, but in no way as offensive as Ayatollah Khomeini's statements.' Very interesting. He would not say that if it did not reflect official thinking.

Saturday 11 March

I come into the office early and keep thinking of extra touches for the opening of the Al Ain office by the Prince of Wales: soft drinks for people as they wait; plastic bags to clear things away in; access to loos; a UAE flag to fly alongside the Union Jack.

At 10.00 am, I go to the Embassy to rehearse the reception for the royal couple at the Ambassador's Residence. The Prince and Princess will meet all the Embassy staff in ten minutes, and then (in the sitting room) the British Council staff. For us five minutes are allotted. Then they will go to the terrace for the file-past of the British community. I calculate that each person will have between six and seven seconds with them. The Defence Attaché enters into the whole business with enthusiasm as if it is a Salisbury Plain manoeuvre. I ask awkward questions like, 'What if it rains?'

Sunday 12 March

I drive to Al Ain and go to the new centre. For two hours I go through every detail of the Prince's visit. There will be no need for flowers in the garden – 100 people ought to provide enough colour. There will be a security sweep on Tuesday morning, and I receive a call from four police officers. On the day of the visit there will be ten policemen on duty on the premises. With Sue and Gary, who are to be in charge of the Al Ain Centre, I go through everything: drinks, glasses (we veto mugs), where we will stand, the placing of furniture.

Monday 13 March

At a meeting at the Embassy we hear that a security committee in London has advised against the Prince and Princess coming to the Emirates. There is discussion on this. Number Two was in Lebanon in 1982 when the Princess Royal visited Beirut. The decision on her going there during the civil war went right up to the Queen. 'The Royal Family takes risks,' she said, overriding the faint hearts of ministers.

Theresa will get an invitation to dinner with Sheikha Fatima and the Princess of Wales. For this she will have to get a long dress.

Tuesday 14 March

I go to Dubai and rehearse the expected visit of the Prince of Wales to the office there. Then lunch with Shirley and Jolyon Kay. The guest of honour is the archaeologist Beatrice de Cardi, whom I first met in

Jordan in 1970 when I took her to Petra. We discuss sources of funding to support archaeology in the Emirates.

I return to Abu Dhabi, and go to the Residence to join a convoy of vehicles to the Palace of Sheikh Khalifa bin Zayed, son and heir of the Ruler. We pass lots of armed policemen and are ushered into a room where 60 ambassadors are seated around a majlis. After a while we are escorted to a banqueting hall. Some of the sheikhs come in. Then Sheikh Khalifa bin Zayed, looking frail, comes in with the Prince of Wales. It is an all-male function. The first thing I notice about the Prince is his bald patch. He looks like a paleface who has caught the sun. There is no applause, no speeches. I am seated between the Dutch and Italian ambassadors. Afterwards we file out, to shake hands with a stony-faced Sheikh Khalifa and a nonchalant Prince of Wales.

Wednesday 15 March

We get to Al Ain in good time and have three hours to wait around. I check again on everything and read a few pages of H W C Davis's *England under the Normans and Angevins*, on the reign of King Henry III. I am in regular contact with the chief of the Al Ain police, Ali Mubarak, who is monitoring the movements of the Prince of Wales.

The Prince is being delayed at the camel races.

He is on his way and we hear the sound of escorting police cars. There is an exquisite tension. I have planned the 30 minutes he is to be with us in as much detail as possible; aesthetics, practicalities, security, public relations, fairness of access. The courtyard of the British Council centre is crowded, as is the street outside the compound – nationals and British. There is nothing more I can do. The visit takes over.

But right at the beginning there is an unplanned dilemma. His car drives into the compound and I am on the wrong side to greet him. I have to shuffle round quickly to his side of the car, to greet the Prince with 'Good morning, Your Royal Highness. I'm Peter Clark.' We walk slowly through the garden and the Prince talks to some of the children who have gathered. Then into the building and I invite him to unveil the plaque. Gentle applause and the flashing of cameras.

'If you had been unable to come, Sir, we would have put a "not" between "was" and "opened".'

'I wonder how many plaques there are like that around the world,' he says with a laugh.

I take him into the Shell room and tell him of our policy of getting businesses to sponsor rooms. I suddenly see Sheikh Nahyan and the Ambassador in the background, and tell Sheikh Nahyan that I would like him to visit us and see what we are doing. The sheikh says he would like to see us involved more in the university.

I take the Prince into the room where colleagues are gathered to meet him. He is very good at asking interesting questions and listening to the answers. We go back into the garden and the Prince talks to others. Our son, Natty, presents him with a posy. The Prince passes it on to an equerry, who gives it to someone else, who gives it back to us. The Prince is then manoeuvred into his car, which flies his standard, and – whoosh! – he is off. We have a sense of happy anticlimax. Nothing went wrong.

We return to Abu Dhabi after a snack, and then to the Residence for the reception. Embassy and British Council staff are in the living room when the Prince and Princess of Wales arrive. We file past. She seems to be an inch taller than him. She has a three-second handshake and looks through me, moving me along so she can deal with the next person. We are a conveyor-belt.

I slip away to change into dinner jacket, bow-tie and cummerbund, and then back to the Residence for dinner. The first to arrive is David Douglas-Home, chairman of the Committee for Middle East Trade (COMET). He looks like his father, the former Prime Minister, like a fly-catcher with a mobile neck. I tell him about my classroom sponsorship idea and he undertakes to talk to Muhammad Al-Fayed to see if we can get a Harrods sponsorship. The Prince of Wales arrives, and then the principal UAE guest, Sheikh Khalifa bin Zayed, with Zaki Nusseibeh as his interpreter. Sheikh Khalifa is taciturn and looks like a hooded owl. I talk to the bespectacled Sheikh Muhammad bin Zayed, who is head of the Air Force and interested in paintings. Sheikh Nahyan is a bubbly man, the youngest of the UAE guests, totally at home. His uncle, Sheikh Surur bin Muhammad, is there, alert and full of controlled energy.

I talk with the Prince, Sheikh Muhammad and the Defence

Attaché. The Prince, a gentle man, disliked the rigours of Dartmouth and hated doing bombing exercises over Wales. 'I felt I was about to vomit into my oxygen mask.'

At dinner I am seated next to Ahmad al-Khalifa al-Suwaidi – a delightful man. I talk with him mostly in Arabic, about Tunisia and Yemen and the Cultural Foundation.[18] David Douglas-Home is asked about his father, who is fit, 85 and 'spends all his time fishing'.

After dinner, Number Two brings in a case. It is a hunting rifle, a gift from our Heir Apparent to the UAE's Heir Apparent. We have a group photograph and the Prince and sheikhs depart.

'Hope all goes well,' are his last words.

The rest of us feel a sense of relief, especially Number Two, whose duties are now over.

The Ambassador says with modesty and dignity, 'None of us will be at such a dinner again in our lifetime'. He then suddenly realises he forgot to get the Prince to sign the Embassy's visitors' book.

I shall be seeing the Prince again on Friday, but I am impressed by his professional interest in people and his approachability.

Kenny Ball is playing at the InterContinental Hotel. The Defence Attaché proposes and the Ambassador seconds the idea that we all go off to hear him. Which we all do. I stay for half an hour and drink a glass of champagne.

Thursday 16 March

I hear that some children regularly stationed themselves outside the door of the hotel – a special entrance bypassing the central lobby – used by the Prince of Wales.

'What school do you go to?' the Prince asked them.

'You asked us that yesterday,' replied one of the children.

'But you've changed your clothes since then.'

I phone my sister, Stella, who tells me our mother is not well. She is in a retirement home and has had cancer – she is 91 in a few months – but can still quip. She has to take tablets each day.

'Are these to prevent me from having a baby?' she says.

---

18 Ahmad's son, Muhammad, was Secretary-General of the Cultural Foundation.

She can also run upstairs and is always first at the dinner table. I hope to go to England and see her next month.

Friday 17 March

The Prince of Wales is due to see the British Council office in Dubai today.

I go to Dubai early, getting to the office by nine. Within half an hour heavy security arrangements become all too apparent. Armed police are on all the neighbouring rooftops. The roads by the British Council are closed and totally cleared of traffic, and even of pedestrians. All who enter the British Council building are carefully searched, their invitation cards checked against their identity documents.

There was going to be a polo match. That has been cancelled and journalists have come to the British Council instead.

One of the first to arrive is Easa Salih al-Gurg. I tell the journalists the story of Easa and the Tooting landlady, and Easa holds his own personal press conference.

The Prince of Wales arrives and stays for 40 minutes. He apologises for being late – he was looking at wind tunnels – and introduces me to Sheikh Buti bin Maktoum, who was at Cambridge at the same time as him. Allen, who is in charge of the Dubai operation, and I take the Prince to the exhibition illustrating our work. We give him a seven-minute briefing about what we do – finance, culture and sponsorship. He then meets the teachers and the local staff. He puts them at their ease and asks questions. He asks the Pakistanis if they had voted for Benazir Bhutto. I escort him to his car and a British lady journalist calls out, 'Are you disappointed at missing the polo, Sir?'

'Yes, of course I am,' he shouts back.

Saturday 18 March

The Ambassador gives a press conference about the royal visit: the British Council was placed second in the order of achieved objectives, before high-level contact-making, and ahead of defence and commerce.

I have a letter from Robyn Davidson, whom I invited to come and talk about camels. She is lying low. For three years she was living with Salman Rushdie, including during the period he was writing *The Satanic*

Verses. The media have not picked up on this, but she is somewhat fearful.

Sunday 19 March

I attend a self-congratulatory prayer meeting at the Embassy and show the Ambassador the letter from Robyn Davidson.

I calculate that since I arrived we have raised £22,000 in commercial sponsorship. We could, I reckon, double that.

Monday 20 March

I attend a meeting of the British Businessmen's Group. The Ambassador speaks of the success of the Prince's visit. 'He was intelligent, well-briefed, easy to deal with and treated everyone well. We had a photograph taken of the dinner party with the Prince, Sheikh Khalifa and others, looking like an Oxbridge dining club. I was inordinately proud of that picture – with Sheikh Muhammad bin Zayed kneeling on the floor.'

Monday 27 March

I have a phone call – 'This is Jack Butterworth'. I have been advised that he may turn up. He is Lord Butterworth, the former Vice-Chancellor of Warwick University. I go and see him at once. He has been called to Abu Dhabi by Sheikh Nahyan to advise on the appointment of a new Vice-Chancellor for the United Arab Emirates University. We discuss the kind of person he should be. He should be an Arab and a Muslim, with a reputation as a scholar and as an administrator. He should preferably be a scientist. He should not be seen as part of one of the existing mafias: that might exclude Egyptians, Sudanese, Jordanians, Palestinians and Iraqis. He could be from North Africa. We get on well together. He is 71, stocky and fit. He obviously enjoys influence and the House of Lords. I take him to see the Ambassador. Their paths crossed over 30 years ago at New College, Oxford, when the Ambassador was an undergraduate and Butterworth was Bursar.

Wednesday 29 March

We go to the Queen's Birthday Party at the Ambassador's Residence. He gives a speech to the people attending the party, thanking everyone for their support over the royal visit, and is about to propose the loyal toast. He is floundering about in search of his glass, any glass, and I hand him mine.

Friday 31 March

I go to the local supermarket. It is Friday, the end of the month and shortly before Ramadan: three factors that make the place crowded and chaotic. I tell people off for jumping the queue, and quote from the Holy Koran (in Arabic), 'Allah is with the patient, if they show patience'. They cannot but agree with this, and get into line. One woman is buying 60 packets of Opal Fruits.

'That'll ruin your teeth', I tell her.

'They're not for me, they are for my pupils; I'm a schoolteacher.'

Tuesday 4 April

Katie has been with us. We have celebrated her 21st birthday, and Theresa has taken her to Fujairah.

Samih Qabbani invites them to the Flying Club. There they meet Sheikh Salih, brother of the Ruler of Fujairah. He takes Theresa and Katie in his four-seater plane and they fly over the ships waiting to enter the Gulf. The sheikh loves flying. He has a jet, another plane at Coventry and a farm near Lewes. He is charming and great fun.

We go to a party given by the British manager of a stationery shop. It is full of precious people, including two sewerage engineers who have the reputation of being very funny, a nice Keele graduate and her bumptious husband. There are aspects of Abu Dhabi I do not enjoy.

Wednesday 5 April

I take Karen to the university, where she sets up shop as 'Education Adviser'. She is very conscientious, able and pleasantly relaxed about it all.

A Tunisian academic takes me off to his flat for a lovely Tunisian meal. They tell me of fundamentalists at the university. They represent a mild version, simply a pressure group with access to Sheikh Zayed. They recently complained to him about a new law lowering the 'pension', the student grant. Reduced income meant postponed marriages and a threat to virtue. It therefore encouraged prostitution! I am told of the arguments of Abdul Fattah Muru, one of the Tunisian Islamist leaders, about Ayatollah Khomeini and Salman Rushdie. Khomeini was acting against the tenets of Islam in presuming on the will of God. If God wishes to punish Rushdie, he has his own ways of doing it. It does not require incitement to murder.

We go on to a party hosted by Mike Hall of Shell. I talk French to a banker and English to everyone else. There are no non-Europeans present.

Thursday 6 April

I am reading Wilfred Thesiger's *Arabian Sands*. It is beautifully written and tells more about the Arabs of the desert than about Thesiger.

Sunday 9 April

One of my female locally engaged colleagues has had an offensive phone call from an old man and a boy, who called her a whore. I ask what was the word in Arabic that was used and she is too embarrassed to tell me. I phone the man and he starts shouting at me, calling me a *qawwad*, a pimp. I put the phone down and reassure my colleague that she is not being picked on. He is abusive to everyone.

The Defence Attaché drops in and unwinds. He tells me I have had a great impact: 'a streetwise academic', he calls me. That is as nice as being 'the Representative that reaches the parts that other Reps cannot reach'. He can't stand Number Two, but we both appreciate the Ambassador.

Theresa takes me to the airport to catch the plane to London. I get on the plane at midnight and settle into an uncomfortable seat between two schoolboys for the eight-hour flight. I see nothing, but read more *Arabian Sands*.

Monday 10 April

I arrive at Heathrow at dawn, and go into central London and check into the Travellers Club. I walk up to the YHA shop to buy some maps for our summer holiday. Then I browse among bookshops, and in Hatchard's Piccadilly see Wilfred Thesiger. I have written to him suggesting lunch but he has not received my letter; we arrange to have dinner.

I meet him at the Travellers. He is tall and looks a little frail – he was

79 in June. Indeed, he gets muddled and a little confused but I spend a tremendous three hours with him; he talks about all sorts of things – the Emirates, Sudan, Yemen. He tells me of women who pursue him through letters, including one recent persistent lady from Devon. He drinks tomato juice and Perrier water with his dinner. He is touchingly vain, and enjoys praise of his books, especially when I can quote from them.

'The success of my books,' he says, 'allows me to travel club class.'

He wants to help his old Darfur friend, Idris Daud, with funding for a cataract operation, if needed. I listen to him talk. He once met Wendell Phillips, the American millionaire and Yemen archaeologist, who invited him to lunch at the Dorchester Hotel. Wilfred felt irritated at his style. Phillips only drank mineral water and ate toasted cheese. Wilfred ordered the most expensive dishes and the most expensive wine. I ask him about Ethiopia.

'I will only return to Abyssinia,' he says, 'in order to witness the public hanging of Mengistu.'

I ask him to sign my copy of his book of photographs.[19] He has, he tells me, 65 volumes of photographs and a file of correspondence that he calls 'mad letters'.

I see him into a taxi and feel quite elated at the experience of meeting and getting to know a great man.

Peter spent ten more days in Britain, calling several times on his mother, seeing Paul, and having a few days to himself, staying at youth hostels in Sussex, walking the Downs and visiting remote country churches.

Monday 17 April

It is again a wonderful day's walking. It is not as wet as yesterday, though rain threatens and there is a bit of a headwind. The cliffs of the grounds of Arundel Castle are off to the left, the meadows of a bird sanctuary to the right. Then onto a footpath by thick woods and onto marshy ground – ah, the English squelch as you tread onto soaking land. Squirrels race up trees and I see, with excitement, bluebells and primroses.

---

19 Wilfred Thesiger, *Visions of a Nomad* (Collins, London, 1987).

I walk up onto the Downs. I plod along with the utmost tenacity. It is a hard slog going up, and the views to the south I am sure should be lovely but for the mist. There are folds in the Downs and occasionally superb extensive views. I drown my eyes in the sight, storing it all as a contrast to the aridity of the Gulf. On and down to the main road, with its pollution of speed and sound.

Back in Abu Dhabi.

Thursday 27 April

During the evening Theresa and I go to the opening of a new branch of British Home Stores in Khalidiyah. In a shop full of overpriced ladies' underwear, ambassadors and senior businessmen talk of this and that. A maternity-wear section called Pre-maman is opened by the Belgian Ambassador.

Saturday 29 April

I receive my performance assessment. Apparently I am 'not up to the demands of the job'. Last year I was 'beyond the demands of the job'. Extraordinary.

Saturday 6 May

The Eid marking the end of the holy month of Ramadan is on us. I go to call on Muhammad Ahmad al-Suwaidi. He has a large, newly built place next to Sheikh Surur's house, on reclaimed land. I am ushered into Muhammad's majlis and seated to his right. He has a house in Findon, near Worthing, and another in London. He is reading Proust in Arabic and asks me what I think of his work. We talk about Flaubert, our favourite Muhammad al-Murr stories and the best time to be in England – autumn.

Sunday 7 May

On the few occasions that I have been to Ras Al Khaimah, I have often looked left to Al Jazira Al Hamra, a low-lying attractive-looking village, undeveloped and gently fringed with palms. I indulge my curiosity and we drive off past breeze-block shops and garages round the village. It is completely deserted! Nobody – not even a cat – is in the place. Bungalows are all boarded up. It is a ghost town, and looks as if it has been hit by the plague.

Monday 8 May

Returning from Ras Al Khaimah we stop at Dubai and go to the Yum-yum Centre. It has a vast café in a mall, with sections for pizzas and buffet food. Staff have badges on their lapels with 'Hi! I'm Lena' or whatever. There is canned music and non-stop cartoons on televisions for customers to see as they eat.

Friday 12 May

There is a Heads of Mission conference in Abu Dhabi. This consists of all the British ambassadors in the Middle East, plus people from London, including the Minister of State at the Foreign Office, William Waldegrave, and my line manager, Jeremy Barnett.

I take Jeremy to Al Ain. We see the Ambassador travelling in his Jaguar with William Waldegrave. Everyone else is in a bus. I join the visitors to the conference at lunch at the farm of Sheikh Nahyan.

Later there is a dinner at the Ambassador's Residence. I am sitting next to a man from the Ministry of Defence. He is very interesting on the management styles of successive ministers. Michael Heseltine was demanding and had the answers first, before he asked the questions. He would be tough on staff, in contrast to Sir George Younger, who was always courteous and most appreciative of all that was done.

Saturday 13 May

I attend the opening of the Heads of Mission conference in the Ambassador's dining room. It is chaired by William Waldegrave, who must be the youngest person in the room. He talks first and is very low-key and unimpressive.

In the evening we host a dinner party for some of the visitors, including Mark Marshall, Ambassador in Sana'a. He is a godson of Charlotte Bonham-Carter, whose husband was Legal Secretary in the Sudan in 1899. She was a secretary at Versailles in 1919 and is today 95 and becoming gaga. I met her a few years ago.

Sunday 14 May

I attend all the conference. It is fascinating to observe the group dynamics. Waldegrave is very much in charge. His low key disguises great authority. There are no stars. The Minister does not seem to take advice from anybody but listens to everybody. He and the senior Foreign Office official, David Gore-Booth, have an interesting relationship. They both give an impression of effortless superiority. Both are Hons, both went to Eton, David Gore-Booth being three years older than the Minister. Could the latter have been the former's fag? Both went on to Oxford. Most of those present are meritocrats, having attended minor public schools or grammar schools. Rob Young is bright and almost a star. He went to a grammar school in Norwich and Leicester University. Only the Etonians say 'bloody' in formal sessions.

Over lunch Peter Hinchcliffe, our Ambassador in Jordan, tells me that when he was in Dubai there was a cricket match between the Ancient Britons and the Ancient Asians. Anyone over 40 was able to add the number of years over 40 to his score. When Peter faced the bowling, he found he was facing Imran Khan.[20] He was out second ball.

In the afternoon session I listen to the round-up. There is no mention of our European partners or our American allies. It is as if the Gulf is an Anglo-Japanese lake. Nor is there any mention of the investment from the Gulf in Britain – especially in property and finance.

Monday 15 May

I go to a meeting of the Monday Club. Alan Briggs of British Airways talks about civil aviation in the Gulf. He says duty-free shops should only be available at the journey's end. There was once an emergency landing in which people grabbed their duty-free booze and slid down the exit chute. At the bottom there was a pile of broken glass and a pool of spilt alcohol.

Wednesday 17 May

I call on Abdul Rahim Mahmud, the extremely well-dressed Under-

---

20 Former captain of the Pakistan cricket team; later went into politics.

Secretary at the Cultural Foundation. He asks me about hotels in Brighton, more modest than the Grand. He cannot turn up there in jeans, he says. It is hard to see the spruce, be-dishdasha-ed Abdul Rahim touring England in jeans.

Thursday 18 May

There are celebrations in Abu Dhabi to mark the wedding of Sheikh Hazza bin Zayed to a daughter of Muhammad bin Buti. Near the parade ground scores of tents have been erected and food provided. There were portable loos and a mosque area. People have come from all over the place to celebrate. There is spontaneous tribal dancing. People drift around happily and purposelessly.

In the evening we stroll along the Corniche. Scores of families are enjoying the cool evening air. Some have brought rugs, chairs, even hubble-bubbles.

Friday 26 May

I take the boys for a walk and we chat to a Sudanese guard at a big house. He tells me that Yusuf Husain Yahya, the guard from Darfur who indirectly introduced me to Wilfred Thesiger, is now guarding the US Embassy. I go there to see him. He tells me that Idris Daud's son, Mustafa, is a doctor and that the father is comfortable. It might be too much of a dislocation for him to have a cataract operation. Yusuf talks of 'Mr Moore' again. 'Mr Mubarak' (Wilfred Thesiger's Arabic name), though also remembered, did not have the impact that 'Mr Moore' obviously had. I show Yusuf the picture of Idris Daud in Wilfred Thesiger's *The Life of My Choice*. An American comes out of the Embassy, curious about my intimacy with a security guard. Am I bribing him to throw a bomb over the wall? I explain that we are old friends from Sudan: the truth is too complicated to unravel.

Sunday 28 May

I have lunch at the American Ambassador's Residence to meet some visiting educationalists. The Ambassador, David Mack, is very good at explaining local cultural sensitivities. With Muslims there is a 'shame culture'; with us a 'guilt culture', derived from Protestant ethics.

Muslims, he says, are concerned with what people see and say. But both shame and guilt are public matters.

Tuesday 30 May

I am planning an exhibition of photographs taken by Wilfred Thesiger in the Emirates in the late 1940s. I will call it 'Mubarak bin London', the name by which he was known to the ruling family and the local tribes here 40 years ago. Today I receive a phone call from ADNOC to say it will sponsor the exhibition. The exhibition can mark Wilfred Thesiger's 80th birthday next year.

British Homes Stores has agreed to sponsor a classroom in Dubai.

At a dinner party I talk to John, father of one of our teachers. He was at Oxford with Alan Bennett, who was a smart, shy Yorkshire lad who could amuse friends. John and others persuaded him to do his amusing acts to the whole Junior Common Room. It was a success and things took off – sermons, headmasters' addresses, the plays.

Wednesday 31 May

Our friends Robin Thelwall and Rebecca Bradley are with us. I first knew them in Sudan. They are now working in Kuwait. Robin is a specialist in African languages; Rebecca has been an archaeologist and is now writing stories and novels.

I go with Robin and Rebecca and their young children, Katie (six) and Owen (three), to Dubai. We have lunch with Muhammad al-Murr at the Regency Hyatt, which slowly revolves – one revolution in 90 minutes. Muhammad is amazing. He went to the opera on his first visit to London at the age of 18, seeing *The Magic Flute*. He is familiar with all the latest movements in English literature. He then takes us off to the museum and comments on various artefacts. There are old photographs of the city, the fort isolated with no buildings nearby. We then go on an abra. I would have been content with just the crossing, but Muhammad rents a whole boat for a half-hour cruise. We go up the Creek and back, Muhammad commenting all the time. He talks of the young women of one wealthy family who live in a gilded cage. They cannot marry because nobody is good enough for them.

'The servants are Indians selected for their ugliness, so the women will not be tempted. If they had been handsome Greeks or Italians, on the other hand …'

Thursday 1 June

We all have lunch with Frauke Heard. Robin is fascinated by the Shihuh, a tribe on the Musandam Peninsula. In the plains, says Frauke, there are all sorts of myths and legends about them being descendants of Portuguese. Look at their fair hair and blue eyes, people say. But the Shihuh do not have fair hair and blue eyes. Nor do the Portuguese.

We have dinner at the house of Zaki Nusseibeh and his wife, Laila. Zaki is one of four brothers, of whom two went to Rugby and two to Eton. One of the Etonian brothers is present. So is Adnan Pachachi.[21] And Jamal Ghusain, President of the Palestine Fund, and his wife, an aunt of Zaki; they have a house in Curzon Street. And David Mellor MP, who is popular with Arabs in general and Palestinians in particular for his public rebuke of some Israeli soldiers in Gaza. I ask him if his outburst was spontaneous or premeditated. 'A bit of both,' he acknowledges. He says that support for Israel is a generational issue. People of his age in the government no longer give Israel the benefit of the doubt out of a sense of guilt. He became a QC not because of legal work in the courts but as a result of his work as a junior Minister in the Home Office. Zaki takes us to see his study, full of books, carefully arranged. He has three of Salman Rushdie's novels, as well as some manuscript Korans.

Saturday 3 June

I have a visit from Brenda Walker and her husband, Jolyon. She has been a teacher and headmistress and got involved with translation and poetry. She now has her own publishing company, Forest Books, in Chingford. She has contributed to books translated from Romanian and Urdu. They invite Theresa and me for lunch and we meet her Syrian son-in-

---

21 Born 1923, Iraqi Foreign Minister 1965–7 and Ambassador to the UN between 1967 and 1969. He became an exile in the UAE, and in 2004 publicly declined the role of President of the Iraqi Interim Government.

law, a businessman, Georges Pandeli. His grandfather was an Austrian engineer who worked on the Hejaz railway.

At the Italian National Day party, I chat to the Chinese Ambassador in Arabic.

Monday 5 June

It is my mother's 91st birthday. My sister has phoned to say she is declining and this will probably be her last birthday. Seventy years ago, a gypsy told her fortune and said she would live to the age of 91. In the last year or so she has referred to this prophecy. Contrary to custom, I do not phone her as I do not wish to remind her of her age, or this significant milestone.

Zaki Nusseibeh phones me and invites me to the diwan, the offices of Sheikh Zayed. I go up and have a chat. Sheikh Zayed wants to see Wilfred Thesiger when he is London, and the head of the diwan, Ali al-Shurafa, wants his address. I talk to them of my idea of having an exhibition of photographs Wilfred Thesiger took of the Emirates.

Theresa has been offered a job at the Emirates Private School as a teacher of Mathematics.

Monday 12 June

We depart Abu Dhabi for leave. We are taking the boys for a few days in Tunis before going on to Britain.

The TunisAir plane is full of migrant Tunisian workers returning home. As they check in, they are carrying a lot of consumer goods; one actually carries a kitchen sink.

Peter was away for three months. The time was spent catching up on friends and relations. He saw people in his headquarters and went on a training course. He, Theresa and the boys drove to Scotland and stayed at youth hostels. Peter walked up Ben Nevis with Gabriel. In England he visited his old mother several times.

One day was spent at Wilfred Thesiger's flat in Chelsea – Wilfred was away – going through his 65 volumes of photographs, all carefully labelled. Theresa and Peter selected 30 for an exhibition. Peter arranged for them to be copied and enlarged for exhibition display purposes. He stipulated that he had a postcard-size copy of each one; he had the idea of trying to identify the people in them.

Theresa returned to Abu Dhabi before Peter to start her new teaching job. Peter flew back with the boys on Saturday 9 September.

Sunday 10 September

I do not sleep well. But on my desk in the office is a bowl of flowers and a card saying 'Welcome back'.

In today's paper there is an article attacking the British Council for being a Jewish conspiracy. Apparently in an English-language test paper there were references to Charlie Chaplin, a girl called Sharon and Yehudi Menuhin. Chaplin may or may not have been Jewish. But so what? Sharon, with the emphasis on the first syllable, is a common English girl's name, and Menuhin's father was a ferocious campaigner against the State of Israel.

Tuesday 12 September

We may have to move premises in Abu Dhabi. I discuss the issue with the Ambassador. Sheikh Zayed gave a site to the French Cultural Centre. He could give one to us. But it might be inconveniently sited, although it would be an embarrassment to decline. The Embassy compound, centrally sited and well known, would be ideal. The Ambassador says, 'It would be ideal, but I had always thought that you chaps did not want to be too closely associated with us chaps'.

Wednesday 13 September

I go to Dubai and catch up on things there. The Vice-Consul in the Consulate-General has been arrested in London. Apparently, he was very close to the Iranian community and may have received presents from them. Earlier this year he and his wife had gone on an elaborate holiday in the Far East that was clearly beyond the means of a Vice-Consul's salary. What intrigues me is the investigation of him that led to his arrest. To some extent he was doing his job well, getting to know people. Was he shopped by an Iranian? Was there some element of blackmail?

Sunday 17 September
I ask the Ambassador what I should know or not know about the arrest of the Vice-Consul in Dubai. He has been charged with corruption and not for contravening the Suppression of Terrorism Act. The Ambassador is personally sympathetic. The Vice-Consul is an orphan and has personally done well for himself. He was receiving gifts in kind for services rendered.

Monday 18 September
Our son, Gabriel, aged eight, writes a story on the word processor. He and some friends form a gang. One day Gabriel's dad reads in the newspaper that Sheikh Zayed's palace is on fire. The gang go off and put the fire out and rescue Sheikh Zayed, who is full of appropriate gratitude.

Tuesday 19 September
I have a strange dream. We are to be posted to Queensland in 1991 for a year's study of Chinese and bibliographical studies before I go to be Books Officer for China.

Wednesday 20 September
Frauke Heard tells me that when she left Heathrow on her way back to Abu Dhabi last month, the fields were brown and dry. As she flew into Abu Dhabi, the grass, by contrast, was green and lush.

Monday 25 September
There is a UAE Youth Hostel Association (UAEYHA) and I phone their office in Dubai. I speak to an Egyptian. There are youth hostels in Al Ain, Fujairah, Dubai, Sharjah and Ras Al Khaimah. I shall call on him. Who are the members? Who funds? Who stays at the hostels? Is there an underclass of backpackers in the UAE?

One of the British Council students in Dubai calls. He comes from a boating family, originally from Linga on the Iranian coast. His first language is Farsi. Seven or eight boats – 'booms' – go from Dubai to Iran each day. A smaller number go to Bahrain. I am intrigued.

Tuesday 26 September

I call at the offices of the UAEYHA in Dubai and meet the Egyptian in charge. He is also the warden of Dubai Youth Hostel. Many who stay are non-UAE Arabs working in Dubai; it costs them 10 dirhams (£1.50) a night. Accommodation is mainly for men. If women stay, they have to give advance notice. Some young Western backpackers have stayed. One came on a motorbike, took it on a dhow and went on to Bombay.

I have lunch with Muhammad al-Murr. I ask him about Sheikh Buti bin Maktoum who, according to the Prince of Wales, was at Cambridge at the same time as him. He did not, as I was led to understand, study at the university, but was learning English at the Bell Language School alongside Muhammad.

Friday 29 September

Gabriel wants an operation on his ear – not the one that sticks out but the one that does not. He wants it to stick out so he can look like the Prince of Wales.

Monday 2 October

The postcard-size photographs taken by Wilfred Thesiger of the Emirates in the 1940s have arrived. They are absolutely fascinating. Frauke calls by and she is excited by them. She observes that the barasti huts in the Liwa look like the toilets of a scout camp. Apparently, nomads would roll them up like carpets when they moved on. One picture of Sheikh Zayed has him sitting on the sand, a pen in the breast pocket of his waistcoat, his watch attached to the waistcoat by a safety pin.

Sunday 8 October

I attend a meeting at the Embassy to discuss British Week in UAE 1990. Ideas are discussed. Could we persuade Richard Branson to descend in a balloon over Dubai Creek? The Defence Attaché suggests a re-enactment of the 1819 storming of Ras Al Khaimah Fort by the British, this time letting the Qasimis, the ruling family, win.

I take the Thesiger photographs to the Cultural Foundation and show them to Huda, one of the staff. She is actually a Saudi, born in Beirut and educated in Paris. She points out that in the picture of the Abu Dhabi Corniche women are washing clothes in the sea.

Monday 9 October

A Pakistani taxi driver asks me, I think – in a mixture of bad Arabic, no English and Urdu – if I can arrange for him to have a British wife. I sometimes wonder about a reciprocal request: Can you find a nice Pathan girl for me?

Over the last few months I have translated about twenty-five of Muhammad al-Murr's stories, at the rate of at least one a week.

I give a talk to the Monday Club. I promote commercial sponsorship of arts events that the British Council can manage. I am introduced by the Ambassador, who has read my briefing notes and is most supportive.

Thursday 12 October

We set off before 8.00 am and drive to Sharjah to go to the Cricket Festival there. The national teams of India, Pakistan and West Indies play. I am told that Indian film stars come over for the expensive seats and that the festival is the major event in the Indian-Pakistani social calendar. Theresa drops me off outside the stadium, but I learn that the cricket today has been cancelled because of the death of Sheikh Hamdan bin Muhammad Al Nahyan. I take a taxi back to Dubai and wander along the Creek. Dhows, I learn, go to Mukalla and Aden and even to Djibouti. The boats seem secure and very appealing. It would be fun to take a boat round the Musandam Peninsula to Fujairah.

I ask two policemen for directions, and they are surprised that I know Arabic. I ask them where they are from. Baluchistan, they tell me. They complain about how they are squeezed between Iran and Pakistan.

Friday 13 October

To mark the death of Sheikh Hamdan, the Abu Dhabi English-language radio station is broadcasting nothing but classical music all day. Their range of records or tapes seems limited. I hear Beethoven's Choral Symphony, Dvorak's Cello Concerto, Holst's *The Planets* and

Mendelssohn's *Fingal's Cave* several times during the day. None of the music is prefaced with an introduction, so we move from Beethoven to Mendelssohn to Holst to Dvorak and back to Beethoven without any break.

Saturday 14 October

I work on some of Muhammad al-Murr's stories. I find when I am writing, or translating, like this, the task takes over and the stories almost translate themselves. I also contemplate a 20,000-word book on Thesiger and the Emirates for the exhibition in February.

Monday 16 October

In Dubai I call on Easa Salih al-Gurg and show him the postcard-size versions of the Thesiger photographs. In the 1940s he was one of seven clerks in the Dubai branch of the British Bank of the Middle East when a man in Bedu dress turned up asking, in Arabic, for the *mudir* (manager). 'He walked like a Bedu, kicking his feet sideways as if moving the sand out of the way.' The British manager was in a room divided off by a curtained partition. He came into the office and said, 'Is that you, Wilfred?'

Easa has a flat in Kensington, another in Cadogan Square and a farm in Frinton-on-Sea, Essex. He thinks Dubai is on the brink of a boom and expansion.

I try to trace the places mentioned in one of Muhammad al-Murr's stories, and do locate the Golan cafeteria. Theresa joins me, and so do Muhammad and Jack Briggs. Jack is in his late sixties and comes from Blackburn. He left school at 14 and was apprenticed to a printer. When war broke out, he was 18 and joined the army, then the Palestine police and, after that, the police force in Bahrain and Qatar. He taught himself Arabic and is doing a Master's degree on the Arabic short story. The first poetry he really enjoyed was from pre-Islamic times. He has been a great friend of Harry Aspden, the father of a colleague. Harry was a major cycling journalist who never owned a car, or had a telephone or television in his house until his daughter insisted. Jack is full of vitality and interest in life. He is one of a handful of people who call on the ailing Sheikh Rashid Al Maktoum each day, one of the others being Mehdi al-

Tajir, once reputed to be the richest man in the world. Jack and Sheikh Rashid exchange lines of poetry with each other. Jack turns to me.

'Tell me about structuralism,' he asks.

'Don't bother,' I reply.

Muhammad gives me a copy of the latest collection of his stories.

Thursday 19 October

I work on some of Muhammad al-Murr's stories. I do three drafts when translating them. I also think about the book on Wilfred Thesiger. I could write it all in a month, but I would need to call on people I can identify in the photographs who would have met him 40 years ago.

Saturday 21 October

I have a phone call from Jack Briggs, who has suddenly become a good friend. We talk for nearly half an hour on translation and about Muhammad al-Murr. We discuss the ethics of translating Muhammad's racier yarns. Are they intended for an exclusively Gulf readership? Is there a mystique that would be destroyed by putting them into English? 'We are privileged,' Jack says, 'you and I. We are eavesdropping on local society.' It could all rebound on Muhammad and it is conceivable that an English version could be banned.

I go to see Rabi' al-Qubaisi, the landlord of one of our teachers. I show him the Thesiger pictures. He is an unsophisticated man who seems to be intimidated by affluence, and is squired around by an Adeni (actually, an Abyani), who is uninterested in the pictures.

Sunday 22 October

I call on the only British dean at the university in Al Ain, Iain McLedingham. His Faculty of Medicine is due to expand in the next 12 months. There are already something like eight British professors. They specialise in things like emergency surgery – that is, clearing up after road accidents.

I then meet Samir Rizq, a Palestinian and General Sports Supervisor at the university. He comes from Gaza and is a great swimmer. He lived in a village four miles from his school and swam home from school each day, having given his brother his clothes to carry home. He swam the

English Channel in 1962 and 1963.

Tuesday 24 October
We go to a piano recital hosted by one of the oil companies. It is for the international bourgeoisie. I meet a teacher of English at the French school, a Frenchman who taught at Winchester for four years. I am also introduced to a Christian Turk, Ilyas Halil, who now has a Canadian passport. His family were originally Lebanese and migrated to Mardin in 1860. He writes short stories in Turkish and we chat about Turkey and things Turkish. His wife is also Turkish but went to a French school in Beirut for her education.

Wednesday 25 October
Peter Hellyer, the journalist, takes me to the house of Hadif Muhammad Hawlan Mansuri for lunch. He is Director of the Port and a particular chum of Peter. The house is comfortable but not lavish. Some men are sleeping on settees and on the floor. A couple of hooded falcons squat on the floor. Hadif is fascinated by the Thesiger photographs and has some original comments: 'This man is from the mountains, not from the desert'. He identifies several people in the pictures. His father is a camel owner, and is at Al Wathba preparing for a race.

Thursday 26 October
We take the boys to Al Ain and visit the zoo. The pens for lions, tigers and panthers are very large. The whole place is well kept and it costs one dirham to go in – free for children under eight.

Sunday 29 October
At the Embassy 'prayer meeting' the big news is that the Emirates national football team is through to next year's World Cup finals.

Monday 30 October
Gabriel comes down after he has been put to bed. He comes up to me, puts his arms round me and sits, relaxed, on my lap. This is one of the joys of parenthood. In spite of his sometimes macho ways, he is my child and we love each other.

Tuesday 31 October

I go to a presentation of certificates to officer cadets at the military academy. I give a speech in Arabic full of nicely turned phrases and a couple of lines from the 10th-century poet, Mutanabbi. It includes a highly classical and unusual word for 'lion'. I tell them that they will be lions in defence of their country!

Thursday 2 November

I work more on Muhammad al-Murr's stories. They are lovely. He is very good at exploring and exposing male arrogance.

Friday 3 November

We host a dinner party. One of the guests is a colleague of Theresa at the Emirates Private School, an Iranian called Sara. Her husband, Musaddiq, is Libyan. He was named Musaddiq after the Iranian politician[22] who nationalised BP in the early fifties. He went to Brummana High School, the Quaker school in Lebanon. Neither of them has any sympathy for either Khomeini or Qaddafi.

Sunday 5 November

In one of the smaller emirates, Ajman, there is a university college. The national policy is that there is only one university, the one at Al Ain. It is an example of the smaller emirate twisting the tail of the federation. The situation is aggravated by the presentation of a large sum to Ajman University College from Sultan Qabus of Oman: a provocative gesture.

I show the Thesiger photographs to Muhammad Ahmad al-Suwaidi at the Cultural Foundation. '*Subhan Allah*,' he says when he sees the picture of Khalifa bin Yusuf, bringing in a boat onto the Abu Dhabi beach. 'He is my father-in-law,' he says with excitement.

Monday 6 November

In Dubai, there are big changes in the provision of 'information services' – that is, the library. We are making the librarian redundant. For the librarian, this is a bolt from the blue. I feel as if my hands are

22 Better known in the UK as Mossadegh.

dripping with blood. A Pakistani from Karachi, though born 54 years ago in Lahore, he acknowledges that he is well off and runs two cars, but is also lazy. I undertake to put in a word at the Dubai Municipality to see if he can be employed there, and we do what we can to protect his dignity and spare his feelings. But, in fact, he is dull and pedestrian, has not gained any benefit from training courses, is rude to the public and inefficient, and ignores instructions.

Tuesday 7 November

I go with the Ambassador to the majlis of Sheikh Mubarak bin Muhammad. Edward Henderson is there but most of those present are nationals. I show Sheikh Mubarak the Thesiger photographs. He is excited at seeing one of himself 40 years ago. When he leaves with his son, Nahyan, we follow them to the door. He gets into the passenger seat of a white Rolls-Royce. Sheikh Nahyan gets into the driver's seat and they move off. Apparently Nahyan drives his father round for half an hour or so, and they end up at a mosque for sunset prayers.

Wednesday 8 November

I have a phone call from Dr Mary Malcolm, a specialist in Norwegian and Icelandic literature who teaches at the Ajman University College. She is not happy there and wonders if there is a job with the British Council.

'Does the University College have a future?' I ask.

'No,' she replies directly. There are very few teachers and they teach to classes of 40 or more. Salaries – in spite of Sultan Qabus's generosity – have not been paid.

At Al Ain we are giving private English lessons to three members of the ruling family.

Thursday 9 November

We take the boys to the Liwa. The road is monumentally boring, with nothing to relieve the flatness of the desert. We go past oil installations and through sand dunes. The first European to come to the Liwa was Wilfred Thesiger. We have difficulty finding the rest house where we are staying. Dual carriageways have hardly any traffic but there are gardens on the roundabouts, well tended by Bangladeshis. We check in and go for a walk in the desert behind the hotel, tumbling with the boys in the sand.

Friday 10 November

The Liwa is a strange place. It is hidden away behind the sand dunes, 100 kilometres from the sea. We drive out and wander along the deserted two-lane highway towards the end of the crescent-like string of oases.

On a stretch of ground a cricket match is taking place – presumably immigrant Indians and Pakistanis; there is a happy intensity in the game. A few taxis stand nearby. All in blazing heat.

We allow the boys to indulge themselves in romping about some sand dunes. We tumble down, our feet sinking above the ankles in the sand. We reach a group of palm trees that some Bangladeshis are hacking at. Their boss is Muhammad Abdullah. His sons are in the army. He owns camels, goats and sheep. I ask him about Mubarak bin London. Yes, he remembers him, but he talks enthusiastically about Martin Buckmaster.[23] *He* was *numero wahid* ('number one'). Others join us, including Muhammad's wife. One man complains to me about the bride price – 100,000 dirhams (£15,000), but 200,000 dirhams for a *bint*, by which I presume he mean a virgin.

Natty climbs a palm tree with amazing agility. I suddenly see him ten feet up, picking dates.

Saturday 11 November

I am feeling very tense about my mother. Whenever the phone rings I calculate what the time in Britain is, wondering whether it is a call announcing her death. I am also mentally alert to the idea of dashing back some time.

Sunday 12 November

At the Embassy 'prayer meeting' the Ambassador announces that

---

23 Martin, third Viscount Buckmaster (1921–2007), Arabist and diplomat; Political Officer, Abu Dhabi, 1955–8.

he will be transferred next month. He was at a meeting of European ambassadors and they were addressed by the Papal Nuncio. He spoke of the different attitudes of authorities in the region towards Christian activity. Bahrain comes out best, embracing Christians. Saudi Arabia and Qatar are worst. Ras Al Khaimah is out of step with the rest of the emirates.

At 5.45 pm, I take Gabriel to St Andrew's Church for the Remembrance Day service. It is full of excellent pageantry. The hymns are good and can be sung lustily. There is a panoply of clergy: Michael Mansbridge, the Anglican pastor here; John Brown, the Bishop of Cyprus and the Gulf; Cardinal Gromyko, the Papal Nuncio; Father Butros of the Coptic community; and two people from the Church of Pakistan. A 'Last Post' is played by a bugler from the national army.

Tuesday 14 November

I have not so far spent time in Sharjah looking around to get the feel of the place. I put that right. It is like other cities in the Arab world, sophistication cheek by jowl with tat. A notice on public gardens says that labourers may not gather there. The souk has items of interest and are not expensive – old doors, chests, coffee pots.

Wednesday 15 November

I call on Sheikh Nahyan to discuss a consultancy at the university. His office is lined with books and rifles.

Forest Books has agreed to publish my translations of Muhammad al-Murr's stories. Hooray!

Sue and Garry Evans, who are in charge of the Al Ain office, tell me that they have been showing the Thesiger photographs to Sheikha Sheikha bint Khalifa. She was thrilled. 'That's my grandfather.' And, 'My grandmother told me of the Englishman who came here and stayed with us, dressed like one of us. He kept taking photographs and making notes.'

Sunday 19 November

Celebrations for National Day at the beginning of December will be more elaborate than usual. The Ambassador suggests it is because

Sheikh Shakhbut is no longer alive. Big Brother is no longer watching.

Peter went for a two-day visit to Doha, Qatar, to discuss shared interests with the retiring Director of the British Council office there, Richard Long.

Wednesday 22 November

There are only four passengers on the plane from Doha to Abu Dhabi. The steward announces that the cabin staff speak seven languages between them – English, French, German, Arabic, Farsi, Hindi, Greek and Spanish. (Actually eight.)

Barclays Bank will sponsor the Thesiger exhibition. We will issue a press release next week. Barclays will bring in its Vice-Chairman and Managing Director, Andrew Buxton. The bank's chairmen are usually from the family – the Quaker Barclay/Buxton lot. I phone the office of my Director-General and confirm that he will also come for the opening of the exhibition in February.

Muhammad al-Murr invites me to attend the presentation of the Sheikh Rashid awards. He is chairman of the committee organising it all. The ceremony is in the Sports Stadium in Dubai and is attended by hundreds. I am seated between Iraqi and Kuwaiti diplomats and, looking around, believe I am the only non-Arab present. Muhammad comes in, accompanied by Sheikh Maktoum bin Rashid, Sheikh Muhammad bin Rashid and Sheikh Sultan bin Muhammad Al Qasimi. Sheikh Nahyan is also present. There are speeches, poetry and then presentations to all the Emiratis who have PhDs. At a reception afterwards, I talk to holders of PhDs from Exeter and Durham.

Thursday 23 November

I go to Dubai again for the evening for the opening of the Jaguar-sponsored classroom at the British Council centre. Allen Swales has had the excellent idea of inviting all the students with Jaguar cars to drive them to the centre this evening. So a row of Jags are parked outside – very impressive for the senior visiting officials from the company.

I am driven back to Abu Dhabi, dozing on the way. We pass an accident: a dead camel in the road and the car that struck it well off the road.

Monday 27 November
Sheikh Saeed bin Tahnoun has been in a nasty road accident. The Ambassador tells me that he is a reckless driver. He would drive at 110 miles an hour, talking into his mobile phone in one hand, a falcon on his other arm and Madonna at top volume on the car radio. He drives a yard or two behind the car in front.

Tuesday 28 November
At the Cultural Foundation I talk to Khulud Muhammad Ali, a young lady from Ajman. She is a university graduate and took up painting three years ago. Her work is nightmarish and feminist. A theme is women growing into and out of trees.

Saturday 2 December
It is a public holiday – National Day – and we get away for a couple of nights, staying at Ras Al Khaimah. We drive north, to the fort at Dhaya near Rams. The British took it and imposed a treaty on Ras Al Khaimah in 1819. We park at the foot of the hill on which the fort stands, and clamber up. It is small and made of mud brick. It is unsanitised, unlike so much in the country. It is a struggle to get right to the top and the boys race around fantasising.

In the afternoon we go into the old part of Ras Al Khaimah. In the museum is a new museum dedicated to the ruling family, the Al Qasimis. There is information on the British raids of 1809 and 1819, and a photograph of the castle at Dhaya. The souk is busy and bright. One shop is called 'Rise Stores'. I wonder about this and then see that in Arabic it is *shuruq*, meaning 'sunrise'.

Monday 4 December
The Ambassador and his wife come on a valedictory visit to the British Council. I make a little speech and say, 'I judge ambassadors on two criteria: how far they fulfil the British Council's objectives of making friends for Britain, and how far they are friends of the British Council. Michael Tait scores highly on both counts.'

At the Heards I meet a friend from the Oteiba family, who sees the Thesiger photographs. He sees the one of Zayed with a pen in the breast pocket of his dishdasha. 'What does he need a pen for?' he says. 'He doesn't write. It is only for show.'

Tuesday 5 December

I attend a reception at the Embassy and meet Denys Johnson-Davies. I am a huge fan of his work – he is the doyen of translators from Arabic into English. We talk about Marmaduke Pickthall and my own work as a translator. I then set off for Dubai and meet Ian Fairservice, the boss of Motivate Publishing. We have a long talk and I get to know him for the first time. He is an impressive young man. He came to Dubai ten years ago to work in a hotel, and saw that there was a need for visitors to know what was going on. So he set up the magazine *What's On,* arranged for a copy to be in every hotel bedroom – which accounted for a distribution of 17,000 – and has not looked back. The 'Arabian Heritage' series of books has sold 160,000 copies.

Wednesday 6 December

At the university I talk to Muhammad Safar, who comes from Sharjah. He says he saw Tom Jones in Sharjah in 1967. There was an RAF base there that had visiting pop stars. One night was opened up to 'locals'. He went along as a 12-year-old!

Friday 8 December

I cook for a lunch party. Denys Johnson-Davies is one of the guests. He is 67 and his father worked in the Sudan. He went to a minor public school and was squash champion at the age of 14. A year later he went on to the University of London to study Arabic, and to Cambridge a year after that. He was seen as a child prodigy. After graduating he went to Cairo and worked for the British Council, and was then the representative of an oil company in Qatar in 1950. The company withdrew from Qatar, believing there was no oil in marketable quantities.

Wilfred Thesiger had visited the Emirates in 1977. He hated it, and described Abu Dhabi in an edition of Arabian Sands *as an 'Arabian nightmare'. He never wanted to go to Arabia again. Peter initially had no thought of inviting him to the opening of the exhibition of his photographs in February 1990, preparations for which were well under way.*

I call on Ian Fairservice at Motivate Publishing to discuss the production of a catalogue for the exhibition. Somebody suggests we should have the technical specifications of the camera. Why not get the camera to be on display? I immediately phone the man in London who has been involved with Wilfred's photography. He says he will ask Wilfred, and suggests that if it is on loan there must be absolute security for the camera. Yes, of course, I say. Then he suggests that Wilfred might be interested in coming himself for the opening, provided everything was laid on for him – first-class travel and so on. If he comes, the impact of the exhibition shifts up several keys into a new dimension (to mix my metaphors). I quickly calculate. I know he hates hotels and he should stay at a comfortable private house. When he is here I shall also be entertaining my Director-General and my mother-in-law!

Wednesday 13 December

I talk to David Heard about Wilfred Thesiger. David met him in Abu Dhabi during his 1977 visit. Wilfred had said to David, 'Please ask the sheikhs not to invite me to Abu Dhabi. I don't want to come.' I had heard vaguely about this: hence my reluctance to invite him. But I write a letter to him in Kenya warmly inviting him. I want to be in control of his visit, so it will be purely a British Council event. It will be nice if Sheikh Zayed can take over some things. But the prospect, and even more the certainty, of his coming makes the exhibition at once much more important, a major Anglo-Arab cultural event.

I phone Wilfred's literary agent in London. Yes, Wilfred might like to come. He is interested in the exhibition and has said he would like to see it.

Thursday 14 December

I phone Roger Davis at the British Council in Nairobi. I will fax a letter for Wilfred Thesiger to him. He will get it to Wilfred in Maralal as soon as possible. I hope Wilfred will get it in two days, then telephone Roger, who will telex me. In my letter to Wilfred I tell him that I will let Sheikh Zayed know that he is coming.

Saturday 16 December

I go, by myself, to call on Sheikh Nahyan and Sheikh Mubarak. It is the first time I have gone alone. Hitherto I have accompanied the Ambassador and been in his shadow. I am conscious of my own lower status and apprehensive of being seen as presumptuous. However, as is the custom, everyone stands up as I enter the room. Sheikh Nahyan invites me to sit next to him and calls me Peter. His father is on the other side. I feel increasingly at home and listen to the Gulf accents.

Sunday 17 December

I attend Michael Tait's last prayer meeting as Ambassador. The performance is, as usual, slick and stylish. He thanks us all and makes special mention of me. Sheikh Nahyan had spoken highly of me and he has transmitted this to the Foreign Office. I purr.

I go to a party of expats. I do not usually like these. I talk with David and Frauke Heard. I tell them that my role in life, bringing people together and making connections, is being a hyphen. Frauke says she is a question mark, David that he is an exclamation mark. The BP representative says that John Browne, a senior BP colleague, would like to sponsor the catalogue of the Thesiger exhibition. But Barclays wants to do that. Either way, it will be a saving of £5,000. Terry Adams of Shell offers to arrange a lunch in the desert for Wilfred.

Monday 18 December

I go to the airport early with David Heard to see Michael Tait off. Jolyon Kay from Dubai and Robert Wilson, his deputy, and two or three officials from the Ministry of Foreign Affairs are there. Michael is pleasantly surprised to see us. He behaves in his usual stylish way and we see him right to the aircraft door. He kisses the nationals and seems to be on the point of kissing Jolyon.

I discuss with Jolyon where to house the Thesiger exhibition in Dubai. He tells me that Sheikh Sultan, the Ruler of Sharjah, wants to open up a Sharjah Heritage Centre with the Mubarak exhibition! He is ready to arrange things to fit in with us! This is fantastic! People are running after us.

Sunday 24 December

I am reading Dickson on Kuwait,[24] which I bought there in 1971. Vain, rambling, disorganised, orientalist, fantastic and fascinating.

Tuesday 26 December

I take the boys to Kuwait to stay with Robin Thelwall and Rebecca Bradley. We have a three-hour wait in Bahrain. About fifty young oriental women, apparently aged between 16 and 35, are on the plane. I catch a glimpse of 'Democratic Socialist Republic' on their passports and fail to work out where they are from; it turns out to be Sri Lanka. I help one or two of them filling in their Kuwaiti entry forms. They are going to Kuwait as servants, recruited and transported by some agency.

Peter, Gabriel and Nathaniel stayed in Kuwait for the New Year. Theresa stayed in Abu Dhabi, teaching.

---

24 H R P Dickson, *Kuwait and Her Neighbours* (George Allen & Unwin, London, 1956).

1990

Tuesday 2 January

Back at work with a full in tray. I sometimes reflect how much I would like to be a house husband, writing four hours a day and looking after the boys, while Theresa works. Or would I? I enjoy the semi-diplomatic whirl, fitting into a structured life with recognition and access.

Saturday 6 January

A fax comes into the office, saying that Wilfred Thesiger will be coming from 3 to 15 February. I phone David Heard, who at once takes me to see Ahmad al-Suwaidi. At Ahmad's reception room are some elderly nationals, one of whom is Humaid bin Muhairij. He asks about Martin Buckmaster, Julian Walker[25] and Mubarak bin London. 'Why does *he* not come here?' asks another. David keeps mum. Humaid al-Muhairij tells us he spent three months with Thesiger in 1948. Sheikh Zayed is about to go to Pakistan for a month. He will certainly be back for the latter part of Wilfred's visit. But he could insist that Wilfred be flown to his palace in Pakistan. What a flying carpet!

I tell Peter Hellyer that Wilfred Thesiger is coming but ask him not to make it public. In early February, the archaeologist Geoffrey King is due to give a talk to the Emirates Natural History Group. That could be Wilfred's first appearance. Peter says he will see if Sheikh Nahyan can come to that meeting. Otherwise I aim to keep Wilfred's visit confidential until he is actually here.

Sunday 7 January

David Heard has seen Khamis bin Buti al-Rumaithi, who is in charge of Sheikh Zayed's diary, to discuss Wilfred Thesiger's visit. The government would like to take over all the costs of Wilfred's visit. David declines.

Terry Adams, General Manager of the Abu Dhabi Company for Onshore Petroleum Operations (ADCO), proposes taking Wilfred by helicopter to the desert near the Saudi border. The tribe at a nearby oasis would give him a banquet. My Director-General, Sir Richard Francis, who is coming out at the same time, is also invited. Terry wonders

25 Diplomat and Arabist (1929–). Served in the Trucial States before creation of the United Arab Emirates. Ambassador to Yemen Arab Republic (1979–84) and Qatar (1984–7).

whether the UAE University could give Wilfred an honorary degree.

The prints produced for the exhibition have arrived. They look superb. No detail has been lost in the enlargements, and many fresh details can be distinguished.

I phone Mike Shaw, Wilfred's literary agent, and ask him about any of Wilfred's fads. 'He has weak knees, but does not like to admit it.'

Wednesday 10 January

I spend a couple of hours with Ian Fairservice, the Managing Director of Motivate Publishing. He tells me that, when he started in 1979, the magazine *What's On* constituted 95% of his activity. It is still his main earner, but [now] takes up 17% of his activity. He relies on bulk orders to hotels. He has an office in London, from where he will publish the Arabic version of Wilfred Thesiger's *Arabian Sands*. He takes me off in his Jaguar to the boat he will rent and where he will give a lunch to Wilfred. We go over the programme I have drafted, and discuss a book I will write about Wilfred's visit. I will write it up later this year, perhaps 16,000–20,000 words. I admire Ian's dynamism and appreciation of Wilfred.

Saturday 13 January

I receive a letter from Wilfred Thesiger, dated 21 November, and somehow delayed. I had sent him a copy of my translation of the book on the Battle of Omdurman, which he has appreciated.[26] He also says wistfully, 'Ask Zayid to send an aeroplane to collect me for the exhibition'. So he was already, in November, considering coming here!

Tuesday 16 January

I take the enlarged prints of Thesiger's photographs to the Cultural Foundation and open them up with Abdul Rahim Mahmud. We look at the smaller prints with coos of delight. Then the bigger ones. They are outstanding, and it is like opening a Christmas present. The foundation would like Sheikh Nahyan to open the exhibition, but I am told that

---

26 Ismat Hasan Zulfo, *Karari: The Sudanese Account of the Battle of Omdurman*, tr. Peter Clark (Frederick Warne, London, 1980).

Sheikh Sultan bin Zayed, the second son, is also interested. That is for them to sort out, but it is good to think the sheikhs are falling over themselves to be involved.

I have dinner with Peter Hellyer and his Egyptian wife, Laila, who is a descendant of Zubair Pasha, the slave-trading rival of General Gordon in the Sudan in the 1870s. They have ashtrays made of coins that were minted in Omdurman during the Mahdiya, the period between the fall of Gordon's Khartoum and the Battle of Omdurman.

Theresa's school has a mid-year holiday and she goes to Britain for a fortnight.

Thursday 18 January

I am invited to an evening at the flat of Muhammad Ahmad al-Suwaidi, Secretary-General of the Cultural Foundation. The other guests include his cousin, Khalifa Nasir, Under-Secretary at the Ministry of Labour. Dinner is provided by the Hilton Hotel. We move into Muhammad's superbly equipped video room and we watch a film of Mike Tyson knocking out Michael Spinks within two minutes. Then another boxing match. And then the film *Amadeus,* which is totally absorbing. We are watching it until 2.45 am.

Friday 19 January

I take the boys to Al Wathba for the camel races. The boys protest and claim it is boring, but I think they actually enjoy it. We pass a compound full of camels; all a bit scruffy. People – mostly men – mill around with the latest technical gadgetry, portable telephones, bleeps and so on. One man has a hooded falcon on his arm.

The races are actually very slow. The jockeys seem to be aged between five and ten. They race around a huge track and most spectators are in a grandstand that has two closed-circuit television sets showing us the progress of the race. We see the camels in the distance, closely pursued by two or three lorries with television cameras transmitting it all. The race ends by the grandstand, the camels' mouths pouring out foam.

We return over the Maqta' Bridge and go down to the water's edge. Over 40 years ago Edward Henderson built a causeway here.

Saturday 20 January

I translate one of Muhammad al-Murr's stories, a horrific tale that ends with a Palestinian being dumped in a vat of acid.

Sunday 21 January

At the Embassy prayer meeting, I announce that there will be no culture this week. But early next month we are hosting, in successive weeks, Humphrey Lyttelton and Wilfred Thesiger. I also observe that both are Old Etonians, and that Wilfred was taught by Humphrey's father.

The Embassy spook invites me to meet one of his contacts, Ali Sultan al-Duru', who is about my age and is retiring from the Abu Dhabi army. He was a boy in Ibri when Wilfred Thesiger was there, and his father spent time with Wilfred. Another man joins us, a Siba'i from Saudi Arabia. They talk of Wilfred and his companions. 'This one is still alive. This one is gaga and blind …' and so on. Then they switch to talking of Abu Hunaik, Glubb Pasha. It is amazing that his reputation has crossed the whole of Arabia. Glubb liked to have Bedu in the Jordanian army. When he was recruiting men, he would show them an onion, and ask them what it was. The Bedu would say *ubsula*, and the townsmen *basal*. Glubb recruited the former and rejected the latter.

Monday 22 January

One of the Thesiger's photographs was of a smiling teenage Sheikh Tahnoun bin Muhammad, standing barefoot in the sand with an Omani-style headdress. Peter was advised that this picture could be controversial. In 1990 Sheikh Tahnoun was Sheikh Zayed's representative in Al Ain, a pillar of the state. Would it be embarrassing to have a picture of him unable or unaccustomed to having shoes on his feet? There was also a political problem. In the 1950s there was a huge confrontation between Saudi Arabia and the Trucial States (then under British protection) over the Buraimi oasis. Britain rooted for Abu Dhabi, then one of the Trucial States. A Saudi army briefly occupied one of the Omani villages of the oasis. After diplomatic pressure, the Saudis were persuaded to withdraw, surrendering personally to Edward Henderson. The dozen or so villages that made up the Buraimi oasis were divided between Oman and Abu Dhabi. On the Abu Dhabi side, the villages became the town of Al Ain. The picture of a senior Abu Dhabi personality wearing an Omani headdress might be seen as giving sartorial authority to the Omani claim to the whole of the Buraimi villages.

I go to the majlis of Sheikh Mubarak bin Muhammad and his son, Sheikh Nahyan.

'What's in the envelope?' asks Sheikh Nahyan.

'I want your advice,' I say. 'It's a picture of your uncle, Sheikh Tahnoun. I want him to agree to it being shown in the exhibition.'

'He will agree,' says Sheikh Nahyan at once, before seeing the photograph.

He takes the picture and shows it around.

'Guess who that is,' he says.

They laugh and joke at the photograph, suggesting that it was taken just a few years ago.

Wednesday 24 January

The Argentinian Ambassador calls on me. He is learning Arabic in one of our classes. He is actually Lebanese in origin, and has forgotten the Arabic he knew as an infant. I ask him about the food he had as a child. He reels off the names of a whole lot of Lebanese dishes, eyes bright and with perfect pronunciation. His president, Carlos Menem, he tells me, is from a Syrian family originally called Abdul Mun'im.

Thursday 25 January

It is Natty's seventh birthday and I take him to a café that organises children's parties. It is also the first birthday of Christina, daughter of Marie-Reine, my Lebanese PA. The boys and I go to her party at the Marina Club for a lovely Lebanese evening. Little girls do splendid Gulf dances, tossing their hair back flirtatiously.

Friday 26 January

At Gabriel's suggestion, we go to the Dhow Restaurant. This is my favourite eating place in Abu Dhabi. The clientele is not the international bourgeoisie, but a mixture of Arabs. After we eat, the boys wander round the ship. There appears to be a cafeteria downstairs where people just sit and watch the waters of the Gulf. It is a family venue, grandmothers and small children all gathered together: a contrast to the childless, alcoholic occasions of European, and especially British, socialising.

I take the boys for a walk along the Corniche. I am utterly happy when I am out with the boys, running, exploring, playing, imagining. They are happy too.

Saturday 27 January

I have a call from Abdul Rahim at the Cultural Foundation. All stops are being pulled out for Wilfred Thesiger's benefit. The government will reimburse the British Council for Wilfred's air fare, and will make a government car and driver available for him. We ask if we can have a driver from the Hadramaut or from the Rashidi tribe – these were his companions when he crossed the Empty Quarter.

Sunday 28 January

Tim Mackintosh-Smith phones.[27] He is in Muscat, but we talk of Yemen. 'We miss you,' he says kindly. 'Yemen needs you.' He talks of joining the British Council.

'No, don't,' I tell him. 'Those of us who believe in the importance of cultural relations and of people are keeping the flame alight; but it is as if we are under occupation. Wait a little while.'

He will be coming to Abu Dhabi and I arrange for him to have dinner with Wilfred Thesiger.

I go to a reception in honour of the Lord Mayor of London. I chat to his Swordbearer, a retired army officer who got fed up working for the Ministry of Defence.

Monday 29 January

The word is getting round that Wilfred Thesiger is returning to the Emirates. My office phone rings constantly. One Englishman, ex-SAS, rings to say he was in Sudan and Iraq; he admires Thesiger enormously and would love to meet him, or even just set eyes on him. Another Englishman, who works for the Dubai Petroleum Company, knew

---

27 Writer and historian (1961–). Teacher at British Council in Yemen from 1982, when he was recruited by Peter Clark.

Thesiger in the 1940s and would like to meet him.

Tuesday 30 January

I go to the Police Headquarters and see Yusuf Hasan Yahya, the Darfuri nephew of Wilfred's old friend. I arrange for him to meet Wilfred next week. It is thanks to Yusuf that the whole Thesiger business started!

Humaid bin Drai, Head of Protocol to the Ruler in Dubai, phones. On behalf of the Maktoums he is offering car, driver, accommodation, dinner, everything. Once again, the sheikhs are falling over themselves to be involved in a British Council event.

A hitch! Wilfred's books are banned in Dubai. I will ask Humaid. All I want is an order suspeng the ban. In return Humaid can host Wilfred for lunch.

Wednesday 31 January

Our friends from Kuwait, Rebecca Bradley and Robin Thelwall, are here and I take them to Sharjah. I call on the Deputy Ruler, Sheikh Sultan bin Saqr. He is a quiet, friendly, unassuming man in his early forties with two passions – archaeology and shooting.

We go on to Ras Al Khaimah to the site of Julfar and see Geoffrey King and Beatrice de Cardi, immaculately dressed and made up. Geoffrey takes us over the site. They have excavated a lot of the mosque but are unable to date it with any confidence. Most of the site could be from the 14th or the 18th century. It is good to have Rebecca, as an archaeologist, with us. For her it is a relatively simple site compared with Qasr Ibrim in Egypt. The Ruler would really like a Jerash to be discovered! The Lord Mayor of London was here yesterday. Could the City of London be tapped for sponsorship money?

Thursday 1 February

I phone the British Council in Nairobi. Wilfred has left his home in Maralal and is on his way. He is staying two nights in Nairobi as the guest of the British High Commissioner.

I collect Theresa from the airport at 3 am. She has returned from a short stay in England and is with her mother, Phillippa, and we hear the dawn call to prayer when we reach the house.

Friday 2 February

In 1982 Peter was British Council Representative in Yemen and managed a visit from Humphrey Lyttelton and his band. One day, Humph and the band were hosted by Theresa and Peter at their very Yemeni house. People took off shoes and sat on the carpets in the reception room. Gabriel was nine months old. Humph has described what happened:

While we sit, Baby Gabriel is on the move again, cruising round the room as if by high speed clockwork. On one circuit he stops and crouches over my stockinged foot with his back to me. 'He's taking a great interest in your feet,' someone says jokingly, at which point I am racked with a sudden piercing pain in the big toe. I should have remembered that babies investigate the world with the mouth before hands and fingers – he's taken enough of my big toe into his mouth to give me a nasty nip in the sensitive area at the bottom of the nail. Luckily he doesn't care too much for the taste of my sock and lets go quite soon, leaving me with a sore toe and a tricky problem of etiquette. Does one ask a hostess for antiseptic when you've been bitten by her baby? You can't be too careful in this climate but one doesn't want to offend. I decide that Gabriel is more at risk from my sock, so keep quiet. If there isn't an Ogden Nash poem about catching rabies from babies, there should be.[28]

We go to the Embassy club for a party for Humphrey Lyttelton and his ban, my colleague, the Arts Officer, Maggie Williams met them at the airport and has brought them to the club. Humph's first words are, 'Is your son here?'

We talk about Gabriel and I tell him how much I have been enjoying the collection of correspondence between his father, George, and Rupert Hart-Davis.[29]

'Some of the family,' he tells me, 'were miffed at Rupert's presentation of George as being stuck in Suffolk, with nobody to talk to. We were looking after him and constantly visiting him.'

---

28 Humphrey Lyttelton, *Why No Beethoven? The Diary of a Vagrant Musician* (Robson Books, London, 1984), p. 140.

29 Rupert Hart-Davis (ed.), *The Lyttelton Hart-Davis Letters* (6 vols) (John Murray, London, 1978–84).

I tell him of my appearance in the Letters[30] and how I am dismissed as 'some ass'. He confirms that this was his father's familiar term of disapproval. I am in the company of, among others, Matthew Arnold.

Saturday 3 February

We all go to Humph's concert. David Heard and I slip away at 10.00 pm, collect Edward Henderson and go to the airport to meet the plane from Nairobi. Abdul Rahim Mahmud is waiting for us. The plane is late, coming in after midnight. We see Wilfred, who has been collected from the plane by Haitham Ibrahim of the official protocol department. Wilfred is gaunt, frail but alert. He is rather shabbily dressed and is clutching a Robert Ludlum thriller. We sit in the VIP lounge as Haitham looks after formalities. Abdul Rahim, Wilfred and I travel in the government car to our house. Wilfred is very happy to be back, but regrets deafness and a confused memory. He will not write any more. We reach the house, where Theresa, her mum, Robin and Rebecca have been waiting up for us. Wilfred retires.

Sunday 4 February

Wilfred Thesiger's closest companions in the 1940s were Salim bin Kabina and Salim bin Ghubaisha. He crossed the Empty Quarter twice with them. They were from the Rashidi tribe of Dhofar, the western province of Oman. Wilfred's classic account of his Arabian journeys, Arabian Sands, *was dedicated to these young men, who were barely out of their teens in the late 1940s. Peter had arranged with Shell for Bin Ghubaisha to come from Salalah in Dhofar to Abu Dhabi for the official opening of the exhibition.*

I take tea into Wilfred, who wears only a loin-cloth in bed. He joins Robin and Rebecca for breakfast and charms them before they set off overland for Kuwait. Wilfred would like it if Bin Kabina could come to the exhibition. I phone my PA, Marie-Reine, and she phones the British Council in Salalah to see if Bin Kabina can be found.

I take Wilfred to the Documentation Centre in the Old Fort and

30 Hart-Davis, entry for 21 August 1959.

Ahmad al-Suwaidi comes out to meet us. Compliments and anecdotes are exchanged.

'When I came here in 1977,' says Wilfred, 'I was full of resentment. I was looking for the past. I now accept the present.'

I go to my office. There have been non-stop phone calls all morning about Wilfred.

At lunchtime I receive the message that Sheilkh Zayed would like me to take Wilfred to dinner with him this evening. This is most unfortunate, for Jocelyn Henderson has to abandon the dinner party she was arranging.

David Heard and I take Wilfred and Edward Henderson to the majlis of Sheikh Surur bin Muhammad. He greets us with a big smile. We are joined by Abdul Rahim Mahmud, and in government cars move on to Sheikh Zayed's Sea Palace. We wait in a reception room. Others there include Humaid of the Mahra tribe, who was one of Wilfred's companions 40-plus years ago. Another is Ali Khulfan of Gulf Air. And Sheikh Saqr, the deposed Ruler of Sharjah. We all talk together. And wait, and wait. The Bedu who are present slip from the comfortable armchairs and squat on the ground as if they are in the desert. Sheikh Saqr goes out and then returns. '*Al-shuyukh jāyin*,' he says – 'the sheikhs are coming'; but he is referring just to Sheikh Zayed, using the plural. Sheikh Zayed joins us, looking shorter than I had expected, but with a big grin for Wilfred.

We move into a room with comfortable chairs, and Sheikh Zayed and Wilfred sit together on a sofa. Long residence in Kenya has made his competence in Swahili wipe out much of his Arabic. So I find myself sitting on the floor facing them and acting as interpreter.

Wilfred is full of appreciation for the modern Abu Dhabi. What a change! He is graceful, gentle, enjoying it all. Sheikh Zayed invites Wilfred to make his home in Abu Dhabi. 'We can give you a house, a car and servants.'

We move into a dining room. The table is in three parts, with two wings making it like a giant 'U'. Sheikh Zayed and Wilfred sit at the centre. There must be 20 or more at the table and conversation is difficult. I am modestly seated lower down, so cannot interpret. But next to Sheikh Zayed is a man kneeling on the floor, reading aloud. I learn later that he is reading news from a newspaper.

Monday 5 February

I bring Wilfred some tea at 7.30 am, and soon after we go to the palace of Sheikh Mubarak and his son, Sheikh Nahyan, for breakfast. We wait a few minutes before the sheikhs appear. Greetings and coffee, then we move into the huge dining room, where the table groans under the weight of traditional goodies. Among the other guests are Abdul Jalil Fahim. Wilfred receives adulation. As we leave the room to go to the lobby to chat over coffee, a side door opens and there is a rush of servants, Baluchis and Pathans, to the breakfast table to eat up our leftovers.

We talk of Bin Ghubaisha and Bin Kabina, who are due to come to Abu Dhabi.

'There is one man who I would dearly like to meet, and that is Musallim bin al-Kamam,' says Wilfred. Nobody knows whether he is alive or not. I pass the message on to the Embassy spook, who is looking after Bin Kabina when he arrives.

We move on to David Heard's house and sit in the garden. Wilfred goes to the Cultural Foundation to see the photos. There is a phone call from the Embassy spook to say Musallim bin al-Kamam has just walked into his office asking for Mubarak bin London.

I dash to the Embassy and meet Musallim, a spry, lively Bedu. I take him to the Cultural Foundation and say to Wilfred, 'You asked an hour ago about Musallim bin al-Kamam. May I present him to you?'

Wilfred is amazed and delighted. They embrace and perform the triple nose kiss. They have not seen each other for more than 40 years. Wilfred has, in his Chelsea flat, a camel stick that had been fashioned by Musallim. We all look at the pictures, identifying people. One man is standing alone in the sands. Wilfred and Musallim look at each other with amazed pleasure and Musallim murmurs, '*Ana*' – 'That's me.'

In the evening, we take Wilfred to the Cultural Foundation for a meeting of the Emirates Natural History Group. The patron is Sheikh Nahyan; he takes the chair, for the first time in the group's history. He lauds Wilfred to the skies. The actual lecture by Geoffrey King is a bit of an anticlimax. Afterwards people crowd round Wilfred and he signs some of their books. It is all very emotional.

Wilfred Thesiger in the late 1940s.

Sheikh Zayed bin Khalifa Al Nahyan in the late 1940s; photographed by Wilfred Thesiger.

Tuesday 6 February

The hospitality car comes to collect Wilfred and me, and we go to Dubai.

On the way, he talks about the writing of *Arabian Sands*. He had written an article, and Graham Watson and Mark Longman persuaded him to write it up as a book. He went to a hotel in Denmark to do the writing.

'Why Denmark?' I ask.

'There would be no distractions.'

We go straight to the Rashid School, which has 125 boys and 25 teachers. It is funded totally by Sheikh Maktoum bin Rashid. Two of his sons, Said and Rashid, are pupils and are among the audience as Wilfred talks for 20 minutes. He is absolutely happy in this environment and listens carefully as boys ask intelligent and direct questions. One asks about Sheikh Shakhbut. A teacher tells me the boy is a son of the Ruler of Ajman. His mother is a Nahyan.

We have lunch with Suzie and Allen Swales. It is, they tell me, the most exciting event in their professional lives. Among the other guests are Bill Duff, who has worked in the Customs Department in Dubai since the 1940s, and Ali Safar, who when he was a boy knew Wilfred. Wilfred gives one interview to a stringer of *The Sunday Telegraph* and another to a totally unbriefed journalist from the *Khaleej Times*. I have to rescue Wilfred, who comments peevishly, 'I've never met a stupider woman'.

We go on to the British Council and arrange a book-signing session. The books have been cleared through the censors after a dramatic few days. People gather and at one stage there is a queue of 40 waiting for a signing. He signs patiently, his full name. I reckon he signs about three hundred times. At one stage I suggest a respite.

'No,' he says. 'I'll go on until I drop if I have to.'

But we run out of books. Wilfred is cross. They are also mostly paperbacks. I phone his literary agent in London to pass on his complaint.

We have dinner with Jolyon and Shirley Kay. He looks at Shirley's book on Saudi Arabia.

'Superficial,' he observes tartly.

The other guests include Easa al-Gurg, Muhammad al-Murr and Jack Briggs.

Wednesday 7 February

Jolyon Kay and I take Wilfred to call on the Ruler of Sharjah, Sheikh Sultan bin Muhammad Al Qasimi. Wilfred and Sheikh Sultan chat for half an hour and the Ruler presents Wilfred with a copy of his book, *The Myth of Arab Piracy in the Gulf*. He has to check the spelling of Thesiger as he writes a dedication. 'The book,' he says, 'explains that my family were not all pirates.' As he says this, his round, smiling bearded face is lit up with sparkling eyes; nobody could look more piratical. I can almost see a parrot on his shoulder and a ring in one ear.

We return to Dubai and have lunch at the home of Muhammad al-Murr. He has brought in some younger nationals of Dubai. They are curious and respectful.

The hospitality driver takes us back to Abu Dhabi. I am exhausted and so is the driver. He tells me he was drinking gin in Sharjah for most of last night, and appears to be nodding off. Wilfred is most alarmed. I go into the front seat and talk to him continuously in order to keep him awake.

We go to the Cultural Foundation for a press conference. Tim Mackintosh-Smith joins us. A small group of sedate journalists sit round a table, and questions are politely asked and answered. Then there is an interruption, a clipped cry of '*As-sa-lam- a-lay-kum*'. In walk four Rashidi tribesmen, headed by Musallim bin al-Kamam, followed by Salim bin Kabina and two others. They sit down, and the press conference collapses in gleeful farce. Wilfred and Bin Kabina exchange the triple nose kiss. The bourgeois journalists look spare.

We adjourn to Frauke and David Heard's house, where we have a Bedu meal in a tent in the garden.

'The only thing wrong with Mubarak,' says Bin Kabina, 'is that he did not have a family.'

Wilfred tells the story recounted in *Arabian Sands* about when, at the end of an exhausting day crossing the Empty Quarter, a hare was caught, which Bin Kabina cooked. They had not eaten meat for a month and were full of anticipation. Then three Bedu turned up. Wilfred, Bin

Frauke Heard-Bey and Wilfred Thesiger.

Wilfred Thesiger having dinner in the Liwa, flanked by Sir Richard Francis, Director General of the British Council, and Suhail Faris Mazrui, head of the Abu Dhabi National Oil Company; on the far right is Salim bin Kabina .

Kabina and the others insisted that the guests eat the meat and refused to join in. Wilfred was hungry and admits that he felt murderous.[31] We ask Bin Kabina for his memory of the incident. He talks of another tale of a hare being caught and escaping and then being shot on the top of a sand dune. Wilfred observes that generosity was so common that there was nothing exceptional in the story of the hare and the guests.

Among the Rashidi, Wilfred was known as Mubarak bin Miriam, son of Mary, the name of his mother. It was the Rashidi custom to add the name of the mother rather than the father.

I have to leave the party to go to the airport to meet my Director-General, who will be replacing Wilfred as our house guest.

---

31 This story is told in Thesiger, *Arabian Sands*, pp. 166–7.

Thursday 8 February

Reveille at 5.45 am. I wake the Director-General, Sir Richard Francis, with a cup of tea. The British Council driver collects us and we meet David Heard with Wilfred Thesiger, Musallim bin al-Kamam and Bin Kabina at the airport. We take off in a 20-seater propeller plane, a Twin Otter. We shoot up into the sky and fly long, low and slow alongside the island of Abu Dhabi and along the coast, then inland, and descend onto a dusty airstrip in the Liwa. A banner proclaims 'Welcome to Mubarak bin London'. The head of ADNOC, Suhail Faris Mazrui, is on the tarmac to greet us.

We check into a rest house and all go off in four-wheel-drive vehicles into the desert to an area full of lofty dunes. Two drivers give spectacular displays of sand-dune driving, performing U-turns at speed on 45-degree slopes. Wilfred must be horrified at this invasion of noisy machines polluting the silence and beauty of the desert.

At the rest house a marquee has been erected and a banquet awaits us. I ask David to tell Suhail that Dick Francis is a very big cheese. The hint is taken and my Director-General is seated with Suhail and Wilfred.

A dagger is presented to Wilfred and hardback copies of *Arabian Sands* to all the guests.

Friday 9 February

My Director-General is not the centre of attention as he usually is on an overseas tour. One national wonders if he is Director of the British Council in Dubai. That may not do my career any good, but I reflect that UK-UAE relations are more important than my professional prospects.

Wilfred and the rest of us are taken to a garden in a Liwa oasis and Wilfred gives a television interview to Peter Hellyer. Wilfred is flanked by Musallim bin al-Kamam and Bin Kabina, while the lone and level sands stretch far away to Dhofar. Wilfred is graceful but says he feels a bit of a fraud, coming back like this.

We are flown back home and we host a small dinner party for Wilfred, my DG and the newly-arrived British Ambassador, Graham Burton, and his wife, Julia.

Peter introduces Wilfred Thesiger . . .

. . . to his audience. The man with the stick is Musallim bin Al Kamam; to his left Salim bin Kabina; two to his left Sheikh Nahayan bin Mubarak Al Nahayan; at the right endof the front row, Salim bin Ghabaisha.

Saturday 10 February

I take my DG to Dubai to meet staff. He has been pushed away from the limelight that he normally enjoys. It has been clear that I regard Wilfred Thesiger as a more important visitor than my Director-General.

In the late afternoon, I go to the Cultural Foundation to check up on arrangements for the opening of the exhibition of the Thesiger photographs. There is intensive activity. Tables are brought into place. Sheets are being ironed. Catalogues are laid out.

People start gathering at 6.00 pm and the Cultural Foundation is soon crowded. Theresa brings the DG. Wilfred arrives with David, and Sheikh Nahyan with an armed guard. Nobody at the Foundation seems to be in charge or ready to welcome and look after Wilfred. The latter would like to say a few words, and Peter Hellyer and I decide to take over a lecture room. I have to fight my way through crowds, nationals and foreigners, to the hall. I am pushed forward to introduce Wilfred, which I do in a few words. I have had to abandon the DG to the good-humoured chaos of the crowd. Wilfred speaks in the lecture hall, which is packed out with people standing in the aisles and outside the doors.

Sheikh Nahyan then takes Wilfred through the crowds to the exhibition hall. There is spontaneous applause. The tape is cut and the exhibition room becomes immediately packed. Police have to hold people back and give Sheikh Nahyan and Wilfred space. I hear people have come from all over the Emirates. We had invited 500 people, but there are well over 1,000 at the opening.

Sunday 11 February

The DG is full of compliments. He says he has experienced a similar event only once before. That was a Byron bicentenary exhibition in Greece. 'But you brought Thesiger here. You struck a bell. It was spontaneous combustion.' We have fired an interest among the circles that the British Council does not normally reach.

Well, the months of preparation have been justified. It could have all gone wrong. I have been managing a superstar. Indeed, last night, in the face of the acclamation, Wilfred turned to me at one point and said in his high-pitched, reedy voice, 'I feel like a pop star. I feel as if I am Boy George.'

I take the DG to call on Sheikh Nahyan, who says, 'The Mubarak exhibition has been the talk of the majlises for the last two weeks'. That is the most gratifying remark I have heard since I have been here.

The DG says he will write to Sheikh Nahyan.

'I follow the Ambassador's advice,' I say, 'and address him as "Your Highness".'

'I'll follow DG practice and write "Dear Sheikh Nahyan".'

Monday 12 February

I take the DG to the airport and see him off, returning to my office to deal with a huge in tray.

I join Wilfred for lunch at David Heard's house. Bin Ghubaisha has arrived from Salalah. Wilfred crossed the Empty Quarter with him and Bin Kabina. Both of them – and Musallim bin al-Kamam – are also present.

'You should settle down and take a wife,' Musallim tells Wilfred.

'It has to be a Rashidi girl,' says Wilfred gently.

He goes on to talk about the Nuer in southern Sudan, among whom he worked as a District Commissioner – a colonial administrator – 50 years ago.

'They never wore any clothes, men or women,' he recalls.

'Aaaah,' shrieks Bin Kabina in horror, 'they are animals.'

'But they were totally honest,' says Wilfred. 'They raided but did not steal. And if a man had killed someone and was asked, "Did you kill a man?" he would say "Yes".'

'If I killed a man,' observed Bin Kabina, 'and was asked if I had killed him, I would not say "Yes".'

Wilfred's three companions are leaving tomorrow and I say farewell to these dignified Bedu.

An American friend says the Americans feel they cannot compete with our cultural efforts and say I am conducting a cultural scorched-earth policy.

Tuesday 13 February

David Heard, Wilfred and I drive to Al Ain and Dubai. David points out a tree that used to be the only tree on the island between the bridge and the fort. In the years before he first came here in 1963, the journey to Al Ain/Buraimi used to take four days. People would camp on the dunes just on the mainland, then at Khatim and then at Hazarat al-Bush.

Thursday 15 February

David Heard, Edward Henderson and I take Wilfred off to the airport. Sheikh Nahyan sent an envelope for Wilfred, containing 40,000 dirhams – just over £6,000. That will help, for Wilfred is not rich. He has an overdraft and has had to sell some valuable paintings. He has also been generous and given money away to friends. We see him off. Well, that has been one of the most interesting, absorbing and exciting fortnights in my life.

Theresa and I have dinner with the Defence Attaché. I receive a stream of congratulations on the Thesiger visit – and on the British film week, which has also been going on under British Council auspices. I have been unable to see any of them.

Saturday 17 February

David Heard phones. He has thanked Sheikh Nahyan, on Wilfred's behalf, for the money.

'It will help with the cataract operation he has to undergo,' he explains.

'But we'll pay for that,' says Sheikh Nahyan.

Monday 19 February

I have a phone call from Christopher Dickey, an American journalist based in Paris, who has written a book called *Expats*, which is due to go to press in a few days' time. It is about European and American communities from Tehran to Tripoli. A few years ago he interviewed Violet Dickson and Wilfred Thesiger. Wilfred had said he would never return to the Arabian Peninsula. Friends in Dubai had phoned him last week to say, 'Thesiger is here'. He is having to rewrite a section of the book, which is due out in June. I brief him and fax some local press articles.

I hear from a colleague in London that the DG was 'over the moon' about the Thesiger exhibition. Perhaps my star in London is glowing.

Tuesday 20 February

I go to a dinner hosted by the Faculty of Education at the university in Al Ain. I look at the faces of some ageing Egyptian academics. They are grey, self-satisfied, bored and uninterested in anything around them. How right Taha Husain was: they have a colonialist bullying attitude, with no interest in the local culture.

My mother still lives. I am managing very well with all this intensive activity and limited sleep. For a month I have rarely had more than six hours' sleep at night, or any day off. But I am looking forward to April and a break. The Downs beckon. A trip to France, seeing new places and old buildings, all that I miss so much here.

Friday 23 February

I go to the Abu Dhabi Music Institute for their tenth anniversary and presentation of awards. I am the guest of honour. It is great fun, being graceful and charming and having everything done for me. About 30 little boys and girls are all dressed up as concert pianists. I talk to them (without notes) about the universality of music, and how in Abu Dhabi we have available all sorts of music from all over the world. Then lots of photographs and forced smiles. At the recital a Lebanese boy called Ziyad plays the piano and a national girl called Sara plays the flute.

Saturday 24 February

I go to Sharjah for the Thesiger exhibition there. It will be opened by Sheikh Sultan, the Ruler. I get there early, just as Maggie Williams is polishing up the prints, which look lovely against the white background. Sheikh Sultan's security people come in and throw us all out as they do a check for hidden bombs. Then Sheikh Sultan comes in. He cuts the tape, and he and I process round the pictures. We then adjourn to sit in comfortable chairs drawn up in a circle. Sheikh Sultan talks to Jolyon Kay and I talk to Muhammad, the Ruler's 17-year-old son, who is studying at a private school and expects to go on to

Sandhurst. He has read *Arabian Sands* in English three times. I urge him to write to Wilfred, who he missed meeting this month. As we all chat, the picture of Sheikh Zayed falls down and the glass shatters. None of us makes any comment as local staff clear it all up.

Saturday 3 March

The London Shakespeare Group, led by Delena Kidd, is here and puts on *Macbeth* at the Cultural Foundation. Nobody seems to be in any authority there, but a lot of schoolchildren attend as arranged. They are poorly supervised. Hoots, whistles and catcalls start when Macbeth and Lady Macbeth embrace. Every opportunity is taken to cheer and boo. But many of the children are paying close attention and there is a satisfactory turnout, including some of the children from the Emirates Private School, where Theresa teaches.

Sunday 4 March

I attend Embassy 'prayers'. Robert Wilson[32] is in the chair. He tells me that Graham Burton is due to present his credentials to Sheikh Zayed tomorrow. 'Would you like to come?' he asks, almost casually. Of course I leap at the opportunity. I really love pageantry and am happy – as I would not have been 30 years ago – to take part in it all. I wear my diplomatic hat with pride and pleasure.

I have a letter from Wilfred. 'I cannot tell you,' he writes, 'how grateful I am to you for all you did to make the Exhibition such a success. It was magnificently done, everything from the way the pictures were displayed and lighted to the programme. Above all for all you did to look after me. I really did enjoy my visit and this was largely due to you, and the way that you looked after bin Kabina, bin Ghubaisha and Musallim – I was so happy to see them again and I shall never forget the way you produced Musallim out of the blue at an hour's notice.'

Monday 5 March

I have been reading Edward Henderson's memoirs. I see his wife,

32 Dr Robert Wilson, former Lecturer in Arabic at Cambridge; Head of Chancery at the British Embassy, Abu Dhabi, 1989–93.

Jocelyn, and mention that the book does not mention her.

'He's a typical Arab male,' she observes dryly.

I go to the Embassy soon after 9.00 am and wait. At 10.00, government hospitality cars turn up and six of us are taken at high speed to the palace on Al Ras Al Akhdar. The Ambassador goes in the first car with the Head of Protocol, the rest of us in other cars. Traffic is held up for us and the first car has three motorcycle outriders. Sirens sound but not with any sense of conviction. We arrive at the side of the palace and disembark. Graham Burton is invited to review the Guard of Honour, who wear bright blue-and-red uniforms. The rest of us stand to attention as the national anthems of both countries are played. We then go into a huge majlis and wait. For two hours. A screen partition separates us from a group that includes the Belgian Ambassador and the Crown Prince of Belgium. In our majlis, the ambassadors of Mali and of Somalia are also waiting to present credentials.

Eventually we are ushered into another huge room, where Sheikh Zayed waits to receive us. We take our places respectfully behind Graham Burton, who launches into a beautiful speech in classical Arabic, without a note. He brings a personal message from the Queen, and says how pleased he is to be back, and how Abu Dhabi means a lot to him because his only son was born here. (Sheikh Zayed smiles and nods at this.) We are then all presented to him and sit to one side as the Ambassador and Sheikh Zayed chat for half an hour while Zaki Nusseibeh interprets. It is informal and cosy and there are smiles. Friendships need to be kept in good repair, says Sheikh Zayed. We leave. The Ambassador is relieved – he hates having to talk Arabic in public – and we return to the Residence. The Second Secretary points out that my trousers are falling apart at the seams. I am filled with embarrassment.

Thursday 8 March

The Thesiger pictures have moved to Al Ain and we have arranged for Sheikh Tahnoun bin Muhammad to open the exhibition there at the British Council centre.

Sheikh Tahnoun turns up on time and I greet him as he arrives. He was a favourite with Sheikh Zayed, who regarded him almost as a son. Sheikha Hissa, the mother of Sheikh Khalifa, the son and heir of Sheikh

Zayed, is a sister of Sheikh Tahnoun. I show Sheikh Tahnoun round the pictures. He stares quizzically and without comment at the picture of himself as a boy, barefoot in the sand. We withdraw to another room, drink orange juice, chat and watch a video about Thesiger.

The party disperses and I see Sheikh Tahnoun off. Four armed bodyguards get into the back of his Range Rover, which he drives himself.

Friday 9 March

We go to dinner with Theresa's Iranian colleague, Sara, and her Libyan husband, Musaddaq. They have a house in St John's Wood, where they really belong. Another guest is Ziyad al-Askari, nephew of Qais and grandson of Ja'far Pasha al-Askari, former Prime Minister of Iraq. His father was invited here by Sheikh Shakhbut in 1960 and has UAE nationality.

Peter had invited the London Shakespeare Group – 11 performers – to come to the Emirates and put on Macbeth. *The British Council in London had a drama policy and arranged tours by companies they approved of. The London Shakespeare Group was regarded by British Council London as old-fashioned. Peter managed to bypass this by meeting all the costs of fees, transport and board through local commercial sponsorship. There were international schools whose parents often had well-paid jobs in key companies. They were happy to arrange for sponsorship of a theatre group that put on plays that helped to educate their children.*

Peter had a constant dialogue with his headquarters about cultural activity. He was told that UAE nationals were his major target, and the many Egyptians, Indians, Pakistanis, Iraqis, Palestinians, Jordanians, Syrians, Sudanese and Syrians were not. Peter argued back that the nationals in Abu Dhabi made up only 10% of the whole population. Therefore, if there was a cultural activity attended by 300 people of whom 40 were nationals, there was a disproportionate number of nationals in the audience. And, moreover, the non-nationals would be priority targets in their own countries.

Delena Kidd was passionate about taking Shakespeare to the people. She gathered actors who were competent and dedicated professionals. She was ready to accept whatever constraints local censorship or practice might require.

Saturday 10 March

We go to the Hilton Hotel to see the London Shakespeare Group perform *Macbeth*. We talk to Abdul Rahim Mahmud and his daughter, Dina. Frank Barrie, who plays Macbeth, fractured his kneecap in Dubai and appears on crutches. But it is a good show. The audience consists mostly of our sponsors and potential sponsors. At the end, Delena comes on and makes an excellent speech appealing for support. Four thousand people have seen *Macbeth* in the last few days. This has only been possible with support in cash or in kind from sponsors.

Sunday 11 March

One of the actors has an eight-year-old passport that has no more pages. Crisis: he needs an Iraqi visa for the next stage of the tour. We collect him and take him to a photographer and then to the British Embassy. The staff of the consular section are excellent, and a new passport is issued within 20 minutes. The Iraqi Embassy stays open till 2 pm and we are in time to get there, fill in forms and get the necessary visa. The group is due to fly to Baghdad tomorrow.

Robyn Davidson is due to arrive. I met her in London a few years ago and we have kept in touch. I have invited her here to demonstrate that Arab males do not have a monopoly in the management of camels. She is a former girlfriend of Salman Rushdie and was living with him when he was writing *The Satanic Verses*. I have been accused of lacking judgement in not rescinding the invitation, but I have a feeling of loyalty. If there is the slightest hint of trouble, I will have to send her back to London, but I hope and expect there will be no problem.

Wednesday 14 March

I have lunch in Dubai with Jack Briggs. He lives in a house provided by the Dubai authorities and has a job with the local Special Branch. He combs through about thirty English-language papers from India and other places in Asia for any information that may be of use to the Dubai police, especially on matters relating to smuggling or dealings in drugs or gold.

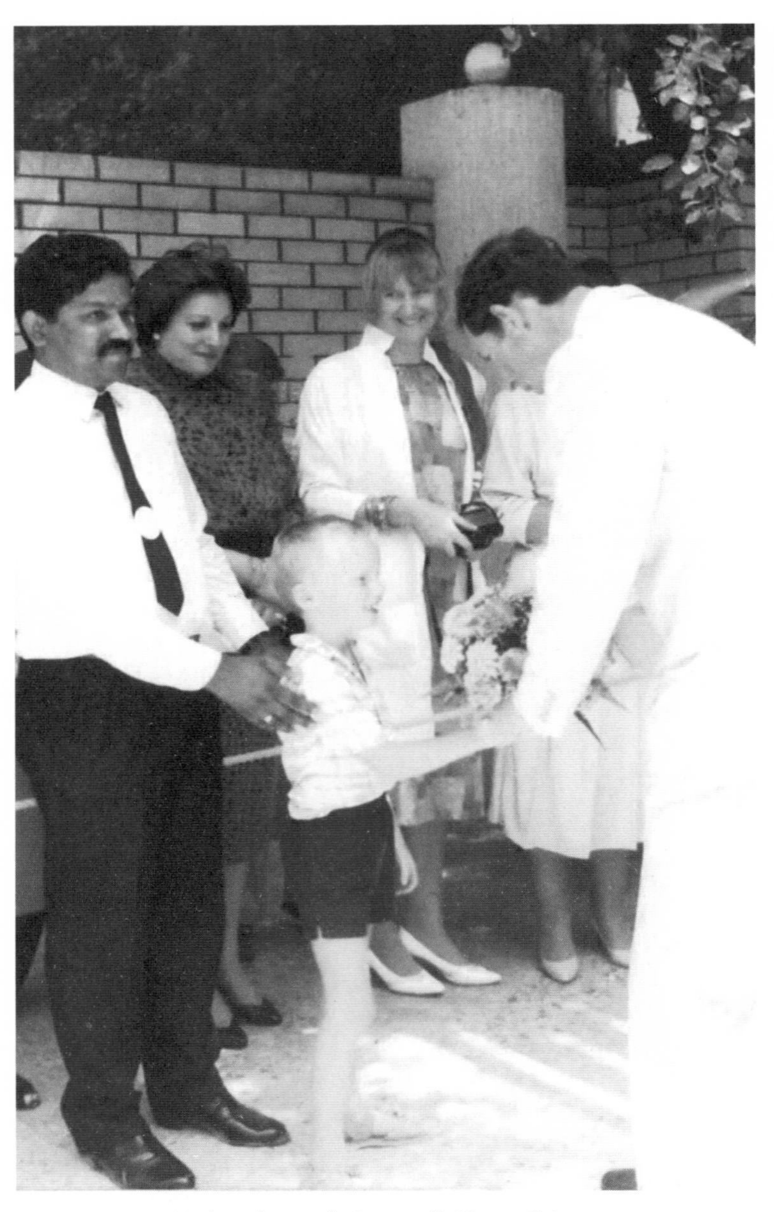

Nathaniel meets the Prince of Wales at Al Ain.

Thursday 15 March

At the airport at midnight I meet Robyn Davidson, sensitive, nervous, anxious and willowy. She has one case and a carton of her books. I have reflected that we will have to bluff our way through customs with the latter. If challenged we can say they are presents, but if we have to surrender them to the censors, so be it. I smile and flash my diplomatic card, and there is no challenge.

Friday 16 March

I take Robyn and Gabriel to Al Ain. Robyn is interested in everybody and everything. We meet the Bangladeshi Sanwar ul-Karim, who is dressed as an Omani. We get into his Toyota and drive into Oman and off on a track to the middle of nowhere, and come upon a group of camels and cars. Carpets are laid out on the ground and we are greeted by Jum'a Ali al-Darmaki, a retired policeman. He trains slender young

Dinner with the sheikhs. The Prince of Wales is flanked between Sheikh Khalifa bin Zayed Al Nahyan and the British Ambassador, Michael Tait. Mrs Kirstin Tait sits between David Heard and Sheikh Nahyan bin Mubarak Al Nahyan.

camels for racing, and recently sold one to Sheikh Sultan bin Zayed for a million dirhams. We sit and join him in a late breakfast. Robyn quizzes Jum'a and rides a camel. So does Gabriel.

Sanwar ul-Karim takes us to lunch at the house of Hamid al-Badi, who was a young man in one of Wilfred Thesiger's photographs. It is only at the end of the meal that Hamid focuses on Robyn and her desert travels, asking questions.

'Nine months travelling in the Australian desert? What did you do for food?'

'I shot rabbits and kangaroos. And wild camels.'

'You shot wild camels? They sell for millions of dirhams here.'

'Yes.'

'And you ate them?'

'Yes.'

Hamid smiles with appreciation.

'What kind of gun did you use?'

'One rifle for camels, and another for rabbits.'

Then more questions about carrying and finding water and so on. In conclusion he says, '*Dahiya*'. I have to look up this word later. It has the meaning of 'shrewd, sly, cunning, resourceful'.

Saturday 17 March

I take Robyn to Dubai. Muhammad al-Murr collects us and takes us to the camel-racing track, even though he 'hates camels'. We meet a friend of his, Shaiba, who takes us to see some Australian camels recently purchased by Sheikh Muhammad bin Rashid. We meet a couple of Australians who are looking after them and immediately recognise Robyn as 'the camel lady'. Then Sheikh Muhammad turns up, driving his own Range Rover, registration number Dubai 1. Muhammad greets him as the cousin he is, and Sheikh Muhammad takes us in his car to see his racing camels, beautiful slender beasts like giant greyhounds on stilts. Sheikh Muhammad enthuses about one called Mihna. He is breeding them and is interested in the details of their feed and their skin. He asks Robyn about her journey.

Tuesday 20 March

I take Robyn to see Zaki Nusseibeh at the Emiri Diwan. We spend an hour with him. Although he too 'hates camels', he asks lots of questions – about camels, hunting, the trip and writing. He says Sheikh Zayed and Sheikh Tahnoun would be interested and immediately phones to ask about entry into the Ruler's enclosure at the Al Wathba camel-racing track. No tickets are needed. We should just turn up at 3.

In the afternoon, I drive to Dubai and join Jack Briggs. We go to the award ceremony of the Sultan Owais prizes for Arab literature. Speeches and a poem from Sultan Owais. There is great applause for the Palestinian poet Fadwa Tuqan, a little old lady, as she takes her prize. The prize-winning playwright is Sa'dallah Wannus, the Syrian whose play *Evening Party to Celebrate 5 June* I saw in Damascus in 1971. I mingle with writers afterwards and introduce the poet Sheikha Maysun Saqr Al Qasimi to Jack. With a big smile and absolutely no rancour, he says, 'It was my job to put your father on the plane when he was deposed. I had to search him physically.'

Jack and I have dinner at the Iranian restaurant. He is loudly abusive of the Iraqi government. Afterwards I comment on his outspokenness.

'The restaurant is probably bugged by the Iranian secret police. That's why I was talking so freely about Iraq.'

I raise my eyebrows.

'Oh yes, they're all wired. Why, twenty years ago, I personally wired the Carlton House Hotel.'

Wednesday 21 March

Theresa and I take Robyn to the Queen's Birthday Party in the Ambassador's garden. The guest of honour is Major General Muhammad Said al-Badi, the nephew of our host last Friday. He invites Robyn back and offers all the facilities of the Abu Dhabi army to help her.

Thursday 22 March

Robyn joins us on a trip to Al Ain and beyond. We go to a wadi known among the Emirates expatriates as 'Fossil Valley'. I sit on a rock, watching other people doing their thing – Robyn walking in the middle distance, finding much in common between this terrain and the Australian desert. Natty collects fossils. Gabriel is looking for temples and caverns.

We find a camp site by some sand dunes and a well, a tree and some bushes. We set up a barbecue. The boys sleep in the tent, the rest of us outside. There is a fantastic pleasure in lying on a mat, totally relaxed and gazing at the stars – a five-thousand-star hotel. When I doze off I sleep profoundly, a pure, clean, deep sleep. I recall my last year in Sudan, when I slept outdoors every night.

In the middle of the night I hear the tramp of camels. I sit up and they immediately make off. To them it must seem as if some monster has sprung out of the ground. I wake up again later and hear a whole lot of camels moving around quietly, but noisily munching the undergrowth.

Friday 23 March

I take Robyn to the camel races at Abu Dhabi, talking our way into the enclosure next to Sheikh Zayed's enclosure. Sweets and cakes are liberally available. Sheikh Zayed arrives and the races commence. There are six races, each of ten kilometres, taking just under 20 minutes each. But it is the razzamatazz that goes with it all that is of interest: the provision of cakes courtesy of the Hilton Hotel, dancing girls in front of Sheikh Zayed swaying their hair to and fro, a Bedu band beating away, poets orating, one man riding up and down on a camel, which he wants to sell, proclaiming its merits. Robyn sees Sheikh Muhammad bin Rashid and gives him a wave. When the races are over we stroll into Sheikh Zayed's marquee and join crowds of people milling near Sheikh Zayed. I try to catch Sheikh Muhammad's eye, hoping he will introduce Robyn to Sheikh Zayed. I fail. In the throng I see Sheikh Sultan, Ruler of Sharjah, who, I am sure, would prefer to be reading a book. Sheikh Tahnoun bin Muhammad seems curiously alone and vulnerable, away from Al Ain and his entourage.

Saturday 24 March

I take Robyn to Fujairah for the opening of the exhibition of Wilfred Thesiger's photographs. Afterwards we sit with notables and Robyn tells her story.

'You should write a book about it,' says a Palestinian who has been in Fujairah since 1960.

We get back to Abu Dhabi in time to go to a farewell party for the Italian Ambassador. The Greek Ambassador asks if I am related to the writer Clark.

'Who?' I wonder.

'He writes on scientific matters.'

'Kenneth Clark?' I venture.

'Yes, that's him. You should take advantage of your time in Abu Dhabi to write a book.'

Sunday 25 March

I attend the Embassy 'prayer meeting' and talk camels.

The Consul mentions that Miss M is here.

'Who is Miss M?' I ask.

'She is the mother of an illegitimate child fathered by a senior national and is seeking money to help with her £186,000 mortgage.'

'That is approximately the price paid for a racing camel.'

Wednesday 28 March

In Dubai I meet Geoffrey King, who tells me Beatrice de Cardi has been in pursuit of money for archaeology. She has been lobbying the Lord Mayor of London, and at a lunch for Sheikh Zayed at Buckingham Palace she tried to get the latter interested in archaeology.

Thursday 29 March

I am preparing for publication the stories I have translated by Muhammad al-Murr. There are 22 Dubai tales altogether, selected from all his books, published between 1980 and 1990. Do I need a glossary? I will rationalise the sequence in which they appear. I am happy to be back writing. I enjoy words. With the stories behind me, I think again of a book on Thesiger that I could write up in the next few months.

Gabriel is 'doing Ramadan', as he calls it. He has something for breakfast but otherwise does not eat anything until sunset. He listens out for the muezzin and eats by himself.

Friday 30 March
I make a late-night call on Sheikh Nahyan. His father is not there, and Sheikh Nahyan comes into the room, a slight but stately figure. Eid Bakhit and three Arab ambassadors join us. We all sit on the floor. I sit next to Sheikh Nahyan as he plays cards with his guests.

Saturday 31 March
Office hours are reduced during Ramadan: we work from 8.30 am to 1.30 pm. I take a flask of coffee in, to spare my Muslim colleagues having to prepare coffee for me.

Sunday 1 April
At Embassy 'prayers' the matter of Miss M is discussed. She is staying at the Hilton and has no money, but the senior national is providing her with a car and driver. What can the Embassy do? The Ambassador cannot walk in on the senior national with a horsewhip. It is concluded that it is a private matter, nothing to do with the Embassy.

Monday 2 April
In Dubai, Ali Rashid Lootah takes me on some Ramadan calls at a late hour. First we call on Muhammad Habtoor, who trained in the United States as an oil engineer and is now an independent businessman. We move on to the majlis of Saif al-Ghurair, cool marble splendour. He has been the head of the Ghurair family since the death of his brother, Majid. A sister of Saif was the wife of Sheikh Saqr, Ruler of Ras Al Khaimah. There are two prominent sons of Sheikh Saqr, Sultan and Khalid, from a wife who was an Al Qasimi cousin. At the majlis I also meet Muhammad Khalifa Bakhit, Under-Secretary at the Ministry of Education. Also the erudite Dr Rashid Mukhawi, a former Ambassador to Germany. He is discussing with our host the poll tax that the British government has introduced. Our third and last call is on Abdul Aziz Obeidallah, Deputy Chairman of the Bank of Oman. (Saif al-Ghurair is the chairman.)

Tuesday 3 April
I drive to Ras Al Khaimah and have a good hour with Michael Edwards, Technical Adviser to the Ruler, Sheikh Saqr. Michael has been in Ras Al

Khaimah for 15 years. The Ruler is a conservative gentleman who used, from seniority, to chair the meeting of the Rulers in the 1960s before the establishment of the UAE. Since then he has been bypassed by the bigger Emirates and by Sheikh Zayed, with whom he never exchanges the intimate nose kiss. The 1970s were boom years and Ras Al Khaimah had its own police and army. Then funds dried up, the police and army were disbanded and the Emirate is now poor.

At 9 pm we call on Sheikh Khalid bin Saqr, who is 48 and was educated in the United States and at Loughborough. His third wife is the sister of Sheikha Maysun bin Saqr of Sharjah. Sheikh Khalid is the first sheikh I have met who is clean-shaven. I am invited to sit at his right and he talks of his house at Geneva. We plan for the Thesiger exhibition to come to Ras Al Khaimah at the end of May. I hope the Ruler will be able to open it. We adjourn to a less formal room and carry on chatting, sitting on the floor.

Wednesday 4 April

Ras Al Khaimah is like a developing country, trapped into partnership with the rest of the Emirates. It lacks the sanitised smoothness of Abu Dhabi and Dubai.

Michael Edwards takes me to call on the Ruler, Sheikh Saqr, a small man but alert and quick in his movements. I talk to him of the Thesiger exhibition and how we have neglected Ras Al Khaimah in the past. With his permission, we wish to embark on a series of cultural activities in Ras Al Khaimah, starting with the exhibition. I show him the catalogue. He then takes me into an adjacent room. We sit together on the floor and he rummages through some files and photographs. He shows me a portrait of his father, who died at the age of 97,[33] with Ras Al Khaimah notables. He then presents me with a framed picture of a group of Sharjah notables. One of them is the Sharjah Sheikh Saqr, who was deposed and whom I met when I took Wilfred Thesiger to call on Sheikh Zayed.

I go on to see his son, Sheikh Khalid, who has a very modern office in contrast, with framed portraits of his children.

---

33 Sheikh Saqr himself died in 2010, aged 90 or 92.

From 10 April Peter took some leave in England.

Friday 13 April

I call on my mother at the nursing home in Long Melford. I hardly recognise her at first. She is flopped in a chair, dozing. Her cheeks are sunken and her complexion seems yellow. I have to bellow to her who I am. I sit on the floor holding her hand, and have to repeat everything two or three times. So does she. The staff at the nursing home tell me that she never complains and seems quite happy. She has no memory of anything. The doctors say she could go on for two or three years. She has defied the doctors and thrown off cancer.

Saturday 14 April

I have Abu Dhabi reactions to things in England. A sound I heard made me think for an instant that it was the call to prayer. I have a half-second of shock when I see someone eating or smoking in public – in Ramadan. A puddle makes me think: there has been heavy rain here.

Peter took a train to Hereford and stayed with Hugh Leach[34] for a night. His quarters are a waggon at the end of the garden – rather like a train carriage. He then set off walking northwards and stayed at Glascwm youth hostel. He was the only one staying there.

Tuesday 17 April

I phone my sister, Stella. Mama died this afternoon. She had a haemorrhage on Sunday night, and was weeping and in pain. She was vomiting black blood. On Monday morning she was rushed to hospital in Sudbury. Stella spent much of the day with her. 'Am I on the way to Heaven?' she had asked on the way to hospital. She was put into the small ward where my father died in 1971. She sat up in bed, looked out of the window and said, 'What a nice view'. She asked after me, and was reassured by Stella's presence.

I spend the evening alone by the fire and reflect. In 1971 I came back to England from Lebanon a few days before my father died. In a

34 Soldier, spook, diplomat, explorer and writer (1934–2015).

similar way, I saw my mother just four days before she has died. I feel calm and relieved, but no doubt there will be a delayed reaction.

Wednesday 18 April

I have ten miles to walk to the nearest public transport, for I must see get back to London or Suffolk and arrange with Stella our mother's funeral.

As I walk I reflect on my mother's 92 years. She never was unkind to anyone. She had a relaxed but nonetheless strong sense of duty, and never complained about her role in life, or indeed any adverse circumstance. She was resourceful, systematic, cheerful and rarely moody, a compulsive compiler of lists, and an acute observer of flowers, trees and dress. She wrote well about her experiences in diaries and letters. She was well read and familiar with much English literature, classical and modern. She was careful with her money but unconcerned about gain or wealth. She gave happiness to those who were near her.

Monday 23 April

I have dinner with Wilfred Thesiger at the Travellers Club. I talk of the exhibition going to the Women's Association and he gives a sort of snort. Later he says how he is opposed to women priests: 'It goes against all tradition'. When women were proposed as members of the Travellers Club, he was ready to resign and move to Brooks's. But he is immensely proud of his 59-year membership of the Travellers.

'Have you seen the photograph?' A photograph portrait of Wilfred hangs in the lobby of the club.

'Yes.'

'I'm awfully proud of that. It is the only photograph of a living person who is not royalty.'

We go upstairs and pause by the Roll of Honour for members of the Club who were killed in the Second World War. His brother, Pilot Officer Thesiger, is named.

'He was killed on the day he got his commission.'

We talk books, and it is clear he has all sorts of possessions. He recently sold a Tiepolo painting, and has valuable books going back to the 16th century – Portuguese books about Ethiopia, or 'Abyssinia', as Wilfred calls it. He obviously enjoyed his recent visit to the Emirates and has written a new introduction about it. I hope he mentions the British Council.[35] We drink wine. He drinks a lot, and seems a little unsteady afterwards. I have to steer him to a taxi.

Thursday 26 April

In Sudbury I go to the Chapel of Rest to say farewell to my mother. She is laid out, in white, at peace. The skin of her face is tight and drawn back and she has a canine – almost lupine – look. She has a lot of whiskers and there is a characteristic family twist to her left nostril – her brother Dick has it – which I have not noticed before. I kiss her on her forehead and say goodbye. Stella arrives as I leave. I am pleased to have been alone with Mama. It is strange how frightened we are of our own emotions.

Back in Abu Dhabi.

Tuesday 1 May

I attend the ninth graduation ceremony of the University at Al Ain.

I am there in good time and doze off as we wait. I am woken up by a bugle call outside, and a band starts to play. The sheikhs process in. A reading from the Koran and a speech from Sheikh Nahyan. Several hundred students, all identically dressed, sit in rows behind their deans. Then a long procession of people going up to receive their degrees from Sheikh Zayed. Two of his sons, Nahyan and Saif, are among the graduands. Some visiting dignitaries are received by the Ruler, including Dr Abu Bakr al-Qirbi, a friend from our Yemen days. I catch up with him at tea, where we are joined by Fuad Qa'id Muhammad, who was Minister of Development during my years in Yemen. He is now head of the United Nations office in the Emirates. When he hears I am going to Dubai this evening, Abu Bakr asks me to take some Yemeni *qat* to his sister-in-law. I agree, with some misgivings – a Yemeni was recently imprisoned for possessing qat. It is also strange, for Abu Bakr was not a qat-chewer in Yemen. I take it, but feel self-conscious whenever I see any

35 He does.

policemen; I do deliver the goods.

Thursday 3 May

I settle down to some writing. I prepare my translations of Muhammad al-Murr's stories for publication. Rebecca read some first drafts and made some useful comments. For example, I do not have to say 'he said' or 'she said' all the time. That is implicit in the flow of the narrative. I also sketch out for Motivate a synopsis for a book on *Thesiger's Return*. It will only be about 18,000–20,000 words.

Later on, all the family go to Al Ain. We go straight to the zoo, the layout of which is impressive. We linger in the aquarium, which houses walruses, penguins and a wide range of fish of different shapes, sizes and colours.

Monday 7 May

I am lifted out a spell of boredom and depression at the office by a phone call from Musallim bin al-Kamam, who is at the porter's lodge at the British Embassy. I immediately go round, and bring him to the office. He hesitates about entering the building but I persuade him. We look through photographs of Wilfred's visit and I suddenly have the idea of phoning Wilfred at his Chelsea flat. It is about 9 am UK time. He is a bit taken aback, but he and Musallim greet each other over the phone. I tell Wilfred that we will look after Musallim and he apologises that when he was talking to him Swahili kept breaking in.

I ask David Heard to come along and we all go to the house. I arrange to have a Syrian takeaway meal. Gabriel and Nat join us. I impress on them the sense of occasion and they greet Musallim in Arabic. Musallim has brought presents for Theresa and her mother.

I take Musallim back to Bani Yas, a suburb of Al Wathba. We enter a bungalow where a man, old, bald and wearing just a loin-cloth, is fast asleep. He wakes up and gets dressed. When Musallim is out of the room, the man indicates in sign language that Musallim is not to be trusted and would put a knife in your back if it was turned. When Musallim is back and the old man is out of the room, Musallim tells me that the old man is crazy. When they are both in the room, the old man asks Musallim, pointing at me, 'Where did you find him?'

'In the street. I knew him before. He's a good man. He's a Rashidi.'

'A Rashidi from where?' the old man asks.

'A Rashidi from England,' I say. 'Musallim is my uncle [*'ammi*].'

I am given a bowl of dates as I leave.

Tuesday 8 May

I write a few hundred words on Thesiger. It is nice to try a different mode of writing, a mixture of journalism, reminiscence and reflection.[36]

Thursday 10 May

In the office, I have a phone call from somebody who wants Buti. I explain (in Arabic) that he has the wrong number. He says something in English and we continue in that language.

'You speak very good English,' he says. 'Did you go to school in Kenya?'

I tell him I am English, but he refuses to believe me and insists that I am Sudanese, or perhaps have an English mother and an Arab father.

I go to a reception at St Andrew's Church for Bishop Brown and his wife, Rosemary. We talk of Sudan and of mutual friends like the missionary and language expert, Roland Stevenson, who was a great friend of his. They used to travel abound the Nuba Mountains together in the early 1960s. I also talk to Mike Hall, who has lived in Sudan. We talk about characteristic Sudanese words. He asks me what the Kordofan word for lion was. '*Dud*,' I recall. I regret that I did not keep a diary during my six years in Sudan.

Saturday 12 May

I call on Fu'ad Qaid Muhammad, director of the United Nations office here. He has the doddle of a job here. He is originally an Adeni and was for 20 years a career international civil servant, before being seconded from the UN to be a Minister in Yemen, the reverse of the usual pattern. He is switching places with Abdul Rahman Abdullah, whom I knew in Sudan when he was Minister of Public Service and Administrative Reform. He has been in Qatar and has not been well, and the medical

---

36 Published as *Thesiger's Return* (Motivate Publishing, Dubai and London, 1992).

facilities in Abu Dhabi are better than those in Doha.

Monday 14 May

I have a visit from a sheikha from the Sharjah ruling family. She has a first degree from Ain Shams University in Cairo and a diploma from the University of Reading. I ask her, 'What next?'

'I want to do a PhD at the University of Sussex, because I have a house in Brighton.'

'It must be curious, being a sheikha in the Emirates and a student in Britain.' She smiles. 'Which do you prefer?'

'Being a student in Britain. There's more freedom.'

Tuesday 15 May

The British Council office in Dubai has received a threatening letter. I think it may refer to Salman Rushdie, but when I am faxed a copy I see that it is about Sulaiman, whoever he is, and his lack of faith. Otherwise the letter is the ravings of a lunatic. But lunatics can lob bombs and at present we have a lot of people whom we do not know sitting exams and leaving bags in corridors. I ask for a police check of these bags.

Thursday 17 May

We go to a party hosted by the Embassy for the British community in Al Ain. There are 350 people connected with the Tawam Hospital, a very self-satisfied group. I talk to a few people whom I know or have heard of. One very elderly medical man. A Pathan, married to a British lady of uncertain age. A nice Welsh girl from Merthyr Tydfil, married to an Egyptian who speaks English with a Welsh accent. A nurse from Jeddah who finds it all a bit quiet here. The smart Deputy Head of the English school, a Cockney.

Friday 18 May

I sometimes fantasise about leaving the British Council. I do not see enough of Gabriel and Nat. I would like to share their development more. I would like to be with them and watch the course of nature, see things grow, learn new things and old things with them. Streams, hills, woods. I would happily be a house husband, and spend four hours a day writing. There are several books in me struggling to get out.

Sunday 20 May

I go to the Embassy 'prayer meeting'. The Ambassador starts by publicly dressing down those who did not go to Al Ain on Thursday.

'When the Ambassador invites you, that is an order. You cancel previous engagements and come. There was nobody from the commercial section and only one from Chancery: he had done the right thing and cancelled a prior engagement. I am the Queen's representative.'

The Chancery man and I exchange smug glances.

Monday 21 May

I go to Ras Al Khaimah to make arrangements for the Thesiger photographs to be exhibited here. Things are very informal. It is like a developing country, with power cuts and policemen behaving casually. I see the Syrian historian Ahmad Tadmuri (from Tadmur or Palmyra), whom Mike Edwards calls 'Ted Murray'. He takes me to call on Sheikha Mahra, former wife of the Crown Prince, who is off to Britain 'until October', she says with a smile of complicity.

Wednesday 23 May

I am reading Wilfred Thesiger's *Arabian Sands* for the second time this year. It is particularly interesting now I know Bin Ghubaisha, Bin Kabina and Musallim bin al-Kamam. Musallim is ten years older than the others and was a reconciler of conflicting tribes in southern Arabia in the 1940s.

Thursday 24 May

I am writing about Musallim bin al-Kamam when he turns up in person. We have coffee and I am fascinated by his life story. According to *Arabian Sands,* he was already a man of some stature in the late 1940s. Thesiger describes him as being middle-aged – I reckon he was in his late twenties or early thirties – and quotes a man talking about 'the Christian who travelled to the Hadramaut with bin al Kamam'. Musallim has been all over the Arabian Peninsula and has just been in Qatar, where he has two sons studying. I take him to see Frauke Heard, who would like to get

Sheikh Saqr bin Muhammad Al Qasimi opens the exhibition of Thesiger photographs at Ras Al Khaimah.

Musallim talking on tape. Frauke and I talk in English. Musallim ticks us off, accusing us of being like the Mahra,[37] lapsing into our own language and cutting him out.

Saturday 26 May

I drive to Ras Al Khaimah for the opening of the exhibition of the Thesiger photographs. I pay a courtesy call on the Ruler, Sheikh Saqr. I tell him Musallim bin al-Kamam will be coming to the exhibition. As we talk, the lights go out, and I leave as a Saudi delegation arrives.

The Ambassador arrives half an hour before the exhibition is to be opened by Sheikh Saqr at the hotel. The tape is ready, catalogues available. Frauke Heard arrives with Musallim, and Sheikh Saqr arrives at 5, bang on

37 A southern Arabian tribe that has its own language, a survival of one of the pre-Arabic languages.

time. The tape is cut and I start to talk to Sheikh Saqr about the pictures. But Musallim takes over, and he and Sheikh Saqr get on fabulously, laughing and talking together in an Arabic that I find incomprehensible. Three of Sheikh Saqr's sons are with him – Sheikh Khalid, Sheikh Saud (who is married to a daughter of the Dubai merchant, Jum'a al-Majid) and Sheikh Faisal, whose wife is a daughter of the Ruler of Ajman.

Thursday 7 June

We go to Fujairah and visit the English school, which was founded in 1955 and so must be the oldest English-medium school in the Emirates.

I call on Saeed Raqabani, the federal Minister of Agriculture. He is the Fujairah man in the federal cabinet. He is very affable. We discuss what the British Council can and cannot do in Fujairah. He invites us to visit his farm tomorrow.

In the hotel later, I write up the section of my Thesiger book on his personality – the paradoxes, the mixture of toughness and gentleness, the blazing integrity, and the touch of savagery in him.

Friday 8 June

Muhammad Atiya, the Egyptian farm manager of Abdul Aziz al-Raqabani, collects us from the hotel and we drive, following him, 30 miles up the coast, past Khor Fakkan, and swing off left to the farm. We are given a guided tour: 400 mango trees, some with other branches grafted on to them. There are citrus fruits, dates and a few pawpaw. Overlooking the garden is the men's house, with two bedrooms, a majlis, a swimming pool, a tennis court and a football pitch. More secluded is the women's house. The Minister does not sell the produce but either uses it or gives it away. Muhammad Atiya has been in Fujairah since 1972 and speaks to the workmen fluently in their languages – Baluchi and Bengali. Next door is a fine palace belonging to Sheikh Muhammad bin Rashid Al Maktoum of Dubai, and nearby is a farm belonging to one of the Dubai merchant families. We leave loaded with mangos and limes.

I have dinner with two of the teachers of the English-medium school. One of them, Jan Brettingham, has had an interesting career. She has been a global auditor for Peat Marwick and checked accounts in Marib in Yemen. She has taught at Dubai College and in New Zealand, and been married. We talk about all sorts of things. Jan says that men in the Emirates accept the professionalism of women far more readily than Europeans. The Ruler of Fujairah, I learn, is married to a granddaughter of Sheikh Rashid of Dubai.

Saturday 9 June

I am invited to the graduation day at Al Worood School. We have an hour of elaborate pageantry. The Police Band plays the National Anthem, and then a pipe band comes in. The teachers, all dressed alike, parade in, to applause. Then the graduates. The guest of honour is Ahmad al-Khalifa al-Suwaidi. Four ambassadors are present. One of the teachers, Erika Hodeib, tells me that Ibrahim al-Nur, a relation of her husband, Abdul Hamid, is staying with them. I knew Ibrahim very well when he was Under-Secretary in the Ministry of Education in Sudan. We are invited to dinner straightaway. Ibrahim and I chat away, reminisce, gossip and joke. When he was studying medieval European history in Britain he was nearly converted to Catholicism by the monks of Caldey Island. He is witheringly contemptuous of the fundamentalists. Our host has given up drinking alcohol but Ibrahim, with the authority of an older male relative, insists that beer and whisky is on the table.

Sunday 10 June

Frauke and David Heard, their daughter Theresa, Gabriel, Nat and I have been invited to see Musallim bin al-Kamam at Al Wathba. We are warmly greeted. Camels wander outside in the unmade streets. David and I sit with Musallim. Frauke and Theresa go to the women's quarters. My sons wander to and fro. I ask Musallim what he means when he refers to 'Frankish piastres'. They are Maria Theresa thalers. Thesiger was a better man, he tells us, than Abdullah Philby[38] (whom he knew). The latter used to have rages.

---

38 H St John Philby (1885–1960), traveller and author, former public servant. He settled in Saudi Arabia and became a Muslim – adopting the name of Abdullah. Father of spy Kim.

Wednesday 13 June

I speak to Muhammad al-Murr by phone. He is weary from sleepless nights with a new baby, called Baiat, named after a great-uncle who was killed by 'Awamir tribesmen. Baiat is one of a hundred names for 'lion'.

Saturday 16 June

I call on Zaki Nusseibeh. I give him a copy of Marmaduke Pickthall's *Oriental Encounters*. He refers to a recent book on Pickthall by …

'By me,' I say.

We talk books, Islamic fundamentalism, the Koran and Arabic historiography.

Tuesday 19 June

The British Council driver takes me to Fujairah, and I see George Bajk, the Lebanese general manager of the Private Affairs Bureau of the Ruler. He takes me along to the Ruler's *diwan* and I chat to various members of the ruling family, and to Muhammad Rashid al-Amiri, a Dubai businessman, who remembers seeing Mubarak bin London at Tawi Hasan.

'Why do you need a car to go hunting?' Wilfred had asked him. 'What's wrong with a camel?'

I then go and see the Ruler, Sheikh Hamad bin Muhammad al-Sharqi. He is in his early forties, and has a farm near Lewes and an honorary KCMG. He has forgotten to thank the Queen for this honour. We talk about the possibility of extending British Council activity in Fujairah. Step by step, I argue. His office is spicker and spanner than that of the Ruler of Ras Al Khaimah. As I enter the anteroom, a man looks up from his telephone and suddenly asks me, 'What time is it in Tokyo?' He is conducting some commercial transaction.

As I am driven back to Abu Dhabi I read some of *Arabia, the Gulf and the West* by J B Kelly, a detailed indictment of British policy. Whew! He has a fine style. I am totally absorbed in it when there is the most violent jolt and clash of metal. A car, driven by a Swede, has run into the back of us at speed on one of the speed humps. He immediately acknowledges responsibility. I am in the back and am not wearing a safety belt. My head hits the roof and I feel as if my windpipe has been twisted. But above all, I am shaking from shock. It is my fifth road accident and I do not seem to be getting used to them. The police come along, and we go to the police station at Mafraq and are then free to go. I feel totally drained by the incident.

Sunday 24 June

I take Nat to a party. We take a taxi and, unusually, the taxi-driver is also the owner of the car and a UAE national. Most of the taxi-drivers are Pathan, with a minority of Goans and a number of Syrians – all from Dera'a. The owners of the cars are often UAE widows. I ask the driver where he is from.

'Al Ain,' he tells me.

'And your tribe?'

'Baluch,' he says. He is a most engaging man.

Monday 25 June

I take a taxi. The driver is, as usual, a Pathan.

'Pakistan good,' he says.

'What about Benazir?' I ask.

'She no good. She woman, not good for Muslims.'

'Is a good woman better than a bad man?' I ask.

'Yes,' he has to confess.

Wednesday 27 June

I meet Said Ghobash, Minister of State for Supreme Council Affairs. He is from Ras Al Khaimah, in his mid-forties; a delightful man, who graduated from the University of Cairo in 1969, and was first Ambassador to Lebanon and then to the US. His uncle was assassinated when Minister of State for Foreign Affairs. He wants to do some study or be attached to a British university, not to get a degree but to write something of lasting value.

'You can have a block of flats but it comes down after twenty years. A work of scholarship would be on library shelves for ever.'

Sunday 8 July

I see Zaki Nusseibeh, who is planning to go on an intensive Italian course this summer, followed by time at Bayreuth, but between the two he has to interpret for Sheikh Zayed when he meets Benazir Bhutto.

Theresa and the boys went on leave, and Peter followed on 8 July to take two months off. He flew out to Aden for a few days, staying with the Ambassador, Douglas Gordon, then on to England for Kate's graduation from the University of York. Theresa and Peter were based at their house in Brighton but in late July, with the boys, took a fortnight's holiday in Provence.

While they were in France Iraq invaded and occupied Kuwait.

Peter returned alone to Abu Dhabi in late August, Theresa and the boys joining him later.

Wednesday 22 August

I touch down at Abu Dhabi at 9 pm local time, 5 pm London time. The British Council driver meets me.

The situation in Abu Dhabi is tense. People are stocking up on rice in case of trouble. There are more road checks and a rumour that Palestinians, whose loyalty is suspect, may be purged. People are glued to the BBC news.

Thursday 23 August

I see David Heard. He hands me a report on terrorism in the Gulf that shows how Saddam prepared the way for his invasion by terrorism and sabotage in Kuwait. Abu Dhabi could be vulnerable. Power stations and oil installations depend so much on foreign labour, some of which is Iraqi. Such people could be suborned with threats to their families in Iraq. Sheikh Zayed was once personally insulted by Saddam at a conference in Cairo. Before that he had seen Saddam as a rough diamond, a leader of men. Now he feels the UAE, his creation, is under threat. A causeway is being built between the island of Abu Dhabi and the mainland as a safeguard against the bridges being blown up. One official who had been sympathetic towards Iraq commented ruefully as he gazed at the gardens, 'Saddam wants to destroy all this'.

Sunday 26 August

At the weekly Embassy meeting, I hear about comments made by

Sheikh Zayed after the invasion, full of wise and pithy observations, such as:

'You can recognise a wise man, but it is impossible to figure out a fool,' of Hussein (King, not Saddam).

'He has Syria, the PLO and Israel between him and his clothes.'

'It is not wrong for a man to be frightened of a snake'.

I call on Zaki Nusseibeh on my way to Dubai. I bought him a book in London. He was recalled from his leave by the crisis and had to miss Glyndebourne. And Salzburg.

'What do I owe you for this?' he asks.

'Your friendship,' I reply.

He is upset and angry with Saddam and the pro-Saddam Palestinians. He comments that many Arabs want to be either a hero or a martyr, with little in between. He also talks of Leslie McLoughlin[39] and how good his Arabic is.

'He is our Zaki Nusseibeh', I say.

Thursday 30 August

I go through the final proofs of *Dubai Tales,* my translation of the stories of Muhammad al-Murr.

On security advice, I no longer leave the car on the road outside the house but bring it in to the compound.

Saturday 1 September

The British community in the Emirates were, under Embassy guidance, divided into groups headed by a 'warden'. The wardens were the link between the Embassy and everyone else. Peter was a warden and his responsibilities were for the British Council staff and teachers.

I discuss security with a visiting Foreign Office expert who is out from London. Many terrorist incidents have been averted by vigilance. Seventy-five per cent of attacks are made when people are going to or coming from their offices. Cars are particularly vulnerable.

I go to the Embassy clubhouse, generally known as the Rabbit

---

39 Arabist, interpreter, teacher and author (1935–).

Hutch, to join other British wardens – the links between the Embassy and British subjects – to meet Douglas Hurd, the Foreign Secretary. We sip orange juice. One man has beer. Hurd comes in, thin-faced, looking drained. He tells us that he is impressed by the way business is being carried on as normal. Whatever emerges from the crisis, Saddam (which he rhymes with 'madam') will not come out of it rejoicing.

Sunday 2 September

There is no weekly prayer meeting and I go to the Embassy in vain. Instead I watch a flotilla of cars, mostly UAE hospitality cars with motorcycle and police escorts, set off with the Ambassador and Douglas Hurd. I feel, curiously, a glow of patriotic pride seeing the flag flying and witnessing this cooperation between two countries.

I hear a broadcast of a press conference given by Douglas Hurd: calm, authoritative, comprehensive. He is good.

In the afternoon I brief the British Council teachers on the situation and about contingencies. I emphasise the need to avoid both complacency and paranoia. Being aware of dangers and being alert are the best safeguards.

Monday 3 September

I have dinner with Muhammad al-Murr in Dubai. He tells me that when Dick Cheney, the US secretary of defence, was here last month, he was very cross that a Palestinian, Zaki Nusseibeh, was interpreting.

He tells me about a friend, a UAE-based Iraqi at the university, who met up with a US-based Iraqi with whom he had been at school.

'What happened to So-and-So,' asked one.

'He was accused of being a communist and was executed.'

'What about So-and-So else?'

'He disappeared.'

And so on. It turned out that half their classmates had disappeared or been executed. As Muhammad says, quoting his Iraqi friend, 'An air of sadness hovered over the room.'

He also tells a story of a Kuwaiti businessman in Kuwait after the Iraqi occupation who had food and water in the house and kept low. An Iraqi officer came to the house and said, 'Why don't you come out? If you have any problem, come to me. I'm in the police station over there.'

A few days later two or three Iraqi soldiers came to the house and asked for some water. He gave it to them. The next day they came again and asked for some fruit juice. He went to fetch some. When he returned, the Iraqi soldiers were helping themselves to the television set. They left, and the businessman went to see the officer at the police station to complain. The officer summoned some soldiers.

'Is it these?' he asked.

'No.'

More were summoned, with the same exchange. Eventually the businessman said, 'Yes, it's them.'

The officer immediately shot them dead.

Muhammad tells the story simply, eloquently, directly, like one of his own short stories.

Saturday 8 September

There have been some significant deaths in the last few days: Lord Caradon, brother of Michael Foot and father of Paul; Sir Len Hutton, a sporting hero; and A J P Taylor, an intellectual hero whose biography of Lord Beaverbrook actually reduced me to tears.

Wednesday 12 September

The crisis continues to dominate news and conversations. One newspaper predicts war in the second half of this month, another that the Americans will strike in October. I meet my American opposite number, Sami Hajjar, a political scientist of about my age, Lebanese in origin (from Souk al-Gharb). He reckons the crisis is now a public relations exercise. I put forward the theory that, in the global village, the cable news network is like the village coffee shop, with people coming and going, with rumours and news, seeking to influence public opinion.

Thursday 13 September

I take the boys to a circus. It is in a big tent with one entrance, and I tremble for the fire hazards. A smell of animal urine prevails and we have to wait for half an hour. It is called a European circus but most of the performers seem to be Filipino. We have jugglers and unfunny comics and clowns in Laurel and Hardy masks. Dogs are dressed up and perform antics. A belly dancer gyrates with a snake and another with a couple of bears. A Filipino family come on and throw themselves about, tumbling all over the place. A small boy comes in, aged about seven, and twists himself into all sorts of amazing contortions. Then younger brothers come in. The youngest must be four or five. He stands on his head, on his father's hand.

Friday 14 September

There is a T-shirt on sale with the slogan 'Visit Iraq before Iraq visits you' and the picture of a tank.

Sunday 16 September

There are Kuwaiti refugees here. Some are not making themselves popular by being unappreciative and demanding. There is a joke going the rounds, about a newspaper ad: 'Sri Lankan family seeks Kuwaiti maid'.

Monday 17 September

Robert Wilson from the Embassy comes to talk to British Council teachers. The potential war zone is as far away as London is from the French–Italian border. The Iraqi missiles do not have a good aim. If an evacuation of the British is recommended, it might be that we should take a commercial flight out, or go to Fujairah or Oman. A boat may be available. But we would have to pay. He recommends that everyone should register with the Embassy.

Wednesday 19 September

I call on Abdul Rahman Abdullah. He is the uncle of Abdullah Ahmad Abdullah, who was head of the University of Khartoum in my time and is now Sudanese Ambassador to the United States. Abdul Rahman is now head of the United Nations Development Programme here. He was Sudanese Ambassador to the UN at the time of the Falklands crisis. He talks of his career. Before Sudanese independence in 1956, he was a junior official in Fanjak in Nuer country (where Wilfred Thesiger had been in the 1930s), one of the most backward parts of the whole of

Sudan. He learned the Nuer language and loved it there. From Fanjak to New York! The years in Fanjak were the best of his life. He talks about Numairy, and how he lost his sense of reality. There are enough of Numairy's former ministers (such as Ma'mun Abu Zaid and Fatma Abdul Mahmud, and Abdul Rahman himself) in the UAE to form a cabinet in exile.

Thursday 20 September

I hear that there are anxieties about sabotage. An Iraqi police chief in Iraq has a son in a senior position in the oilfields here. There are cars at Musaffa on the mainland, loaded up with food, ready for a quick getaway to Oman. Boats are moored, stocked with food and water, ready to cross to Bandar Abbas in Iran.

Sunday 23 September

At the weekly Embassy meeting there is talk of war, rumours of war, preparations and contingencies, such as commandeering the Embassy swimming pool (20,000 gallons) for drinking water. People in Qatar and Bahrain have been told to come to Abu Dhabi if the balloon goes up.

I have a phone call from a woman who wants to do a PhD on some women's subject. What should I advise her? I suggest exogamy and endogamy in the UAE in the last 40 years or so. Are people from Sharjah, say, more likely to marry people from another Emirate since the federation in 1971?

Saturday 29 September

In a Zeal-of-the-Land Busy mood, I decide to have a fire drill in the office. It is arranged at a time of minimal inconvenience – just before the end of a lesson. But we learn from it. The alarm is not loud enough for everyone to hear. And we need to have a hammer by the alarm to break the glass. It is the first time anyone can remember having a fire drill.

Tuesday 2 October

After lunch I go to the Passing Out parade of the army volunteers – about 5,000 of them. I join a busload of diplomats and we go to the parade ground, which must be two miles long. Sheikhs, ambassadors and visitors are all in place. Then the president of the country, Sheikh Zayed, turns up, arriving in a car with Muhammad Said al-Badi. They tour the whole of the parade ground, passing by the troops. Speeches are followed by a spectacular fly-past with the dropping of what seem like 200 or more parachutists. People seem to be tossed out of planes and take two minutes to reach the ground. Most fall into the desert nearby. One falls onto the parade ground. Presentations are made to the most outstanding volunteers, the youngest of whom is ten years old, the oldest 60. Then poetry. Indeed, this is the longest element, and is interrupted by the call to sunset prayers. Darkness falls and I make my way to the diplomats' bus. In the light of the current Gulf crisis, there is a new-found seriousness about the whole ceremony.

Wednesday 3 October

I have a call from Sharjah from Sahib Ali al-Habshi, who wants to study in England. I ask him about the origin of his name Habshi, which means 'Abyssinian'. He tells me that his forebears were swarthy and were told they were black, like Abyssinians.

Saturday 6 October

I spend a couple of hours going round Abu Dhabi, checking out where each of our teachers lives.

Sunday 7 October

At the Embassy meeting there is more gloomy talk about preparations for war. There are other bits of gossip. Benazir Bhutto's husband has business interests in Dubai, and turned up in a flash suit and a Rolls-Royce at a charity cricket match, joining the Indian and Pakistani film stars who are there to be seen.

Zaki Nusseibeh drops by. He is pessimistic. He thinks the Americans need a war before people get bored or before there is a political movement against war.

Monday 8 October

There is a rumour going round that Saddam may withdraw unilaterally from Kuwait. He will have taught Kuwait a lesson and shown that the Gulf states are dependent on the West. He will have removed the *casus belli* and the *raison d'être* of the presence of the US troops in the region. He will have given a spur to the Palestine issue and will summon an Arab summit conference in Baghdad, to which most Arab states will go. Meanwhile the stories from Kuwait continue to be awful. It is a capital offence to possess a Kuwaiti flag or a portrait of the Amir. People have been summarily executed for refusing to display pictures of Saddam.

Theresa phones me at work to say Sheikh Rashid, Ruler of Dubai, has died. There is an unspecified period of mourning. The heir is Sheikh Maktum bin Rashid, although his brother Sheikh Muhammad has been very much more in the public eye as federal Minister of Defence. He has been meeting all sorts of people from overseas and has developed a close relationship with Sheikh Zayed.

I receive copies of the cover of *Dubai Tales*, my translation of a collection of the stories of Muhammad al-Murr. Printing may take up to two months, so I may have copies by Christmas. Hooray!

Tuesday 9 October

I send a telegram of condolence, to be published in the local press, on the death of Sheikh Rashid.

Thursday 11 October

I pack various precious items into a suitcase to be sent to England: things we would hate to lose. Family photographs, my diaries, and some books and papers relating to Pickthall and Thesiger. It is improbable that Abu Dhabi will be either bombed or occupied, but the loss of these things would be incalculable. Clothes and other books can be replaced.

I have lunch at the house of Abdullah Abdul Rahman. It is in honour of Muhammad Abdullah al-Nur, the Sudanese head of the FAO office in Alexandria and brother of Ibrahim. One of the other guests is Dafa' Allah al-Hajj Yusuf, whom I used to know when he was Minister of education in Khartoum. He was a right-wing lawyer working with the Sudanese entrepreneur Khalil Osman. A chain-smoker and valetudinarian, he went on to become Numairy's chief justice, presiding over 'Islamic justice' in 1983, including the severing of the hands of people found guilty of theft. He is very cordial. He is now practising law here.

'The Sudanese government and the Egyptian opposition are united over Kuwait,'[40] observes one Sudanese, 'and the Sudanese opposition and the Egyptian government are also in agreement.'

Monday 15 October

The office has a demolition order. We have to quit the premises in six months. The office is in a building built in the 1970s and looks old.

Thursday 18 October

We are guests for dinner with the parents of Reem Metwalli, a talented artist. Her parents are exiles from Iraq. It is a family occasion with some other guests, including Jennifer, who is housekeeper for Sheikh Muhammad bin Zayed. She tried to get a job with the British Royal Family but was turned down because, she suspects, she was divorced. She sorted out the London home of Sheikh Khalifa bin Zayed in Hans Crescent recently. He does speak English.

Friday 19 October

We have a lunch party. One of the guests is a sulky Northern Irish lady who seems to be at war with the world. She comes up with all sorts of conversation-stoppers, such as:

'I wouldn't marry that man if you paid me,' on being told she looked pensive.

'You'd look pensive if you hadn't spoken to anyone since two o'clock yesterday afternoon.'

'You've been married twice, Theresa, and I haven't even been married once.'

'You've got everything, Theresa: a husband, two children, a nice house.'

It is hard – nay, impossible – to cheer her up.

---

40 They supported Iraq.

Sunday 21 October

The British Minister of State for the Armed Forces, Archie Hamilton, has been here. He called on Sheikh Muhammad bin Rashid and barked, all six-foot-eight of him, 'Sorry about your father. Great friend of the family and all that, rah rah. Looks as if we're going into Iraq. Might as well not delay, rah rah.'

A national friend calls. He applauds what Saddam has done, though he acknowledges there has been a lot of suffering.

'The Amir of Kuwait has promised to restore the liberal constitution of 1962. That would not have happened but for Saddam. Things are settling down in Lebanon. That would not have happened but for Saddam. The Americans have cast a veto at the United Nations against Israel. That would not have happened but for Saddam.'

Thursday 25 October

The office manager, Jamal, a Keralan Muslim, calls at the house. The office driver was – at Jamal's request – driving Jamal's car and knocked a child over. The driver took him to the hospital and the traffic police are being heavy; Jamal fears that the driver may be imprisoned. I go with Jamal to the traffic police and talk to the Omani officer. He bonds more easily with me, as an arabophone, than with Jamal, as a fellow Muslim.

We drive to the bungalow that the Embassy owns at Al Ain. We have a dip in the greasy irrigation tank that is called the swimming pool. Then we prepare for guests for dinner. We provide the drinks and arrange for the Hilton Hotel to do the food. Our guests are mainly the Tunisian staff at the university – Mongi and his wife Yumna, Abdul Razzaq, and Hedi and Laila. They are totally at home. Another guest is Richard, a sixties American radical who finds it difficult to adjust to the current Gulf crisis. He is from an American university that has always been radical – they were among the first to offer degrees to women and to admit black students. He has a shadow, Catherine, who seems to have no existence independent of him.

Saturday 27 October

Twenty copies of *Dubai Tales* arrive. I am overjoyed. They look good.

I phone Muhammad and persuade him that he should be ready to autograph books at the Ghurair Centre bookshop. He will arrange for me to be interviewed on the English-language channel of Dubai television. I send Muhammad 12 copies, some for review, some for the censors and some for promotional purposes. I give one to my PA, Marie-Reine (who typed the drafts), and one to a friend who will see the Abu Dhabi censors tomorrow.

I come home and we drink a bottle of champagne in celebration. I drag the boys away from the television. They have a sense of occasion and I want it to be a family celebration.

Monday 29 October

I have a call from a Mr Joskurian, who asks permission to translate my translation into Malayalam, the language of Kerala. I have no objection, but pass him on to Muhammad for his approval. There is a local Malayalam weekly for which he will write it.

Thursday 1 November

The *Gulf Weekly* has the fourth and final extract from *Dubai Tales*. I have had good publicity. People are talking about it. The *Khaleej Times* has a supplement on the British Council in the UAE, with a nice selection of photographs: Douglas Pickett, a former Director, with Sheikh Rashid at the opening of the British Council in Dubai in 1972; me and the Prince of Wales; Sheikh Nahyan and Wilfred Thesiger.

I go to the Embassy to attend a briefing from a Major Roberts. It is excellent. The audience is all male. Would wives have been welcome? He gives a tremendous survey of Iraq's military capability and the defences in Kuwait. Berms have been erected to check the progress of tanks. The Iraqi army is hierarchical and relies on command, not leadership, and leaves nothing to initiative. There are, in fact, four armies: the Republican Guard, the regular army, the militia, and Palestinians. The latter two are mainly responsible for the looting in Kuwait. The talk is peppered with military abbreviations: CW, BW and KP (chemical warfare, biological warfare and key plants). The Iraqi army is often idle, with only ten of 60 divisions actually in combat at any one time. Morale is low, supply lines are tenuous and the whole lot could collapse under pressure. The hostages are well looked after. He is reassuring about the missiles. The longer the range, the smaller the payload. The effectiveness of chemical weapons is dubious. They need a sophisticated and mobile launcher, and contaminate those who deal with them. The first stage of the war will be a battle for air supremacy, which could be settled in between 36 hours and six days. The overrunning of Kuwait by the infantry could be costly and messy, especially if oil installations are damaged. It could end up with our saying, 'Here's Kuwait back. Sorry it's a bit singed.'

Friday 2 November

I have a phone call from Musallim bin al-Kamam. 'You must come and see me in Bani Yas.'

He calls at the house in the afternoon. He prays, removing his headdress and tucking up his *jallabiya*. The boys are good and culturally sensitive, and do not stare or giggle. We then drive off, Musallim in the passenger seat, his feet folded beneath him as if he is squatting in the desert. At the Rashidi house in Bani Yas, we drink coffee, eat lots of fruit and watch cartoons on the television.

Saturday 3 November

Two people come from the Hilton Hotel with an enormous cake to celebrate the 21st anniversary of the British Council in Abu Dhabi. What a nice surprise!

I go to Dubai to be interviewed by the English television station. I compare Muhammad al-Murr to Somerset Maugham and talk tactfully about how well he deals with the role of women.

Later I have dinner with Muhammad and at his house we see the local news. There is a four-minute item about the publication of his stories in English.

Peter went to England for two weeks. He spent a couple of days walking on the Sussex Downs, saw his sister and her family, and attended a course on negotiation, during which he amused himself with making anagrams from the names of his colleagues: 'No rent boy I' for Tony O'Brien and 'Heil Tory peasant' for Stephanie Taylor.

He returned to Abu Dhabi on 20 November.

Wednesday 21 November
I call on the majlis of Sheikh Mubarak bin Muhammad and his son, Sheikh Nahyan, who has been appointed Minister for Higher education. I give him a copy of *Dubai Tales.*

Thursday 22 November
We spend the evening with Sara, Theresa's Iranian colleague, and her Libyan husband Musaddiq. We go to the Japanese restaurant at the Hilton Hotel and are served by kneeling Thai girls dressed as Japanese geishas.

Monday 26 November
One of our teachers in Al Ain tells me they are giving private lessons to a young sheikha, a graduate of the university. She has never left Al Ain, not even to go to Abu Dhabi or Dubai. Her English is good and she talks with the teacher about a fantasy life – taking the children to school, doing housework, playing tennis. All things that would seem tedious in England but which she is unable to do here.

Tuesday 27 November
Dubai Tales, I hear, has not been cleared by the Abu Dhabi censors. The introduction (by me) is all right, but the censors' office is troubled with the idea that Gulf people might drink alcohol and commit adultery. One bookshop is selling copies, even though the book has not yet been cleared.

Wednesday 28 November
I have a call from Ali Nasri Hamza, who I knew in Sudan 15 years ago. He was one of seven or eight bright brothers from Kawa. The historian Ma'muna Mirghani Hamza is his cousin and sister-in-law. He is 61 and single. I remember when his brother brought a young British bride to Sudan. She was miserable, and Ali came to me to see if I would talk her into liking Khartoum. It was very touching, but I had to refuse.

Ali and I talk Sudanese history and Sudanese historians. There was a fine generation – people like Mekki Shibeika, Muhammad Ibrahim Abu Salim and Yusuf Fadl Hasan. He adds the name of Muhammad

Sa'id al-Qaddal from a younger generation: he is *marxisant* and currently in prison in Port Sudan.

Thursday 29 November

Britain has restored diplomatic relations with Syria. I immediately contemplate a posting there. I have thought I would not want another Arab posting, but I will make an exception for Syria.

I phone my line manager and say that if the British Council opens up in Syria I would be interested.

'I do not regard Syria as Arab,' I say. 'It is Byzantine.'

'So are you,' he says.

Friday 30 November

Jack Briggs phones. He was at one of Sheikh Maktoum bin Rashid's majlises and one elderly man asked him, 'Are you still cycling?'

'Oh, yes,' said Jack.

'Doesn't it affect ... the other?'

'Not at all,' said Jack. 'On the contrary, if people knew how good it was for ... the other, every mother's son would be out on their bikes all day.'

We drive to Al Ain and visit Jahli Fort, where Sheikh Zayed was born. It is a delight, a mud building with towers and lots of space, half-deserted and partly restored. The boys love it. We work out that access to the roof was by stakes projecting horizontally from the mud wall, about two feet diagonally from each other. Next door is a restored tower and a watered garden that we call 'The Ladies' Park'.

Saturday 1 December

We go to the Muwaijih Fort, where Wilfred Thesiger stayed in 1948. It was the home and base of Sheikh Zayed when he was the Ruler's representative in the Eastern Region. It is a square mud fort in a good state of preservation, with a market garden inside.

We camp in the desert just on the Omani side of the border.

Sunday 2 December

I sleep very fitfully in the outer part of the tent. It is cold in the night and very uncomfortable, made more so because I was sleeping on a sandal.

I am physically uncomfortable all the time we are at the camp. Time seems to drag. I cannot sit anywhere at ease. The heat of the sun becomes relentless and the flies irritating. The whole business of camping is labour-intensive and disagreeable, a form of refined Hell.

We escape to the Buraimi Hotel for some tea and coffee, and to empty our bowels. A friend, Harry, joins us to take us to Old Buraimi. There are several false starts and we get lost twice. We find the place eventually. It is a crumbling mud-brick village in the oasis. Harry says it dates from the 13th century; I think it may go back to the 1920s or 1930s. There may have been settlements around that go back centuries. The Buraimi oasis is extensive and we are on an old trade route.

Sunday 9 December

Leslie McLoughlin, who taught me Arabic in Lebanon 20 years ago, is here. I have arranged for him to give a lecture at the Cultural Foundation.

Zaki Nusseibeh is his chairman, and Leslie talks about the translation of Arabic into English, especially of modern literature. He praises the work of Denys Johnson-Davies, and mine. Both of us, he says, live in the Arab community and understand far more than the words. This is in contrast to academic translations. Then an amazing thing happens – Denys Johnson-Davies himself turns up in the audience. He has just arrived from Cairo, where he lives. In his peroration, Leslie refers to Denys's presence. Afterwards there is a joyful reconciliation, for there was some silly misunderstanding between them in 1973.

Monday 10 December

I collect Leslie and we call on Zaki Nusseibeh and together go to see Khalifa Khamis, the Under-Secretary at the Ministry of the Interior, to discuss interpreter training for the ministry. We double back to Zaki's house and the three of us discuss the Arabic for 'bully'. *Baltaji*? *(Q) abadayy*? *Shaqqi*? *Qawwad*? We have lunch, the only other guest being the British Ambassador. As soon as he comes in he says, 'I don't want to talk any Arabic'.

Leslie and I go off to call at the majlis of Sheikh Mubarak. Sheikh Nahyan joins us after afternoon prayers. One of the others at the majlis is an Afghan businessman who sells German desalination equipment. Journalists are making appointments to interview Leslie following his lecture last night.

Thursday 13 December

I take Leslie to Ras Al Khaimah and we call on the Ruler, Sheikh Saqr. I stumble in my introduction and there is an awkward silence. But conversation soon gets going and Sheikh Saqr turns his good eye on Leslie and quizzes him closely about British politics, the recent fall of Margaret Thatcher, and the poll tax. He is curious and asks how it all happened. His son, Sheikh Saud, sits silent and erect at his side. When we leave the Ruler, his son takes us to his office and asks more questions about the Gulf crisis and information technology. He has an American degree in political science and international relations – as is apparent from the books on his shelves.

Saturday 15 December

I take Christine and Leslie McLoughlin to Dubai and we have lunch at the British Council there. The first to arrive is Mehdi al-Tajir, then Khalifa Nabouda, Easa Salih al-Gurg, Muhammad al-Murr, Jack Briggs, Ian Fairservice, Ali Rashid Lootah and Rob Hendrie, the new British Consul-General. Frequently the lunch parties at the British Council are dominated by expatriates who have a proprietorial attitude towards the place; nationals are usually in a minority. This time we have nationals of great weight. I wonder whether the Embassy could get such a turn out.

Jack Briggs talks about his marriage. 'Kath and I got married thirty-eight years ago. I think we both wanted to change the other. She wanted me to be a good Catholic. I wanted her to be a cyclist. We both failed. I nearly succeeded once. We used to take holidays each summer in France and see a stage of the Tour de France. In the mornings I would then go cycling and in the afternoon we would drive over the route I had taken.'

Leslie tells a story of a young colonial official in southern Yemen who acquired a reputation, quite undeservedly, for understanding the local dialect. Someone came into his office and talked at speed in a way that was totally incomprehensible. He paused, and the official said, '*Aywa*' ('Yes'). Then he went on, rattling away, before pausing again. The official did not understand a word, but said, '*Na'am*' (a more formal way of saying 'Yes'). Then another torrent of incomprehensible Arabic. The official guessed he was asking a favour. When he came to an abrupt and interrogative stop, the official said, '*La abadan*' ('No, not all').

Sunday 16 December

Back in Abu Dhabi, I have a meeting with the Ambassador. Eight thousand British soldiers are expected shortly in Abu Dhabi. Could there be military action over Christmas?

Denys Johnson-Davies and I have a pleasant chat. He had published under an assumed name (because he was ashamed of them) two novels – a thriller and a detective story – by the time he was 21.

Wednesday 19 December

Rumours of war. The stories of brutalities in Kuwait make awful news. There is a kind of ultimatum to Iraq that expires on 15 January.

We go to a farewell party. Teenagers are out from boarding schools in Britain. They loll around in armchairs at their parents' boring parties and watch middle-aged folk get progressively drunk.

Friday 21 December

Our older children, Katie and Paul, are with us for Christmas. I am the special guest at a local radio station, The Beach Party Show with special guest for a programme, The Beach Boys Show, at the local radio station. There are three or four snatches of interview about *Dubai Tales,* my other writings and my Middle Eastern career. I am asked to comment on pop music – I really have absolutely no clue – but do choose music for Katie (Bob Dylan) and Paul (Depeche Mode).

Sunday 23 December

We go to an Embassy party, with all the families of diplomats. We sing carols. Robert Wilson does a solo recital on a bicycle pump and Paul falls in love twice.

Monday 24 December

Theresa is working, and I take the four children to Dubai and arrange

Peter with copies of his translation of Dubai Tales *by Muhammad al-Murr.*

for them to go on a helicopter trip. There is room only for the four of them. The pilot is an Australian called Greg, who wears cowboy boots. They are soon up and off, over the Creek, north over Jumeirah and as far as the golf course and back. It all costs 1,000 dirhams. We then drive to the Creek and cross by abra – one dirham for the five of us. And back to Abu Dhabi.

Theresa has invited six of her Filipina colleagues to the house. They are shy at first, but relaxed when they look through photographs and are thrilled to meet Paul. 'I will be your maid, Paul,' says one.

Wednesday 26 December

We go to the Envassy bungalow at Al Ain. The visitors' book includes the names of the Prince of Wales, Wilfred Thesiger, the Duke of Gloucester and Dame Violet Dickson.

I sleep in the open air on the verandah.

Thursday 27 December

I wake up to the call to prayer, with the chaste dawn breezes on my face.

I put on my suit and call on people at the university, then look in at the Al Ain bookshop. To my agreeable surprise, I find a copy of Tweedie on the Arabian Horse,[41] first published in 1894 and reprinted in Beirut recently. It is a ragbag of information, misinformation and curious byways of history and Arabic.

In the afternoon we go to the Jahli Fort. The only person there is an old guard, who asks me about 'Queen' and 'Thatcher'. Otherwise it is deserted, and we have great fun playing around. Gabriel and Nat are police and the rest of us are robbers on the run. The fort is extensive, full of corridors and cubbyholes, ideal for the purpose.

Paul with Filipino admirers.

41 W Tweedie, *The Arabian Horse, His Country and People* (Librairie de Liban, Beirut, 1973).

Sunday 30 December

I read the notes about contingencies in the event of crisis and war. They embrace everything, including the unlikely event of Abu Dhabi being directly involved in war, and how to communicate numbers of British dead and injured. I note, more relevantly, the need for communication lines to be clear.

The Ambassador shows me his report for the year. In it he writes about 'the Thesiger exhibition, which was the brainchild of the excellent British Council Representative'. That goes to Douglas Hurd. Purr, purr!

1991

Tuesday 1 January

I get three and a half hours' sleep. Paul is up all night. He is 'wrecked', as he says. I take him off to the airport and he flies back to London. I go on to Suweihan, where I meet David Heard. We go in his four-wheel-drive over the dunes to an encampment where Theresa, Kate and the boys, and all the Heard family – Frauke and their children Nicholas, Miriam and Theresa – have spent the night. The camp appears deserted and the embers of a fire are still warm. It is the classic beginning of an Arabic pre-Islamic love poem! In fact, they are all hidden in one of the tents. Nat is choking with giggles into his cornflakes.

'You're three months too early,' I tell them.

After a cooked breakfast, we drive into the Omani mountains to a wadi where there are pools of ice-cold water. We all jump in and splash about. We are in Ka'abi country, a tribe that used to have the reputation of being bandits. Men of our age, David tells me, were wary – and still are – when they came here. The Heards are immensely resourceful and I love it when I have no responsibility for the vehicle or for driving or for putting up tents. We idle the day away and drink tea in the dunes as we watch the sun set. A full moon rises magnificently an hour later.

David Heard.

Wednesday 2 January

I am back in the office. I have a fax from Brenda Walker, the publisher of *Dubai Tales*. The BBC plans to broadcast two of the tales in the Radio 2 'Morning Story' programme in March. I calculate that if 1,000 copies are sold in the Emirates, that will represent 0.3% of British exports to the UAE.

Thursday 3 January

We go for drinks at the house of the representative of Gray Mackenzie. One of the older British expatriates is enthusiastic about *Dubai Tales*.

'Normally we only know about the ruling families and the leading families,' he says. 'But in this book there are the lives of people with all sorts of problems: drink, sex and drugs, commuting, making ends meet and so on. Just like the West.'

That pleases me.

We go for a walk in a nearby wood, kept green by a life-support system of irrigation pipes. I walk with Nat, who will be eight later this month. If I walk with Gabriel, two years older, I am bombarded with a stream of consciousness. But Nat notices things, such as a hen with four chicks in tow, or a grasshopper with an infant on its back, or a curiously shaped snail stuck to a blade of grass.

Saturday 5 January

The Embassy provides me with a walkie-talkie set.

We have dinner with Iraqi friends. Our host did a PhD in the United States in the 1950s on taxation and was Assistant Cultural Attaché here. They are all utterly sick of the regime in Baghdad and want the crisis to be resolved, but fear for relatives inside Iraq.

Sunday 6 January

The Embassy is full of military men, slipping in and out of the Ambassador's room, looking serious. My spirits fluctuate daily. Yesterday I was optimistic, thinking both sides wanted a way out of conflict. Today I am not so sure. In 1956, between July and October there was a similar build-up of tension and military might. In the end the victim, Gamal Abdul Nasser, won a political victory though he suffered a military defeat. But the State of Kuwait is not the Suez Canal Company. We are like the proverbial rabbit caught in the headlights, watching the relentless and inevitable approach of something thoroughly unpleasant.

Monday 7 January

War clouds hover. News reporting gets more and more alarming. I must ensure food and water in the house and petrol in the car, understand how the walkie-talkie works, and ensure that the communications network is in absolutely tip-top working order. I fear that there will be war next week. It is hard to see things clearly beyond that, let alone after the end of the month.

Tuesday 8 January

I go to the opening of the Third Gulf Education and Training Exhibition, and talk to people from a Lancashire college. They are louche, inexperienced, suspicious and somewhat absurd. They want to talk to me separately and are afraid of other people pinching their ideas: academic piracy. The two stick together in a conspiratorial way. They have courses from which you can get a qualification even if you fail. It really seems a total corruption of academic standards.

Wednesday 9 January

I walk around the city pondering. Most people actually survive most wars. Our defences are, as far as we can construct them, in place. Channels of communication. Food and water in the house. Petrol in the car. Papers in order. Cash in hand, in case of evacuation, which would be to Bombay. Or we may be advised to go to Fujairah or Oman. I work out that, with teachers and locally engaged staff and families, there are 106 British Council dependants in the Emirates. The largest household is that of Dilawar Husain in Dubai, with eight children. I await the inevitable with as much placidity and determination as possible. I have no influence on the context in which I find myself. British Council London has set up an emergency unit and will be in daily communication.

Friday 11 January

I try to think of every contingency. What I cannot think of is the unexpected, a surprise act of terrorism. I am a target; the British Council is a target. To all I emphasise the importance of vigilance.

Saturday 12 January

I receive a letter signed by all the British Council teachers, requesting the option of leaving before 15 January, when the ultimatum to Saddam Hussein expires. I go to a meeting of the wardens including those from Dubai. Douglas Hurd is on a flying visit and moves around talking to each of the wardens. I show him the letter. He reads it.

'There's no logic in it,' he says. 'In contrast, the rest of the British community is steadfast.'

He talks to us all. The war is not likely to last very long. Nobody can be blamed if they leave now. There is no absolute guarantee of safety: 'I cannot guarantee that in Britain'. He seems to be far more relaxed than when he was here in August. Is it because he no longer has Margaret Thatcher as his direct boss?

Sunday 13 January

I take a visitor to the airport. There are no worried crowds of people anxious to leave. I do see a Royal Air Force plane taxiing, preparing to take Douglas Hurd to Jordan.

I have a meeting with the teachers. They are white-faced and worried. One breaks down. She is scared stiff. I tell them that the security situation is under constant review. Elsewhere advice has changed, but here it is felt that there is no reason to modify the advice given in August. But if people choose to leave they will not be blamed. They will be responsible for their own arrangements and can use the leave due to them. I try to calm them down. There are anxious questions about other communities leaving, about the issue of gas masks. I deal with the questions with as much frankness and confidence as I can muster.

Lithuania is hogging the news at the moment, with the familiar story of Soviet tanks moving in.

Monday 14 January

We are all day in a state of readiness for the shock. I think there will be 24 or 48 hours of extreme tension, when anything could happen. People may drive erratically or be trigger-happy. By Saturday we will know where we are.

At the Embassy meeting my joke – 'Oh, I'm glad I'm not in Lithuania at the moment' – falls totally flat.

I have a meeting with the Under-Secretary of the federal Ministry of Education, Khalifa Bakhit. He locks the door and arranges for no phone calls to be put through. We talk all the time in Arabic. He wants much more activity with the British Council. He wants it free, arguing that Britain neglected education when it was in charge for over a century. I ignore that. He says the Ministry is not an oil company or the Emirate of Abu Dhabi, awash with funds. I make it quite clear that there can be no money to support what he wants. The Minister talks to me of his frustrations. He cannot spend more than 1,000 dirhams (£150) without reference to the Ministry of Finance. A month ago he wanted a fax machine to be installed in his office. The paperwork is still going the rounds. I give him a copy of *Dubai Tales*.

People are hoarding. There is no bottled water available. And stocks of food and booze are being priced higher and higher. I smirk at the thought that I have got all that in advance.

Tuesday 15 January

A joke is going the rounds in Baghdad that a special calendar has been produced in Iraq that only goes up to 15 January.

The atmosphere is tense, resigned, expectant. People are assiduous in their religious observances and the mosques are full.

Wednesday 16 January

The ultimatum expires at 9 am this morning, Abu Dhabi time.

I am a pacifist and the horrors of war are vile. But Saddam is an extreme case of belief in the legitimacy of violence as a political weapon. Most states share the same belief to a lesser extent. My own precious conscience is of no relevance to anybody but myself and God, and I doubt if She (or He) loses much sleep over it. In this conflict, I recall what Bernard Shaw said in 1914: 'They are both wrong-headed, but as I am on one side, I hope my side wins'. Such cynicism appealed neither to the war party nor to the pacifists, but it made some sense.

Thursday 17 January

David Heard wakes me at 5.15 am.

'It's started,' he says. 'Heavy air attacks on Baghdad.'

I lie awake contemplating the awfulness of an American assault on an Arab country. For a few minutes as dawn breaks I feel strangely vulnerable. Then at 6.15 am the Ambassador phones.

'The balloon has gone up,' he says. 'There is no reason to think that this country will be directly involved. Keep quiet. If you go out, take personal documentation with you for there will be security checks. Be patient and courteous.'

We are due to conduct exams. Fortunately, Jamal, the senior locally-recruited member of the British Council staff, lives in the same building as the office and classrooms. He keeps the papers in his flat – so we are able to carry out the invigilation of the exams.

We are glued to the news all day, CNN and BBC.

Traffic is reduced. There is an air of calm normality. But armoured vehicles patrol the streets and police cars stand at crossroads.

Saturday 19 January

The teachers continue to be scared. I have a meeting with them. The fear is collective and even irrational. One teacher has a class mostly of Sudanese and Syrians, some of whom are pro-Saddam. She feels threatened. I find this extraordinary, for if one of them was discourteous, plenty of others would be embarrassed and leap to her defence. I talk as coolly as I can about the dangers. Another teacher becomes confrontational. 'This has not been thought of. Like everything else.'

The Ambassador asks to see me. He tells me that there is a potential threat to the British Council, less so to British Airways and even less to the British-managed primary school. 'You personally are a potential target,' he says. He asks me to consider whether Theresa and the boys should go to the UK. This is quite a devastating bit of news, as if I am terminally ill. I immediately become extremely circumspect. I arrange for the car to be stripped of its diplomatic plates. I am not afraid of dying or death, but the effect on my immediate family would be awful. I share the information with Theresa. I look around at everything and everybody, and wonder whether I am being shadowed. I also reflect on Abu Dhabi's excellent security.

Tuesday 22 January
I have a telephone call from Farihan Shiblak, the wife of my Palestinian friend, Abbas. They have lived in Britain for decades and have a house in Kilburn. He has been arrested and is in prison, threatened with deportation. Farihan is worried and seeks support. I phone Duncan Campbell at *The Guardian*, who comments that the British security people have to justify their existence. There is a three-man tribunal that considers these cases. The detainee can call for no legal support and there is no appeal. Shades of totalitarianism in Britain. Duncan is doing a story on the case.

Saturday 26 January
I receive some faxed articles from *The Guardian*. There has been a leading article about Abbas and he has some friends supporting him. He is the most unlikely threat to anyone's security. He has written for *Jewish Quarterly* and been active in Peace Now. He has also openly campaigned against Saddam's abuse of human rights in Iraq.

Sunday 27 January
At the weekly Embassy meeting the Defence Attaché outlines his expectations of the military situation. He reckons there will be a land battle from early February and that the war will be over by the end of the month. If Iraq uses chemical weapons against our troops there will be massive retaliation against the Iraqi troops, who would have no air cover. Kuwait would be flattened. There might even be a tactical nuclear strike. We all have an intake of breath at that. The word *tactical* seems to make it acceptable and respectable.

Saturday 2 February
I telephone Farihan. Abbas had his hearing yesterday. The Three Wise

Men were actually quite sympathetic, and listened to him. There has been a lot of support, with leading articles in *The Times, The Independent* and *The Guardian*. Their children have been depressed, drawing sad pictures and wanting their Daddy back.

The world of Iraqis, Westernised, liberal or whatever, is crashing. I have an Iraqi visitor and we share our thoughts that what is happening is the worst trauma since Baghdad was sacked by the Mongols in 1258 – betrayal, savagery, sheer nastiness and mendacity. Ugh!

Peter went on a course in London on understanding financial reports.

Tuesday 12 February

I slip into British Council headquarters for a boring course.

In a discussion on inflation, my colleague from Austria says you should get the inflation rate not from official statistics but from the opposition press.

'If you have an opposition,' comments one colleague, to laughter.

'Ah, you naïve Europeans,' observes another.

Our trainer is bright and well-meaning, but is always backing into furniture and does not seem to be in control.

Wednesday 13 February

Abbas has been released. I call on him and Farihan. The whole experience has been terrible. Abbas was believed to be involved in some Palestinian-Iraqi terrorist group. He was seen having lunch with an Iraqi diplomat and whispering conspiratorially, but this was because the Iraqi was a closet dissident. Abbas has worked with Jewish groups in search of a peaceful solution. But the awful time is now over, thanks to publicity raised – not least by Duncan Campbell.

Back in Abu Dhabi.

Tuesday 19 February

Theresa and I go out for dinner, not having done so for months. We go to the Russian restaurant at the Meridien Hotel. The décor is fine, reminding one of a Byzantine church. The wine is Crimean and the food, passable, is served by a Pole and a Filipino.

Saturday 23 February
The war is entering a new and nasty phase. The Iraqi Foreign Minister is making peace moves. Saddam never shows himself as negotiating or suing for peace; he gets others to undertake tasks that look like weakness. The land war is going to be horrible. If it took the Coalition two days to get the Iraqis out of the Saudi town of Khafji, which they held for some days in August, how much longer will it take them to get the Iraqis out of Kuwait, where they have dug themselves in over six months?

Sunday 24 February
At the weekly Embassy meeting says the start of the land offensive is going well – 'dramatically well'. The nightmare of the last six months seems to be approaching an end. Thousands of Iraqi soldiers are surrendering, wondering what on earth they have been fighting for. Discussion turns to the post-war situation and the British role which seems principally to be the selling of arms.

Sheikh Muhammad bin Zayed is having built a huge tower block overlooking the Embassy. It will be the biggest building in the country, and the bottom six floors will be allocated to parking for cars. Meanwhile I announce that I am organising a cultural event – the visit of a group of travelling opera singers led by a lady called Barbara Segal. Will the British Council be the first to stage a cultural event since hostilities began?

Tuesday 26 February
I have lunch with Muhammad al-Murr and we discuss the Kuwait crisis and post-war prospects. Will this mean an end to media self-deception, to the Hero in Arab politics? He tells me a Joha story. Joha was being hassled by children and told them, 'There's a wedding party going on over there'. The children run off to where Joha is pointing. He then tears off after them. 'Where are you going?' asks a passer-by. 'There's a wedding on,' replies Joha. Saddam is like Joha, believing his own propaganda.

Outside the Sheraton Hotel, we see a lot of Kuwaitis celebrating. Police are anxious about a demonstration. The Kuwaiti Embassy is nearby and a youth in one of the cars is leaning out grinning broadly and giving a V-sign. On the car radio, the news tells us that the Iraqi hold on Kuwait has collapsed. Saddam has ordered a retreat.

Wednesday 27 February

I call on the majlis of Sheikh Mubarak. He arrives on the arm of his son, Sheikh Nahyan, and turns to me and speaks in English: 'In London … rain.' I reply in Arabic and talk about snow and terrorism.

Thursday 28 February

I have a phone call from Richard Burge at my headquarters, who wants to come out after Ramadan on a 'marketing visit'. I tell him not to rule out Ramadan. There are advantages: lots of people avoid coming here during that month. Indeed, because so few people do come, those who do come get more attention. I also stress the importance of cultural activity balancing pro-active marketing.

The war is over. The Iraqi forces have collapsed. Saddam is claiming a great victory, with the Americans suing for peace. The gulf between rhetoric and reality yawns wider than ever.

Tuesday 5 March

We are having a lot of rain these days. Pools of water lie about. It makes Abu Dhabi strange, out of character.

Richard Burge arrives. He has seen a piece about me in the Dubai duty-free shopping magazine, and tells me I must be the only British Council officer to feature in a duty-free publication. I take him to call on Khalifa Bakhit, the Under-Secretary at the federal Ministry of Education, who shares with us his frustrations. And jokes, such as one about an Egyptian, a Sudanese and an Iraqi, who are asked, 'What is your opinion about eating meat?'

'What is meat?' asks the Egyptian.

'What is eating?' asks the Sudanese.

'What is an opinion?' asks the Iraqi.

Wednesday 13 March

After looking at the possible site of some new premises, I return to the office to find waiting for me Ahmad al-Suwaidi, the former UAE Foreign

Minister and close adviser to Sheikh Zayed. He often drops in on people unannounced. We have some students learning English from the Abu Dhabi Investment Authority (ADIA), of which he is head. Ahmad is very close to Sheikh Zayed and is one of the architects of the federation that became the United Arab Emirates. He is accompanied by a Syrian, Salah al-Hijazi, who was once Ahmad's teacher, by his secretary, Abdul Karim, a Tunisian from Janduba, and by a bodyguard. We have tea and chat awhile. On my wall I have a picture of the dinner party two years ago when the Prince of Wales was here. Both Ahmad and I are in the picture. I also have a photograph of my call on the president of Tunisia, Ben Ali. We chat in both Arabic and English. We then gather together the students from ADIA. Ahmad greets them all, and talks to them in both Arabic and English.

Thursday 14 March

Frauke and David Heard invite us to go camping, near Al Ain. We erect the tents. Darkness falls. We sit around the fire, and drink and chat while Frauke cooks. There are distant flashes of lightning. They come closer, accompanied by thunder. Both are just behind mountains close by. The winds whirl round and suddenly the rain starts to pour down. Gabriel and Nat have already, at their own request, gone to bed. I gather some fuel and store it in the car so it will not get wet. We fall sound asleep and the rain abates.

At 3.30 am, the rain comes again with a howling gale. The site we have chosen is out of danger of any flash floods, on an elevated and exposed spot. But we suffer the full blast of the storm. The tent sways in the wind. We put the boys in the car while I cling on to the tent to prevent it being blown away. We then dismantle it and join the boys in the car. The Heards' tent collapses.

Friday 15 March

I am first up at 6.30 am and get a fire going with my prudently stored fuel. Tents and sleeping bags are damp on the ground.

There are occasional showers during the morning and the mountainscapes and skyscapes are tremendous. The clouds part suddenly and we see mountains in the far distance, not normally visible from this spot. Theresa cooks breakfast but abandons it when there is a heavy shower of hailstones.

We go to some nearby pools and stroll down a wadi. Gabriel and Nat both swim. Then Nat goes onto a ledge in the rocks and I suddenly see a black snake glide past him, behind him, between him and the rock face, only a few inches from his bare feet.

'Step forward, Nat,' I shout.

He hesitates.

'There's a snake behind you.'

He jumps off the ledge into my arms. I must look up to see whether the snake is venomous or otherwise dangerous.

Sunday 17 March

It is the first day of Ramadan. The Ambassador has taken leave. He is not as keen as his predecessor in energetically making Ramadan calls in the middle of the night.

But I call on Muhammad al-Suwaidi at about 10 pm. He is by himself watching television, but other nationals drop in, including his father Ahmad. (He is a great 'dropper in', observes Theresa afterwards.)

Monday 18 March

I call on ADIA, returning the call – as it were – of Ahmad al-Suwaidi. I see Salim al-Muhannadi, the training manager. He is from Dalma Island and used to live in Qatar. He studied in the United States in the 1970s. Ahmad al-Suwaidi lived in Qatar before Sheikh Zayed came to power in 1966. He brought with him a number of nationals who had also been in Qatar. His family on Dalma Island used to make *muhannad* (swords) and more recently were pearl fishers.

In the afternoon I go to the Embassy to attend a briefing given by Lieutenant General Sir Peter de la Billière on 'How We Won the War'. He is flanked by three junior officers responsible for showing slides with slogans like 'Lessons Learnt'. The general talks of his worry lest the Israelis join in. At one stage they were keen to be involved and there was a fear that they would turn the whole of western Iraq into an 'Israeli military playground'. He talks of his relationship with General Schwarzkopf, whose planning team were officers only with the rank of colonel. General de la Billière seconded a brigadier, but demoted him first and the brigadier donned an American colonel's uniform. The whole war, he observes, could be seen as a trade display for the promotion of arms sales.

Tuesday 19 March

I drive to Al Ain, to the Municipality, and see Isam Hishmat, the Egyptian manager of the municipal theatre. The other day I received a letter from Sheikh Saeed bin Tahnoun (who is in charge of the theatre) wanting the loan of some Charlie Chaplin films. Isam wants much more and I am happy to help. Sheikh Saeed has seen some of the work we have done with the Cultural Foundation in Abu Dhabi and wants some of the action here. So I offer the mounting of the Thesiger exhibition in the summer, a presentation by the London Shakespeare Group, and a visiting opera group in the autumn.

I go on to the English-speaking school and see the head, Mr Crawford. They want to have a 'Thesiger Room', and I undertake to come and give a talk on Wilfred.

I retire to the hotel and read some *Oliver Twist*, a contrast to the heat of the Gulf and the rigours of Ramadan.

Wednesday 20 March

I have a phone call from my headquarters. My colleagues are asking about the planned new premises. Is there a prayer room? I have already thought of this, I explain.

'There are five mosques within five minutes' walk,' I tell her. 'A Baptist mosque, a Catholic mosque ...'; she seems to believe me.

Thursday 21 March

I meet a house guest of the Heards, Joyce Butter. She and her husband used to be in Abu Dhabi and were here when Wilfred Thesiger came through in 1977. She recalls how bitter and negative Wilfred was about everything. She lives in Kenya, in a house (bought from Lord Delamere) built in 1912. Joyce is a portrait painter and has been commissioned to do a series of portraits of old men – the opposite of pin-ups – for a calendar. One is of Musallim bin al-Kamam, which she is basing on photographs.

Saturday 23 March

I spend most of the morning wrestling with a reply to my line manager about a Country Management Policy. He has the impertinence to say that my draft lacks a challenging feel. This is logical nonsense. He is unaware of what has been accomplished since I have been here. But these management exercises are time-wasting scaffolding over a sound structure. It is far more important to meet people, listen to them and get to know them. I despair of the bunch of inadequates in charge of the British Council and hope I never have to enter my headquarters again.

I have a visit from Abdul Rahman Abdullah, the former Sudanese Minister, who is off to St Antony's College, Oxford for a year. He is a close friend of Bona Malwal, a principal opposition figure to the present regime in Sudan, who has been at Oxford for more than ten years.

Sunday 24 March

I drive to Al Ain in the afternoon and, half an hour before sunset, go round to the diwan of Sheikh Saeed bin Tahnoun, who has recovered more or less from the nasty accident he had 18 months ago.

I go into his villa, where a huge meal is laid out under tinfoil in the verandah. I hang around with some others. The sheikh and his immediate entourage come in and we go to a table. I am not well placed, out of the range of his vision. We all tuck into dead sheep, rice and pineapple chunks. After we have our fill we all walk off, following Sheikh Saeed into the garden, where there is a series of kiosks, like a Turkish garden. We move into one of these round kiosks and all flop into armchairs for some coffee. Then 50 of us – one Egyptian, one Lebanese, me, the rest nationals – go into the majlis, another detached building, including Sheikh Saeed's six-year-old son, who snatches off men's headdresses and pours water over people. After a while Sheikh Saeed calls out, 'Mr Peter', and we walk out together back to the main villa and discuss British Council activity in Al Ain, including bringing the Thesiger exhibition here.

Monday 25 March

I go to Dubai to discuss with Allen Swales the opening up of a teaching operation in Sharjah. We hope the Ruler will help with a site and accommodation – he has said he would like us to operate there, and we may be able to sidestep local taxation and municipal regulations. I meet a British teacher who used to be a colleague of Theresa at the school in Tunisia where she taught. He is a mixture of an excellent professional, a drunken boor and a witty, perceptive observer of people. He has left Tunisia because of encounters with fundamentalists. One told him, 'We are going to rule the world. Those who are not Muslims will be killed.' He finds the Gulf far gentler.

Wednesday 27 March

At 10.30 pm I go with Charles Bird of the Embassy to the majlis of Sheikh Nahyan bin Mubarak to pay a Ramadan call. Others there include Sheikh Hamdan bin Mubarak and Nabil Koronfli, a representative of the American University of Beirut. We stay and chat till near midnight. Sheikh Nahyan is Minister of Higher Education but seems to have to act also at all sorts of levels, from Under-Secretary to filing clerk.

Thursday 28 March

Theresa and I take the boys to Al Ain, where we stay in the Embassy bungalow. I like this place more and more. It is a humble log cabin in the middle of two acres, something of an anachronism. The garden is nothing grand. It is all completely out of place in the garden city of Al Ain. It is untidy, poor and down-at-heel. The other day, when the British government Minister William Waldegrave was here, the Ambassador wanted to take him to the bungalow but was overruled by Sheikh Nahyan, who made available his farm, a villa with deep carpets, a swimming pool – rather than an irrigation tank – well-cultivated gardens and a banquet piled high. The bungalow, by contrast, has a touch of the urban European's rural idyll.

Friday 29 March

The boys and I stroll through the oasis made up of palm trees planted close together. We go along the wadi bed and then follow a lane. I fall into conversation with a man building a wall. He is an Iranian and comes to Al Ain for three months a year, building and repairing walls, and then goes back home.

Sunday 31 March

Theresa has invited round the Filipina girls at the school where she teaches. She accompanied them to Catholic mass first. The director of the school exploits them and keeps them fiercely under lock and key. They are made to clean up the Egyptian Club and the houses of his friends. Seven of them share two rooms. One of them is a Muslim, and has to double as the house servant for the Director. They are a sweet lot, bright with lots of laughter.

Monday 1 April

I go into the Embassy and meet Nigel, whom I knew 20 years ago when I was studying Arabic in Lebanon. I thought then that he was an insufferable upper-class twit. Since then either I have become more like him or he has become more like me. Or I no longer care. But we warm to each other.

I go to a Ramadan breakfast with Abdullah Abdul Rahman. The other guests are Sudanese, including the Sudanese Ambassador, who does not like the regime in Khartoum and is lying low overseas. I used to know Abdullah' s nephew when he was Vice-Chancellor of the University of Khartoum. He was a horticulturalist and did his PhD on the dermatology of the onion. He is now the Sudanese Ambassador to the US.

Tuesday 2 April

I go to Dubai and meet Ali Rashid Lootah, who owns a bookshop. Books are not doing well, he tells me. People prefer magazines, and there are high insurance costs on deliveries. We make some late-night Ramadan calls. Saif al-Ghurair has a flat in Harley Street. His first wife was a sister of Jum'a al-Majid, by whom he had five daughters and one son. His second wife is a cousin of Sheikh Saqr of Ras Al Khaimah. With her he has had five sons and one daughter. People address him

With Geoffrey King at the Old Fort, Ras Al Khaimah.

with '*Tawwal 'umrak*' ('May you live long'), a term reserved usually for members of the ruling families.

One of the other callers is Muhammad Saeed Raqabani, the Minister of agriculture, who arrives with a group of Fujairans. Then to the majlis of the jovial, octogenarian Ibrahim Hamid Obeidallah, who quizzes and jokes with me. His son looks older than the father. This is because, I am told later, the son does not dye his beard. Then to the house of the pearl millionaire, poet and patron of the arts, Sultan Owais. He has not one, but two houses in Damascus. Finally, to the house of a Persian merchant, Ibrahim Jaugan. At all of the majlises I am the only non-Arab and at all four there is only one other man wearing trousers. Ali is an excellent guide and companion.

Later on I call on the Ruler of Sharjah, Sheikh Dr Sultan bin Muhammad Al Qasimi. One of his aides tells me that Graham Greene has just died. I meet the Ruler in a spacious, gorgeous sub-majlis and ask him about his researches. He has spent time working through archives in London about the Indian Ocean in the early 19th century, nipping out for a sandwich lunch. I leave him to deal with a dozen petitioners and drive on to Ras Al Khaimah.

Thursday 4 April

Theresa and the boys have come to Ras Al Khaimah and we all go off to see the site of Julfar, which is being excavated by Geoffrey King. He has unearthed a sizeable mosque. Interest in the site is growing. One of Geoffrey's colleagues is Beatrice de Cardi, in her late seventies, immaculately turned out, about to go off and call on the Ruler of Sharjah.

Back in Abu Dhabi we have an *iftar* with our Somali friends, Sabah and Ali. I learn about someone they know, Dave Clarke, who was in Somalia, learned the language and collected oral folktales, transcribed them, translated them and had them published in Mogadishu. The Somali government was having them translated back into Somali.

Friday 5 April

I am dozing at home in the afternoon and hear a strange noise. A goat has wandered in through an open gate and the open front door and into the lounge. It has terrorised our cat. I shoo him out and then clear up three score droppings from the carpet. There is then another visitor, an Egyptian lady, who pleads, '*Dhikr Ramadan*' ('For the sake of Ramadan'), begging for money.

Saturday 6 April

I call on Dr Izz al-Din Ibrahim, an Egyptian who is the cultural adviser to Sheikh Zayed. We discuss possible training for one of the Ruler's sons. He is very interested in Marmaduke Pickthall, and was involved with Denys Johnson-Davies in the taping of the Koran in English, using Pickthall's translation. He and Denys have worked together on *hadith*. He tells me that as a teenager he used to go to lectures given by Hasan al-Banna, the founder of the Muslim Brotherhood in Egypt. Al-Banna would start by reciting a hadith three times, after which he would make a commentary. Izz al-Din tells me that, as a result, he learned the hadith by heart.

Tuesday 9 April

I drive to Ras Al Khaimah to have iftar with the Ruler, Sheikh Saqr. Mike Edwards, his British fixer, and I go to Sheikh Saqr's villa – he disdains calling his home a palace – which has a neat mosque alongside. We enter the majlis, at the back of which is a canopy. The Ruler greets me and escorts me to some armchairs. We are joined by the two deputy Rulers, the Crown Prince Sheikh Khalid and Sheikh Sultan. Then by younger sons, including the youngest, 14-year-old Sheikh Ahmad. The Ruler asks me what I think about the Ras Al Khaimah museum. Unqualified praise. Then, what is the news about Saddam Hussein? I laugh. 'He is like a child,' he says. We then move to the dining room, the floor laden with rice, mutton, fruit and locally grown strawberries. There are two kinds of honey – red and white. Sheikh Saqr explains that the red is from grasslands and the white is from certain trees. We talk about our families. 'Four children from one mother?' he asks me.

Afterwards I go to Mike's house and we drink a bottle of champagne.

Wednesday 10 April

A Sharjah friend takes me to the site of the old RAF base. It is imperial archaeology, full of melancholy nostalgia. The buildings are in an awful mess. They are too big, but the rooms are too small. People are living in them. We note the loopholes in the event of civil unrest and the site coming under attack. We are taken into a room and meet an elderly man called Abdullah Jum'a, who has worked here since 1952. He points out maps and aerial photographs that show the site was really quite extensive. The RAF base was founded in 1933 and extended in

Ras Al Khaimah.

1965, when activity was transferred from Aden. We look round and identify hangars, storerooms and offices. Abdullah takes us along a road, pleasantly lined with trees and officers' bungalows. We go along to a small Christian cemetery with graves of British servicemen and one Armenian. It is still maintained.

Sunday 14 April

At the Embassy meeting the spook reports on a trip he has made to Kuwait. The place is a mess. People are lethargic, waiting for other people to assist them. They have lost their Palestinians, and Asians are less ready to return. Inertia seems to have gripped the Kuwaitis. 'They need a hundred sergeant majors and a thousand Baluchis to sort them out,' he says imperially.

Theresa took Gabriel to England to look at boarding schools. Peter looked after Nat, who missed his brother. His father was no adequate substitute.

Monday 15 April

It is the Eid marking the end of Ramadan. Nat and I go to Fujairah and check in to the youth hostel next to the Youth Theatre. There is nobody there at first but we find and rouse a couple of Bangladeshi construction workers who are staying at the hostel. There are dormitories full of neat beds. It is all reasonably clean. Nat feels nervous. We take a family room, but have to use Pif Paf to chase away the mosquitoes. The hostel has a tattiness that is out of place in the Emirates. We could be in Sudan or Yemen.

Tuesday 16 April

We go to Dibba. There are, in fact, three Dibbas, each quite distinct. All are on the coast, with the Musandam mountains as a backdrop. One belongs to the Emirate of Sharjah, one to Fujairah and one to Oman. I give an old man called Rashid and his son a lift.

'My wife is on holiday,' Rashid tells me. ('*Rukhsa*' is the word he uses.) His Arabic is otherwise pretty hard to follow. He wants an English wife.

'How much?' he asks.

'Lots,' I reply.

We have a swim at the Fujairah Hilton. A tape of Beethoven's Choral Symphony is in the background while a live pianist is playing 'Over the Rainbow'.

Then at 5 pm we go along to the majlis of the Ruler of Fujairah, Sheikh Hamad bin Muhammad al-Sharqi. It is Natty's first majlis. We are ushered into a huge room, lined with uniform armchairs and settees. I go up to Sheikh Hamad and he indicates that I should sit between him and, I guess, his uncle, Sheikh Hamid, who has the same delicate Sharqi facial features. The Ruler is very affable and we talk about his farm near Lewes in Sussex, which he is planning to sell because it is two and a half hours from London. He has known the area from the days when he was a student at Eastbourne, 22 years ago. He also has a place at Chalfont St Giles. I offer to bring *Twelfth Night* to Fujairah under his patronage. Natty plays the part well, bobbing up when a group of gnarled tribesmen come to rub noses with the Ruler. They take their place and we resume our conversation – about traffic jams in Sussex. A few men in suits come in, but nobody I know.

We leave and go to Kalba, where we eat at the Pizza Centre.

Saturday 20 April

Some time before, Peter had checked with the English-language secondary schools in Abu Dhabi to see what Shakespeare play the pupils were studying for their exams. It was Twelfth Night. *He then arranged for Delena Kidd and the London Shakespeare Group to come to the Emirates to put that play on, later in 1990. An attentive audience could be guaranteed. He asked for financial support from his headquarters.*

There is a tiresome telex from Drama Department London denying me access to the drama allocation for use for the London Shakespeare Group. 'The Advisory Committee advises against it.' What do they know about the Emirates?

Sunday 21 April

It is the Queen's actual birthday, and the annual birthday party at the Residence. Julia, the Ambassador's wife, is just back from Britain and tells me that the BBC has broadcast some of the stories of Muhammad al-Murr; the translator was appropriately acknowledged.

The British arrive first. Sheikh Nahyan and Sheikh Surur are among the senior nationals. I hang around, ready to be useful with my Arabic. Another who turns up is Julian Amery,[42] now over 70, with a short beard, rotund and somewhat pickled. He behaves as if the party is for him. I have a cordial chat with him. He is here for two days and spent a couple of hours with Sheikh Zayed. He first came to the Emirates in 1957. The Ambassador gives an excellent speech in Arabic and in English.

Wednesday 24 April

I drive with Natty to Al Ain, where I give a talk about Wilfred Thesiger to a hundred or more children at the English-speaking Primary School. I have brought some of the pictures, and place photos of Wilfred and Sheikh Zayed prominently. I get the children involved.

'Who is this?' I ask, pointing to the Ruler.

'Sheikh Zayed.'

'Wilfred Thesiger only took two things with him from England when he went into the desert. What do you think they were?'

'Water?' says one child.

'No, he took that from wells and Arabian towns.'

'A bed?'

'No, he slept rough.'

'A compass?'

'Well, yes, he may have taken a compass.'

I point to the picture of Sheikh Zayed.

'Who took that photograph?' I ask.

'A camera,' several cry out.

'And what was the other thing?'

'A lorry?'

'No, a medicine chest.'

I survive the ordeal before they get fidgety. Really, they are a very difficult audience, even for 15 minutes.

Back in Abu Dhabi I receive a letter from F T Prince, Frank Prince,

42 Conservative politician and sometime Minister (1919–96).

Peter talking to primary school children in Al Ain about Wilfred Thesiger.

whom I used to know in Yemen when he was Visiting Professor at the University of Sana'a. I sent him a copy of *Dubai Tales* and he is enormously appreciative. 'The stories are gripping, a profound critique of the New Arab Society.'

Thursday 25 April

Nat and I go with Sinwar al-Karim to the Al Wathba camel-racing track. He is a Bangladeshi from a Bengali family that over the generations loyally served the Raj. We are about the only non-nationals present. We see four races. Twenty-five camels with small boy jockeys set off and lope round the eight or nine kilometres in just over 15 minutes. One small boy falls off his camel, and is swept up and taken to an ambulance at hand. We go on to an extended area where there is a camp. Bedu from all over the area come here for the week's camel-racing season. Tents and provisions are laid on. We enter a 'villa' and go into a room presided over by Uwaija Suhail al-Khaili. He rises, and we greet each other. His sister is a wife of Sheikh Zayed.

Saturday 27 April

I hear a story about Sheikh Zayed. He was driving himself round a roundabout where priority was confusing and his car bashed into another car. His police escort got out and were shouting at the poor man driving the other car. Then Sheikh Zayed got out of his car, and explained that it was all his fault. There's nobility for you!

Sunday 28 April

I go to the Queen's Birthday Party at Al Ain. The headmaster of the school I spoke at tells me that at least one child thought I was Wilfred Thesiger.

Monday 29 April

I work on some office figures and discover that 98.5% of the local operating budget for the British Council is revenue, locally earned. In both Dubai and Al Ain it is well over 100%.

Peter flew to London for consultations and some leave.

Wednesday 1 May

At the Travellers Club I am writing a letter to Wilfred Thesiger as he walks in. I hand him the photographs taken at the Al Ain school and letters that some children wrote to him. He immediately writes a letter to the headmaster thanking each of the children by name. I arrange to have dinner with him on Monday, not at the club, but at his Chelsea flat.

'Can you cook scrambled eggs?' he asks.

Monday 6 May

I call at Wilfred's flat. He sits in his intensely masculine living room like an eagle preparing to pounce. He has been making a film with a French company and is to go to Eton College for some shooting. Eton does not usually permit films to be made there but have made an exception in Wilfred's case. We move to the kitchen. Wilfred opens a tin of vegetable soup. I cook some rice and prawns in a bag. We drink some cider and I leave a bottle of Chianti for him. He is vulnerable and forgetful. His housekeeper, Molly, died ten years ago. We talk of ancient parents dying.

Peter returned to Abu Dhabi.

Saturday 11 May

I have another missive from Drama Department telling me that there are some very distinguished people on their Advisory Committee. They have to be obeyed, and the whim of an overseas Director should not challenge their views.

Monday 13 May

A fax comes through announcing the death of the former British Council chairman, Sir Charles Troughton. He wrote to me in Tunisia congratulating me on being awarded the OBE – I had not. I think we exchanged nods in a lift at British Council headquarters once.

I go to Al Ruwais, 240 kilometres west of Abu Dhabi, where there are oil installations. The housing complex is a neat, green, well-watered and well-tended garden city in the middle of nowhere. I go to the Dhafra School and meet the bouncy Glaswegian principal, Mrs Baxter. I go through the whole school with her, meeting staff, mostly Arab, and am as usual thrilled at the brightness of a primary school. They have plans to extend to a secondary school and do GCSE exams. Afterwards she takes me to lunch and talks of her battles with parents, mostly Egyptian. 'They call me Margaret Thatcher, and they don't mean it as a compliment.'

Tuesday 14 May

I am reading *Anna Karenina* – wonderful stuff. You can jog along as fast or as slowly as you like. Familiar people come and go.

Monday 20 May

I go to Dubai for a meeting of the Dubai 1840 Club. This is a gathering for young men (between the ages of 18 and 40), mostly British. The guest of honour is Jack Briggs, who does not speak but shows a film made in 1971. It is absorbing. It focuses on Jack's police work. He was obviously very close to Sheikh Rashid; each was in the other's confidence. Jack is busy greeting and advising, but always in the background. He once taught Arabic at the British Council here.

Friday 24 May

The intense heat is beginning to cause discomfort. I used to be able to cope with the heat in Sudan and even enjoyed the summers, for the greater contact with the Sudanese – unlike the expatriates, most of whom could not escape the summers. Now I find it physically uncomfortable. Is it the ageing process?

I have been quietly fuming at correspondence from my headquarters. My line manager has said I have no vision. Whatever I do is seen in a negative light. Good things are ignored or trivialised. Minor faults are seized on and exaggerated out of all proportion. It makes me realise what it must feel like to be a Palestinian. I found a poem somewhere

> *I see*
> *In many ways an eye that measures me.*
> *The mortal sickness of a mind*
> *Too unhappy to be kind.*
> *Undone with misery, all they can*
> *Is to hate their fellow man;*
> *And till they drop they needs must still*
> *Look at you and wish you ill.*

In the afternoon I go with Theresa and the boys to the Embassy pool. I get enormous comfort and solace from the two boys. They are both developing, in different ways, and fast. They are becoming more responsible. Both are secure and happy, chirpy and self-confident. They are having a rich, varied and free childhood, compared with Theresa's and mine. Gabriel becomes aware of the difference between fantasy and reality. Nat is quite capable of standing up for himself, as the younger brother; indeed, he could become a little thug.

Thursday 30 May

I am taking part in a film about Wilfred Thesiger. Leslie McLoughlin, who has translated *Arabian Sands* into Arabic, is here and we go to the Muwaijih Fort in Al Ain, where Wilfred stayed with Sheikh Zayed in the 1940s. A small Palestinian, Hajj Nimr, turns up. He is from Gaza and came here in 1964 as an agricultural labourer. He talks of the fort with animation and about the herbs growing around, and their culinary and medical uses with even greater enthusiasm. Leslie is interviewed and then filmed walking into the fort. Then Hajj Nimr is interviewed by Leslie.

Saturday 1 June

I take Leslie to call on Sheikh Mubarak and his son, Sheikh Nahyan. Muhammad bin Rabaya is there, old Mubarak from Das Island and Abdul Jalil al-Fahim. Leslie, Nahyan and I talk about the 10th-century Arab poet Mutanabbi, and Sheikh Nahyan refers to Shakespeare as if he is Greek – 'Shake Spiro'. Usually when a visitor arrives, we all stand, and he goes up to the two sheikhs and then falls back to a place appropriate to his station. But then a Very Important Person comes in, with a young man, presumably his son. People go forward to greet him – as we all do. It is Sheikh Saif bin Muhammad. Sheikh Nahyan gives up his seat to his uncle and Sheikh Saif chats to his brother Sheikh Mubarak.

Sunday 2 June

At the weekly meeting, the Ambassador reports on a visit to the Minister of Health. Apparently, 30 percent of the 1.2 billion-dirham budget is spent on medical treatment overseas. People go for medical appointments. They may have to wait for a fortnight, staying in first-class hotels and needing cars with telephones.[43] There are arguments in the cabinet about this, and the Minister wants to change it and is manipulating the press to get his way. Or trying to.

Wednesday 5 June

I have a call from two senior officials from Shell. I present them with a shopping list of possible sponsorship activities, including a scholarship for a Ras Al Khaimah archaeologist. I present each of them with a copy of *Dubai Tales*.

---

43 Rare and costly in 1991.

Thursday 6 June

It is Theresa's 50th birthday. The boys bring in presents before they go to school. I have arranged a party at the Heards' house, and we all go there at 5 pm. I have arranged a birthday cake in the form of the letter 'L' (Roman numeral for 50), and have composed a poem, McGonagallesque in style. I have found a Keralan calligrapher, who has written it out beautifully – which I declaim. The lines come out well with the regular chorus – 'Don't ask me where the time has gone' – which those present join in. There are awful rhymes ('terrace' and 'cherries', 'Yemenis' and 'enemies') and jokes (referring to cooking, 'Don't ask me where the thyme has gone') and private allusions. When I finish, Theresa is in tears. Others comment that there should have been tissues available. I am amused that my mock-heroic theatricality, sentimentality and awful verse can actually move people to tears.

Sunday 9 June

I receive my annual assessment. I am 'average', and my performance is deemed to be worse than last year.

Monday 17 June

With Barbara Segal, who has a small opera touring company, I call on Muhammad Abdul Jalil al-Fahim, who owns or chairs ten companies. He is a charming man, short, lively and radiating intelligence. It is a courtesy call, but implicitly a request for commercial scholarship.

I do get support for Barbara Segal from the Hilton Hotel, who will put the group up. But they want exclusivity – no other sponsors.

Tuesday 18 June

I call on the Managing Director of the supermarket chain, Spinneys. The other day he offered what I thought was a derisory amount of sponsorship money for the opera. I tell him, 'You've been gazumped. The Hilton made me an offer I couldn't refuse. However, we do have a visit from the London Shakespeare Group in the autumn ...'

I get a promise of 30,000 dirhams (over £4,000) and accommodation for the group at the Holiday Inn. In return the group will perform at the (largely British) Marina Club.

Wednesday 19 June

I have a curious dream. I dream that I write a Biographical Dictionary of the Modern Levant. It takes me eight years and I build up card indexes. It traces the history of the area through the lives of people who have been significant in Syria, Lebanon, Jordan and Palestine/Israel.

Barbara Segal and I have lunch with Bharat Jashanmal, Managing Director of a large chain store. He is smooth and well-educated. Born in Kuwait in 1946, with Bahraini nationality, he was educated in Switzerland and is at home everywhere. We talk about taking the opera group to Das Island, which has a fluctuating population that ranges between 1,200 and 5,000 depending on the price of oil. It is multinational and all-male. The oil company would arrange everything, including a fee, flights and accommodation.

Saturday 22 June

The four of us drive to Al Ruwais and to the jetty. We are greeted on a small boat by our host, the Under-Secretary for Education, Khalifa Bakhit, who is with his wife, Nura, and seven children. They are also with a friend, Abdul Khaliq Abdullah, a Lecturer at the university, who has just had a sabbatical year at Georgetown in Washington DC. The voyage is lovely, taking about two and a half hours to Dalma Island. Visibility is not too good and we roll about a bit. I doze and teach Gabriel how to play scrabble. The island comes into view – flat, with gentle hills in the background. It has some modern buildings, dual-carriageway roads and roundabouts, but little traffic or people.

The five-month-old hotel is isolated, and has plans for a swimming pool, chalets and trees in the grounds. The top drawer of the chest of drawers has a prayer mat. There is no licence for alcoholic drinks. Furniture is heavy, wooden and cheap.

Theresa and I go for a walk before sunset, to a jetty full of fishing dhows.

Sunday 23 June

Khalifa invites us to go on a boat trip round the island. We are joined by Abdul Khaliq and his Lebanese wife, and by their and Khalifa's children. The boat belongs to Khalid al-Ghusain, whose father is the Ruler's Representative on the island. He has a crew of three: Ali, an old hand, and two lads. We sail round the island, stopping every now and then to gaze at birds hovering above us. Khalifa takes over the controls and we go fast. I am worried as we bounce violently off the waves.

At one point we hit a wave so abruptly that several of us sitting on the deck tumble over each other. I shout '*Shway, shway*' ('Slowly, slowly'), and Ali cautions. But the fishing is fun. Tackle is produced and Khalifa is in his element; fish are caught and landed on the deck – sheri, pretty little creatures, and a baby shark with small, sharp and ferocious-looking teeth. Theresa and I are concerned about fish-hooks scattered around the deck. But, anxieties apart, the whole voyage is tremendous – exciting, beautiful, an adventure.

Monday 24 June

We leave the hotel and drive to the ferry. Twelve cars are squeezed onto the boat. Everyone is courteous and patient – how unlike comparable experiences in Sudan and Yemen. But the island is part of the Third World: untarred roads, animals. We have only met nationals, and Gulf culture has determined everything.

Wednesday 26 June

I receive my first cheque for *Dubai Tales*: £90 for the broadcast story.

Thursday 27 June

I meet the Ambassador at the Embassy bar.

'Evening, squire,' I say.

'Hello, Abdul,' he replies. 'All well?'

'Tickety-boo,' I reply.

I also meet a visiting businessman. He is divorced. His divorced wife remarried and is again divorced. Her second husband is in Abu Dhabi and the two ex-husbands had a drink together.

'Your daughters' weddings cost me a pretty penny,' said the second husband.

'What do you mean? I paid for them.'

It turned out that the ex-wife had presented the bill both to the girls' father and to the second husband.

Friday 28 June

I am reading a collection of short stories by Emirates writers. They are of varying quality, and I battle with obscure words and pretentious prose. It all shows how outstanding Muhammad al-Murr's work is. Then I come across a sparkling tale by Sara al-Nawwaf. I ponder doing a collection of women's stories. The men are often pretentious and over-write, seeing themselves as Kafka or whatever.

Tuesday 2 July

I am reading *The Viceroy of Ouidah* by Bruce Chatwin. He has an amazing and individualistic style of writing. A sentence is unmistakeably his. He has a mixture of human compassion, utter realism and a readiness to contemplate horror and to document it.

Wednesday 3 July

I phone my line manager, complaining about the language of the guide to the New Financial System. It should be written by an idiot, not by a financial whizz-kid. I offer to be the idiot.

Thursday 4 July

Some bees have started a colony on a tree just outside the house. Nat, of course, is the first to notice this and is thrilled. And the dates on the date palm are rapidly getting ripe.

Theresa and the boys, their school terms over, go to England. Peter is alone in the house for a month.

Friday 5 July

I have my hair cut at the Lebanese barber shop near the fort. The man who cuts my hair is actually a Syrian from Tartus. Awad al-Oteiba comes in for a trim: it is obviously a chic place.

Saturday 6 July
I have another message from British Council Drama Department. I will not get the money allocated for drama in the UAE. The Advisory Committee do not think much of the London Shakespeare Group. And the Chairman has a friend, 'in whom he has much confidence', who saw them and was unimpressed. Whew! What production? And what does he know about the level of drama in the UAE? Why should we take their advice? I feel again that I am marginalised in British Council decision-making. I am not looking forward to another eight years of humiliation. I recall what an old friend said: 'When you lose respect for the people you are working for, you start to lose your own self-respect'.

Sunday 7 July
I drive to Ras Al Khaimah and call at the diwan. Sheikh Saqr is in London. He has a house in Kensington and spends a lot of time walking round London, accompanied by his bodyguards. Sheikh Khalid has been in China, taking his two-year-old daughter to see a medical specialist. Apparently, the little girl upset a bottle of boiling water onto her chest and suffered acutely. In China, they say, you can have treatment that gets rid of disfigurement.

I return to Abu Dhabi via Ajman and see a notice in a shop window: 'The Ajman Chamber of Commerce proudly present a Directory just of Ajman which will have worldwide distribution'.

Wednesday 10 July
I have challenged the low assessment given to my work by my line manager. His line manager confirms the assessment but writes to me kindly. Apparently, I irritate colleagues by my idiosyncrasies and determination to do things my way. I am not an 'organisation man', which may make me a better person. My intelligence and other talents do not fit in with the organisation. Well, now I know!

Friday 12 July
I phone Theresa in England and tell her what my line manager's line manager has said.

'That's the most complimentary thing anyone has said to you for ages!'

Sunday 14 July
Robin Thelwall comes to stay for a day or two. He and Rebecca were on leave from Kuwait when Iraq invaded and occupied the place. Mutual friends, Osman and Mira Dusuqi – he Sudanese, she Austrian – had a nearby villa in the University of Kuwait that was used for three months as a detention centre for the British Airways passengers who were being held. One of the detainees carefully selected items from the house that she thought would be of personal importance to Osman and Mira, and, when she was released, posted them to them in Austria. Another Sudanese friend, Khalid Mubarak, escaped from Kuwait, using the network of Sudanese lorry drivers.

Friday 26 July
In Al Ain, shortly before sunset I go in search of the majlis of Sheikh Mubarak at Al Khazneh. Up a tarred side road on a slight elevation is a farmhouse. Cars are parked in the area outside. I wander in and see white dishdashas in the garden. That is where the majlis is. I pass Awad al-Oteiba as he is leaving and go forward to say hullo to the two sheikhs. Twenty not very comfortable armchairs are set in the form of a horseshoe. It is a complete replication of the majlis in Abu Dhabi, but in the open air among bushes. I sit next to Sheikh Nahyan and talk about our proposed holiday, staying in Hong Kong. He does not know the Far East. I get up to leave as somebody else arrives. 'Why the hurry?' asks Sheikh Nahyan. I must send him a postcard from Hong Kong.

Saturday 27 July
I have lunch with Vichitra, the salesperson of the Al Ain InterContinental Hotel, hoping the hotel will sponsor visiting opera singers and actors. She is Indonesian but her father is British, her mother part-Dutch, part-Indonesian. She was at school at Malvern, then here in Abu Dhabi. Her father, an ex-Lancashire Fusilier, was a martinet but forgot to get a British passport for her. Her parents now

live in Andorra and her father, having bullied the five children all through their childhood, now wants them around to drink with him.

Monday 29 July

My line manager phones. How would I like to go on promotion to Saudi Arabia next year? I pause and say I will give an answer as soon as possible. I toss all sorts of ideas around in my head. I would really like to go to Syria, if that opens up. I would get a higher pension and a bigger terminal gratuity when I leave the British Council in eight years' time. I feel pleased with the offer – I have felt under-appreciated by my headquarters. The offer, I am told, comes from Top Management, and Syria is not definite. 'A bird in the hand …'

Wednesday 31 July

I call on Frauke and David Heard and tell them of the Saudi offer.

'You know how I seek to identify with the people of the country. Well, I will have to revise my views about the Buraimi Oasis dispute between Saudi Arabia and Abu Dhabi in the 1950s.'

'Oh no, you won't,' David laughs.

Peter travelled to England to rejoin the family, and they travelled round the world – Orlando, Vancouver, Hong Kong (staying with Robin Thelwall and Rebecca Bradley), Bombay, Delhi, Nepal and then to Dubai.

After some hesitation, Peter turned down the offer of promotion and working in Saudi Arabia.

Gabriel left Abu Dhabi to go to a prep school – Windlesham in Sussex.

Friday 6 September

We are invited to the opening of the Rajiv Gandhi Cultural Association, run mostly by Keralans. Several diplomats – including us – are ushered into a waiting room. In the absence of the Indian Ambassador, the Italian chargé d'affaires is invited to inaugurate the association. He is selected because of the Italian origins of Sonia, Rajiv's widow. The rest of us outsiders are invited to say a few words. I talk of the Nehru Science Park in Bombay, which we visited only five days ago.

Monday 16 September

I am getting ready for a small opera group, led by Barbara Segal, who will perform *Don Pasquale* at various venues. I enjoy working out all the details. Loos. Flow of people. Who sits where. Special chairs for sheikhs. Ticketing. Accommodation for the group for one night in Dubai. Transport schedules. And so on.

Tuesday 17 September

I go to Ras Al Khaimah to make arrangements for the opera there. A Lebanese, Michel, helps me. He is from Zahle and was there during the summer. The British hostages, including Terry Waite, are held in Baalbek and are moved around from house to house in five Mercedes cars with smoked windows escorted by armoured vehicles. It is gruesome.

Mike Edwards extols Ras Al Khaimah – the ease and the tranquillity. He goes to Dubai or Abu Dhabi from time to time, but he would not wish to live there. 'If we had a Spinneys here, life would be perfect.'

I go on to Fujairah and arrange a performance of the opera with the Tunisian manager of the Hilton Hotel.

There has been a massive pile-up on the Dubai-to-Abu Dhabi road. I count 25 abandoned cars, on both sides of the road.

Wednesday 18 September

The local paper informs us that over a hundred cars were involved in the pile-up in fog at 6.30 in the morning. Three people were killed and ten injured. The road was closed till 10 am, by which time I was in Dubai.

Saturday 21 September

I have been reading Nehru's *Glimpses of World History* with great enthusiasm. It puts global history into a fresh perspective. The whole personality of Nehru's life – his scholarship, style of writing and achievements – are admirable. Only two other 20th-century political figures can compare – Atatűrk and Roosevelt. All were flawed and made colossal misjudgements, but all faced fearful difficulties and gave hope to people.

Monday 23 September

I continue to prepare for the opera visit. Advertising. Programmes. Tickets and ticketing. Then I am asked, 'Have you got permission from the Ministry of Information?' I have forgotten all about this, and feel awful. I need to have an answer quickly in order to put up posters, otherwise I am acting illegally. I immediately think of contacts and hotlines to people in the ministry. I have even called on the Minister. I fortunately have the text of the opera, *Don Pasquale,* and will have to write a crawling letter asking for an urgent answer. But I should not have made a mistake like this.

Tuesday 24 September

Last night I had a strange dream. I dreamt that the British Council in Abu Dhabi had been taken over, but I was protected and was given the job of darts manager at the Dhafra Air Force base.

I make some urgent phone calls. The Under-Secretary at the Ministry of Information, Awad al-Oteiba, phones me back. I tell him the plans for the opera and he says, 'Excellent'. I go to see him with a letter I have prepared, and a copy of the libretto. I see Awad. We chat awhile and he scribbles on my letter, 'No objection. See to the formalities', and passes it on to a colleague. I have to wait for an hour while the formal permission authorisation is typed out. I return to the office before 11 o'clock, feeling triumphant. I reflect that this speedy resolution of a crisis is a consequence of making myself known in the majlises.

Sunday 29 September

I take Barbara and the opera group to Sharjah for their first production of *Don Pasquale*. There are only 80 in the audience, but they are very enthusiastic. Barbara introduces the cast and tells the story of the opera. I translate that into Arabic. Barbara asks me to take a non-singing, non-speaking part as the butler. After the performance, the accompanying pianist, Robin Humphreys, receives lots of notes from girls in the audience, full of love. Commenting on the disappointing audience, I say, 'A best-seller is no guarantee of quality'.

Monday 30 September

Theresa brings home a young Irishman who has been recruited to teach at her school. He has recently graduated from Trinity College Dublin and has never left Ireland before or flown in an aeroplane. He landed in Abu Dhabi, panicked and spent £150 on phone calls last night to his dad, who works at a garage in County Monaghan. He wishes to be a writer, but is totally mixed up and self-obsessed. He will go back at the earliest possible moment.

Tuesday 1 October

Barbara phones from Ras Al Khaimah. Things went well last night, when the company sang songs to the Ladies' Club there. The place was packed with national women who would not normally be exposed to such an experience. The sheikha was gracious and the performers took their bow, the men holding hands, and the women holding hands.

I travel to Ras Al Khaimah in the afternoon and go to the Saqr Hall for the performance of *Don Pasquale*. The hall is packed, with, to one side, a block of Europeans. Facing the stage are rows and rows of young men. I walk into the auditorium with Sheikh Khalid and Sheikh Saud, sons of the Ruler. The young men stand up and applaud us. We sit in armchairs at the front. Barbara and I then introduce the cast and the piece, in English and Arabic. The show starts. The audience is puzzled, challenged and responsive. There must be 300 present. There are catcalls and laughter from the young men. Filipina maids are at the side of the hall. The performers respond and play to the gallery. The audience love it when the young bride lays down the law with Don Pasquale. A few leave at the interval, but not many. The evening is a triumph. The first time that opera has come to Ras Al Khaimah! I feel that I have demonstrated, against conventional wisdom, that you can take an unfamiliar arts medium to a place as unpromising as Ras Al Khaimah. I have needed Mike Edwards as an ally, support from him, as well as local sponsors and the hotel, and a blessing from the ruling family.

Sheikh Khalid tells me that it is actually the third opera he has seen.

Mike Edwards says after the show, 'We would like four of these a year'.

'Fine,' I answer. 'We can provide two. Ask the Americans and the French. Tell them that the British are already in the lead.'

Wednesday 2 October

Theresa's Irish colleague has left.

The buzz from Fujairah is that they want to outdo Ras Al Khaimah.

Friday 4 October

We go to Fujairah for the performance of *Don Pasquale*. They have not outdone Ras Al Khaimah.

At a shop, I fall into conversation with a Sudanese dentist. Her husband joins us. He is a graduate from Bulgaria and Germany. We talk of the fine hotel in Khor Fakkan, which is dry.

'We take our own supplies,' he says.

They are Sudanese of an earlier generation who were dubbed 'communists'. Open-minded, they are interested in the world. Often it was teachers of English who broke out of the Arab-Islamic mould and were ready to add other cultural experiences and modes of behaviour. They have a limited place in the Sudan of today.

Monday 7 October

After disappointing attendances in Fujairah, the group perform at Al Ain. Sheikh Mansur bin Tahnoun attends. He is a bit late, having been hunting bustard with falcons. There is a full house. Lots of nationals. After the show, we all have coffee with the sheikh.

Tuesday 8 October

Wilfred Thesiger has been invited back to the Emirates by Ian Fairservice of Motivate Publishing. Ian is arranging for a house with servants to be available in Jumeirah. Edward Henderson, who is here by himself, will go there and the two old friends will live together. Admirable, but there is also a problem of the publishers sending hardback copies of *Arabian Sands*. Here is an opportunity to sell hundreds, if not thousands, of the new edition in which Wilfred writes gracefully about the modern Emirates, having been reconciled to the new developments.

Wednesday 9 October

There is another production of *Don Pasquale* and I again play the part of the butler. I ham it up, being progressively more drunk each time I appear.

Thursday 10 October

It is the last performance of *Don Pasquale* and I go over the top with my acting. I stagger on with my bow-tie all over the place, leer at the women, knock over a chair and get into a brawl with one of the singers and tumble over the keys of the piano where Robin – unbriefed about my outrageous behaviour – raises his eyebrows and carries on regardless. In my last appearance, I clutch a half-empty bottle of whisky.

Friday 11 October

I am reading *Dubai* by Robin Moore. It was written in the 1970s about Dubai in 1968. Jack Briggs ('Jack Harcross'), Hugh Boustead ('Harry Olmstead') and Mehdi al-Tajir ('Majid al-Jabir') are thinly disguised; Sheikh Rashid and Sheikh Zayed not at all. It is a romp of a yarn about gun-running and gold-smuggling. There is much authenticity about the local situation.

Saturday 12 October

We have a letter from Gabriel. He has discovered conkers, one of those very English customs which, thanks to his deprived expatriate childhood, he has missed.

Sunday 13 October

At a reception, I note that a lot of the expatriate conversation is about eating, slimming and weight-watching.

We go to dinner with the Heards. David introduces me to a construction engineer, Faruq Tuqan, from the Nablus family. He is a nephew of the poet Fadwa and a cousin of the poet and translator Fawaz, and, although he has been an engineer in Abu Dhabi since 1968, he read PPE at Oxford. A son went to Winchester and is now at Yale. He talks of the humiliations imposed by the Israelis on Palestinians at the Allenby Bridge – in his home country! Other guests include Adnan Pachachi and Zaki Nusseibeh. We eat in the garden. It is hot and close. The Italian Ambassador buttonholes me to talk about *Dubai Tales*, Wilfred Thesiger and ... my acting!

Wilfred Thesiger returned to the Emirates as the guest of Ian Fairservice of Motivate Publishing.

Wednesday 16 October

In the office car, we collect Wilfred Thesiger, Edward Henderson and Ian Fairservice in Dubai and drive to the primary school in Al Ain. The headmaster, Jim Crawford, and two children are at the gate to greet us. We go straight to the school hall, where all 150 schoolchildren are sitting on the floor. Wilfred, patriarchally, smiles at them and they ask all sorts of questions. The children listened enrapt. The visit ends with three rousing cheers for Mr Thesiger.

We go to the Muwaijih Fort, where Sheikh Zayed received Wilfred in 1948. Ian takes some marvellous photographs of Wilfred standing in the doorway.

'Where was Zayed sitting?' I ask.

'Under a tree over there,' answers Wilfred, pointing with his stick.

Wilfred and Edward talk about Zayed 40-plus years ago.

'He was tight-fisted,' says Wilfred.

'He hadn't any money in those days,' pleads Edward.

'That's no excuse,' says Wilfred, who goes on to quote amazing examples of desert hospitality.

'You and I, Wilfred, have had this conversation over the last twenty-five years', says Edward with resignation. He then talks of Zayed's nobility in honouring his elder brother Shakhbut after he was deposed.

'What other Head of State would so honour the man he has deposed?'

I take Wilfred to Abu Dhabi. I get a phone call from the Embassy to say that Sheikh Zayed will see Wilfred at 10.30 am tomorrow. The Arabic translation of *Arabian Sands* will be presented to him. I tell Wilfred.

'Damn,' he says. 'That means I'll have to cancel an appointment with the optician.' But he would like me to accompany him.

Thursday 17 October

The British Council driver takes me to Rawdat al-Reef, the palace at an elevation with extensive views over the desert. The guards know nothing about any appointment. They say Sheikh Zayed is not here. He is at another palace. We are about to belt off there, when Ian Fairservice arrives from Dubai in a Cadillac with Wilfred and Edward Henderson, and then, in another car and from the opposite direction, Zaki Nusseibeh, Sheikh Zayed's interpreter. We are then all ushered into the palace; the guards were wrong. We wait for two and a half hours. First we are in a circular majlis-anteroom, and then we are escorted to an open-air majlis that catches the breezes.

Wilfred is a bit testy at the wait, and I tell him even the British Ambassador had to wait.

'He should have walked out after an hour,' Wilfred snorts.

We talk of Eton College, his teacher George Lyttelton and music, for which he has no ear. He has also hated the idea of Israel since he was in Palestine in 1941. Ian and one of Zayed's sons, Sheikh Isa, slip away for a quite smoke.

Sheikh Zayed then turns up, driving himself, and we have 45 minutes with him. He is smiling and relaxed, and splendidly irreverent about other Arab leaders. He speaks warmly of Wilfred, who then hands over a copy of the Arabic edition of *Arabian Sands*, with a fitting dedication composed by Zaki. A photograph is taken of Zayed with Wilfred, Edward Henderson, Ian Fairservice and myself.[44]

We take our leave. Ian is feeling triumphant, and goes to his car and tosses his jacket in the boot, slamming it shut; he then realises his car keys are in the jacket pocket. I arrange for the British Council driver to take Ian, Wilfred and Edward to Dubai, and return with Zaki to Abu Dhabi.

Friday 18 October

Wilfred is now in Muscat with Ian Fairservice. They have met up with

---

44 The picture appears in Peter Clark, *Thesiger's Return* (Motivate, Dubai, 1992), but only includes Sheikh Zayed, Wilfred Thesiger, Edward Henderson and Ian Fairservice.

Bin Ghubaisha and Bin Kabina. Wilfred almost broke down. Wilfred is staying with the Ambassador, Sir Terry Clark, who has asked Ian to move in. He appreciates that Wilfred needs his younger supporters. He is old, nearly blind, a bachelor and unwilling to acknowledge his own vulnerability and helplessness, and needs familiar faces and shoulders around him. Moreover Ian, with the promotion of reproductions of his photographs, is helping to provide Wilfred with some financial security, allowing him to get good treatment for his eyes and so on.

Saturday 19 October

I travel to Muscat for the opening of a collection of Wilfred's photographs. This has been initiated by the Ambassador there and the British Council Oman. I take a taxi to the Holiday Inn, where I am staying, and then a bus to Matrah. Modern Muscat appears as a string of townships to the west of the mountains that shelter the towns of Muscat and Matrah. From Matrah I walk on to the city of Muscat, a sanitised city, apparently a Royal Enclosure. I gaze with admiration at the British Embassy, overlooked by the Jalili Fort.

Elizabeth Rylance of the British Council collects me and takes me to the exhibition centre at Qurm. I meet again Bin Kabina and Bin Ghubaisha and other Rashidis. Wilfred arrives with the Ambassador. Speeches. Wilfred seems less agonised. I talk to Said, son of Musallim bin al-Kamam. His father has been sent by the Omani government to India for medical treatment. I praise his father. 'But,' he says, 'you should have known my grandfather; he was even greater.'

Sunday 20 October

The Residence and Embassy building is large, leisurely and colonial. The Omani government wants to take it over, for it must be the only surviving foreign relic in Muscat. I sit on the balcony with Ian Fairservice and Wilfred Thesiger. The Jalili Fort off to the right is floodlit at night. The Ambassador's Residence has efficient Indian staff, whitewashed walls and a corrugated-iron roof. It is agreeable to hear the plash of the waves of the Indian Ocean, to gaze over this bay, and chat. Wilfred is worried about his eyes. He dreads being alone in his London flat, unable to read. What attractions does London have for him? Poor old man, he has no children to help him share the burdens of life.

I am invited to the house of Kamal Sultan, a Hyderabadi Omani businessman. Some academics are there, as well as Bin Kabina and Bin Ghubaisha and Said Musallim bin al-Kamam. I give Said a 'Get Well' card for his father, and talk to Dawn Chatty, an anthropologist of Syrian origin.

Back in Abu Dhabi.

Wednesday 23 October

I get Gabriel up early. We collect Edward Henderson and drive to Al Ain. There is a gentle mist on the road. I get Edward to talk about Syria, himself and the war. He was in the second batch of students at the Middle East Centre for Arab Studies in 1945 – I went there in 1970. He knew the director, Bertram Thomas, who seems by then to have gone soft in the head and would never know a speaker's name when he was introducing him. He was also forgetting a lot of his Arabic.

We meet Ian and Wilfred outside the diwan of Sheikh Tahnoun bin Muhammad, the Ruler's Representative in Al Ain.

'I've played safe,' says Ian. 'I've borrowed a Rolls-Royce with a driver.'

'Perhaps you should have brought a locksmith,' comments Edward.

We meet some of Sheikh Tahnoun's court and are ushered into his majlis. He gives Wilfred a very warm welcome. Photographs. Then they chat about old times.

'Do you remember the name of the dog you had back then?' asks Sheikh Tahnoun.

Wilfred cannot.

'He was called Warrad,' says Sheikh Tahnoun. 'He used to snatch meat and people had to take it from the dog's mouth. 'We were desperate for meat in those days.'

Edward, Wilfred and Ian set off on the Dubai road. Gabriel and I go to the Embassy bungalow. The phone rings. It is Ian. The Rolls-Royce has broken down five miles outside Al Ain. I dash out with Gabriel. Ian feels a bit humiliated. Wilfred is chortling.

'It wouldn't happen with a camel,' he says. His suspicions about cars are vindicated. 'Anyone who can get it to move can take it,' he suggests. I drive them to Dubai and return to Al Ain.

'Wilfred would be a lovely grandfather,' says Gabriel.

Friday 25 October

I hear that a *qadi* in Oman has decreed that *Arabian Sands* should not be circulated in the country because 'it is not relevant to present-day Oman'. But there will be plenty of opportunities to smuggle it in through Buraimi.

Saturday 26 October

I am working on the 'Country Plan' for my headquarters. Much of it is ludicrous, such as its proposed measurement of efficiency: 'Divide the number of objectives achieved by the number of objectives, and multiply by 100. You will then have the percentage efficiency rate.'

Sunday 27 October

At the Embassy weekly meeting the Ambassador talks about the visit tomorrow of the Honourable Douglas Hogg, Minister of State at the Foreign Office, who will be accompanied by the Honourable David Gore-Booth and the Honourable Dominic Asquith.

'This represents John Major's classless society,' I say.

The Ambassador was at the Sharjah Cricket Festival, where half the Pakistani cabinet were in attendance. The Minister of Justice was receiving some money, and the Minister for Wildlife has given up hunting for as long as he holds that portfolio.

Thursday 31 October

I have a phone call from Julian Walker, who was my Ambassador in Yemen ten years ago. He has retired from the Foreign Office.

In the early 1950s, when he was in his early twenties, Julian was in the Emirates and was given the task of determining the boundaries between the different Emirates. Later the boundaries became significant when it was thought there might be oil under the sand.

Therese and I have lunch with Julian. Sheikh Zayed has asked the British government for Julian to come out and determine a boundary dispute between Ras Al Khaimah and Umm Al Quwain. His links with

Gabriel and Wilfred Thesiger.

the Emirates are extraordinary, for he was consul-general in Dubai at the time of independence. He took Sheikh Khalid, when he was 14, to England, and arranged medical treatment for the then Ruler of Sharjah with his father, Dr Kenneth Walker, who used to write books about sex. His return is a throwback to the world of John Buchan. Apparently, Sheikh Zayed had asked specifically for Julian before, but the Foreign Office had refused. Douglas Hogg has been more relaxed.

Julian tells us how Wilfred Thesiger was seen as a soft touch by the Awamir tribe, who would exaggerate the dangerous reputation of another tribe in order to increase the protection money they were always able to extract from him.

Wednesday 6 November

I call on Sheikh Saqr bin Sultan Al Qasimi, who was Ruler of Sharjah between 1951 and 1963, when he was deposed by the British for being pro-Nasser and (as some say) a drunkard. He lives in a large cuboid villa near the estate of Sheikh Surur. I go up in a lift and am received in his study. The bookcases, wooden inlaid with ivory, are full. The sheikh is alone, not reading. I take the photograph that the Ruler of Ras Al Khaimah gave me, taken in the 1950s. He identifies the others in the picture.

He seems in poor health. He has a house in Cairo. We talk about poetry and translation, and I get him to sign my copy of his volume of poetry. He asks about old British officials who had served in the Trucial States. I promise to bring Julian Walker to see him. Every few minutes, he pops a lozenge or a pill into his mouth. I am prepared to leave as the time for the sunset prayer approaches, but he is happy to chat along.

Saturday 9 November

I work out some interesting statistics. The UAE is, per capita, the tenth-largest purchaser of British books in the world – after Ireland, Norway, Australia, New Zealand, Singapore, Malta, Cyprus, the Netherlands and Bahrain. There is a large potential market of book-buyers somewhere. I also examine the proportion of students to nationals in Arabia. Here there are 12 students for every 10,000 nationals, compared with 20 for Qatar and eight for Bahrain (and 37 for Brunei). I work out an argument for the British Council to target Gulf Indians (South Asians) as a market. Pakistani cabinet ministers come to the Sharjah Cricket Festival, where India and Pakistan can play without fear of disruption. Film stars and popular singers are also there. Such people may send their children to British universities.

I also look at statistics of students in British universities. A Palestinian family here have recently been able to switch their nationality from Mauritanian to Belizean. They have never been to either country. Their two children were students in Britain. When they switched nationalities, the number of Mauritanian students dropped from eight to six (i.e. by 25%) and the number of Belizean students went up from 19 to 21 (i.e. by 10%).

Thursday 14 November

I am reading two books. I am rereading *Bleak House* with huge enjoyment. It is a blockbuster, a soap serial. The murder of Tulkinghorn and the flight of Lady Dedlock are linked. The major leitmotif – Esther's parenthood – and the minor – the pursuit of Smallweed – come together. The police detective, Bucket, becomes a leading character.

And I am reading in Arabic a book by Taha Husain on the 10th-century poet, Mutanabbi. He has a complex simplicity and balance, as well as a superb sensitivity about meaning and appropriateness.

Saturday 16 November

The London Shakespeare Group have arrived to present *Twelfth Night*. This is on the syllabus of some of the English-medium schools here. A year or so ago I asked Delena Kidd, the coordinator of the London Shakespeare Group, if she could bring out a team that could put that play on. I could guarantee full houses. I have arranged with the Cultural Foundation, where they will be playing, for each school to be in reserved places, and for there to be one teacher for every 25 students.

There was also a constraint for the players: Sir Toby Belch was not allowed to clutch a bottle of booze.

The schoolchildren arrive and the theatre fills up to capacity. The performance is excellent. Oscar Quitak is brilliant as Malvolio, bringing a round of applause more or less per appearance. His forced smile is hilarious. All is of a high standard. Ninety per cent of our audience are 'targets'. I feel I have achieved what I wished to achieve.

Monday 18 November

The London Shakespeare Group play at Ras Al Khaimah. I go to the performance of *Twelfth Night*. It is again splendid. Emily Richards is a star, as is Oscar, who had a fit of the giggles at Dubai last night. The archaeologists Geoffrey King and Beatrice de Cardi are in the audience, as well as about two hundred nationals. I sit next to Sheikh Sultan bin Saqr. It is another triumph. A British resident of Ras Al Khaimah, wife of a bank manager, tells me that after the opera here last month she saw a group of young nationals. 'Bravo, Englishman,' one shouted. 'Bravo, Englishwoman. Well done.'

Saturday 23 November

We go to the Marina Club (the British Club) for the performance of *Twelfth Night*. It is the first and only 'public' performance; all the others have been targeted at schools. The production is less restrained than the ones for schools, and Sir Toby Belch is able to carry his bottle.

Delena makes a nice speech at the end and thanks the sponsors – and me. She ends up by saying that Britain's greatest export is the work of William Shakespeare.

Sunday 24 November

I take Nat to Al Worood School to see the production there of *Twelfth Night*. There are over three hundred in the hall. The group have had a busy day, doing workshops and listening to children reciting Shakespeare. Beforehand, I tell Nat the story of the play but he already knows it, having seen it on video. Emily Richard is magnificent and gets round after round of applause. The audience is very attentive, and towards the end there is rapt silence. When Olivia, on seeing the twins, says, 'Most wonderful!' I hear an Arab girl say in English, 'Two husbands'. And there is a gentle 'Aaah' of sympathy as Malvolio finally leaves the stage.

I write a report on the success of the London Shakespeare Group visit. I write in a deadpan and factual way but throw in the remark that I do not think a troupe of puppets – offered by Drama Department – would have had the same impact. I quote what the Director-General has said – that we should be responsive to client demands.

Wednesday 27 November

I visit the Indian school in Abu Dhabi and meet its bearded head and the teachers of English. The school has 3,600 students, who work in shifts, girls in the morning and boys in the afternoon. They work to an Indian syllabus with four Shakespeare plays. Very few go on to the UK for tertiary education. Most go back to India. There are lots of Keralans among the students.

Thursday 28 November

We go camping with Frauke and David Heard. Nat captures a camel beetle and looks after it, feeding it with flies he has caught.

Friday 29 November

I sleep in the open air, and in the night gaze up to the sky. There are lots of satellites. I watch them move about, reflecting on the amount of metal and machinery up there watching us. There is condensation in the night and the duvet cover is soaked.

We move on from our campsite at 9 am, skirt Ras Al Khaimah and drive up a broad Wadi Bih. One road goes (temptingly) to Khasab in the Omani Musandam Peninsula. We turn right and after a while start to climb. It is like a road in northern Yemen. The rock is hard and grey. There are some ruined Shihuh villages. We explore one. The views are fantastic, looking across to Jabal Harim and to the track to Khasab. The villagers migrate for six months of the year to the coast to fish. The architecture is simple and functional, with flattened terraces and loaded palm trees. We push on over the top and down to a settlement – with a helipad! – and through a narrow wadi, a gorge like Petra's *sik*, which goes on for miles. We skirt boulders that fill the wadi bed, and the surrounding cliffs seem fragile and friable. We contemplate the rainy season, when water will pour down this gorge with uncontrollable ferocity. The valley flattens out, we pass another village and eventually sight the sea near Dibba. We reach the sea. Frauke and Theresa swim. Nat and I explore sand dunes.

Sunday 1 December

Nat's camel spider has survived. Frauke tells us that camel spiders can inject an anaesthetic and then devour flesh that it has a taste for. This accounts for the sight of some Bedu without noses or with chunks of flesh missing. Our camel spider is liberated into the garden.

At sunset I go to HMS *Hermione,* a warship that has docked at the Port of Abu Dhabi. We are piped aboard and then a 35-piece military band performs Beating Retreat. It is brilliant. They march up and down alongside the ship, following the man who wields the mace. In the second row are men with cymbals. When they are not being clashed, they are waved around overhead, making the whole troupe look like some huge beast with scales.

Monday 2 December

I go to the airport to help in receiving the Princess Royal. The plane carrying her and her party, and also Julian Walker, is half an hour late and taxis to a red carpet. The Princess emerges, followed by a lady-in-waiting, a wardrobe mistress, a very nice, intelligent-looking secretary

In the Musandam Peninsula.

and a Scot in charge of her baggage. All the passports are dealt with and I am intrigued to see Princess Anne's, which looks like any other but gives her status as 'Member of the Royal House'. The thick passport is full of diplomatic and complimentary visas. There are 16 large packing cases of her clothes, and a hat box. Some of the baggage is piled into the British Council car, and we set off in a convoy, preceded by a police car, half a dozen hospitality cars and two diplomatic cars. We cruise through all the red traffic lights and reach a red-carpeted entrance to the InterContinental Hotel.

Later in the day I go to the Embassy garden, where a fete is in progress: stalls, camel rides, everything. I am presented to the Princess but the Defence Attaché, who is a colonel in the regiment of which Princess Anne is Colonel-in-Chief, hogs all the conversation. I then join the fun of the fete, win a bottle of wine in a raffle, watch the Princess do a walkabout and leave.

Tuesday 3 December

Julian Walker takes Theresa, Nat and me out to lunch and on to the races. We have seats in the grandstand by Sheikh Zayed's enclosure. He arrives with Prince Abdullah bin Abdul Aziz, Heir to the Saudi throne. There are plenty of other sheikhs, mostly from Abu Dhabi. I exchange a smile and a nod with Sheikh Tahnoun bin Muhammad. Nat draws pictures of Sheikh Zayed and wants to show them to him. At one point Sheikh Khalifa removes himself from the presence of his father and sits immediately behind us to have a quiet smoke. Does even he, a grandfather himself, have to defer in this way? The races are short in length and we have exhibitions of dancing girls, a Bedu band and poetry recitations. One of the jockeys is a girl, Miss Caroline.

Thursday 5 December

I meet Hatim Nusseibeh, brother of Zaki, at the British Club, which someone calls 'Butlin's'. Zaki is the oldest of four brothers (and one sister). Zaki and Sari were sent to Rugby when their father was Jordanian Ambassador in London. Hatim and the younger brother were sent to Eton. The youngest brother works in the City (of London) and is married to a granddaughter of Azzam Pasha, the first (Egyptian)

Secretary-General of the Arab League.

Friday 6 December

At a lunch party we host, one of the guests tells me how impressed he was by my quelling '2,000 people' without a microphone on the first night in Abu Dhabi of *Twelfth Night*. Well, actually there were only 800–900 and I had no worries. I did clap my hands for quiet, and the audience (mostly schoolchildren) all applauded. I knew quite well that they would settle down and so they did, though it took a minute or two talking through noise to reach that point.

Tuesday 10 December

I hear that Princess Anne presented Sheikh Zayed with a prepared album of Wilfred Thesiger's photographs. Sheikh Zayed mused about Thesiger and said he was shocked, when meeting him again, how old he looked.

'That's because he is bad tempered,' he says. 'He used to be full of bad temper with the Bedu. But he's got over it though.'

'Well, I get pretty bad tempered at times,' said Princess Anne, 'so I'll age quickly.'

'No,' said Sheikh Zayed. 'You have a beautiful body; you will not age.'

(This was actually translated as, 'You do not have the physique to grow old.')

It had been planned for the Princess to present the album at the end of the meeting, but she saw that the Sheikh was feeling depressed and called for the photos earlier, expecting them to cheer him up. They did. It was absolutely right and she was being magnificently sensitive.

I also hear that, at his London home, Sheikh Khalifa received a letter addressed to 'Mr K B Zayed', summoning him to the Inland Revenue office to talk about income tax.

Sunday 15 December

The first secretary in the Embassy tells me that one of Thatcher's former cabinet ministers is coming to Abu Dhabi. He is being very demanding, expecting the Embassy to get all sorts of concessions and negotiate extra tickets. He has been given one free ticket by the Abu Dhabi government. I suggest that he should be told to stand on his own feet, to pay his way and not to rely on the nanny state looking after him.

Tuesday 24 December

Theresa has invited round the Filipina girls who work at her school again. She takes them to Catholic mass first. Six or seven diminutive and deferential young women turn up, calling me 'Sir' all the time. They are quiet and giggly but charming, and eat well. It is only shortly before they leave that they unwind. We have photo sessions, and two cling on to me. When did they last touch a man? When I ask one of them what her New Year resolution is, she says, 'To think kindly of the Principal of the school'. Another has a boyfriend – more giggles – in the United States. There is hope of a life after the Emirates Private School.

Tuesday 31 December

I have arranged a brief holiday in Oman, taking Nat and Gabriel. We fly over Al Ain to Muscat and fly on from there to Salalah, arriving there at sunset. We are met by Said al-Rashidi, son of Musallim bin al-Kamam, who takes us off in his Mercedes. He prefers to speak Arabic most of the time, but later chooses to practise his English. We go to a Bedu restaurant, sit on the floor and eat fish, rice and salad, followed by boiling-hot milk (camel's?). The décor of the restaurant is a mixture of Bedu culture – rifles – local artwork and tat. We have a coconut-juice drink before retiring to the hotel.

We should see Musallim tomorrow before he goes off to Muscat for a medical check-up.

1992

Wednesday 1 January

Said calls with a friend, Makhbut, whose grandfather travelled with Wilfred Thesiger. We drive out of Salalah. I get that wonderful sense of uplift I always have when we set off on a previously unknown road, as we drive through the banana groves and up onto the plain. This road to Thumrait was built in 1973, and I think of Bertram Thomas and Thesiger as they set out on their great journeys.

Thumrait is 80 kilometres from Salalah, a modern town two or three kilometres from the abandoned old village. We swing off onto an unmade road and reach the modest house of Musallim bin al-Kamam. It has no chairs or tables. In the reception room are many of Musallim's relations – his sons, Mubarak and Salih, sons-in-law and grandchildren. Pretty little girls hover at the door. Musallim looks older, with sunken cheeks, but is as bright-eyed as ever. He gives Gabriel a ferocious-looking rabbit trap. It is inscribed 'Killer. Made in Germany'. Salim bin Kabina comes to lunch, wearing a double belt of cartridges. My boys entertain their boys with headstands and imitations of animals. Their boys do marvellous imitations of camels and cows. Lunch is a sheep on rice and we all tuck in with our hands. The only cutlery in the house are spoons. But Salim bin Kabina has a knife, which he uses to slice off chunks of meat and pass them quietly to me.

After lunch, some of the younger men take me by pick-up truck to a nearby mountain. With one heavy machine gun, taking turns, we all indulge in target practice, firing at a rock placed on a bigger rock. I fire a gun for the first[45] time in my life, experiencing the shock of the recoil and the loud report. The boys spend the hour we are away with the Bin al-Kamam boys.

We return to Salalah and meet Theresa off the plane.

Thursday 2 January

We hire a car and set off to the west. The maps we have are quite unhelpful. But we drive beyond Rasyut and onto a wadi track through clumps of frankincense bushes. We pass by a family relaxing in a cave, meat strung up to dry. Then back to the coast road, to a magnificent

---

45 And last.

beach at Mughsail. A stream nearby has flamingos strutting around and camels plodding in the water. The beach ends with some aggressive cliffs.

We double back and go north of Salalah into hills that remind us of Provence. We reach a shrine, the alleged tomb of the Prophet Ayub (Job). A mosque and a restaurant are close by. The views over the Salalah plain are fantastic: what a place this would be if tourism were developed. The shrine itself is domed, the interior painted a rich green. A starker stone stands outside in a small courtyard that seems to be reserved for praying women.

We drive back to the coast, to see Musallim bin al-Kamam off: he is going to India for medical treatment. He seems to be as at home in a modern airport as anywhere else. Then to the east, to Taqah, where there are acres and acres of sardines spread out on the ground.

Friday 3 January

The four of us drive to Thumrait to see the family of Musallim bin al-Kamam. One son declines to shake hands with Theresa and invites us to take photographs, but not of women. While some of the men are at the mosque, we are entertained by a little old lady whose face is almost completely covered by a brown leather mask. This does not prevent her from chatting away in the men's majlis. Lunch is nothing special this time – dried fish and rice, and lots of tea. We look at the camels in the enclosure and drink first some camel's milk and then some *rabba*, sheep's milk taken just after a birth and heated. It tastes like a blend of cheese and burnt milk. Everyone is friendly, unassuming and naturally graceful. Thesiger is right about their nobility.

Back at the hotel I read the published diaries of Lady Luce. Over the last 25 years I have had four contrasting perspectives of her husband, Sir William.[46] First, Faris Glubb[47] saw him as the personification of assertive British imperialism, carving up the world. Secondly, David Treffry, a

---

46 Sir William Luce (1907–77), Governor of Aden 1956–60, Political Adviser Persian Gulf 1961–6.

47 Journalist and political activist (1939–2004), son of Sir John Glubb (Glubb Pasha), commander of the Arab Legion in Jordan before 1956.

former Adeni civil official whom I used to know, saw him as imposing a Sudanese model on the Adeni colonial service. Thirdly, I met Sir William himself in Omdurman in 1976 and found him reflective and charming. And now his wife's perspective of a conscientious but fun-loving 'Bill'.

We fly back to Abu Dhabi in the evening.

Peter was in London for a few days for consultation with his employers.

Wednesday 8 January

I am told that I am the favourite for opening the British Council in Kiev, but the prospect of a posting to Damascus has re-emerged. The Ambassador there, Andrew Green, has written to the Foreign Secretary, Douglas Hurd, to say that there is no point in him staying there if there is no British Council.

I learn that my Sudanese friend, Mohamed Omer Beshir[48] ('MOB'), has been very ill and is returning to Khartoum to die. The Sudanese government is paying for his first-class air travel, even though he has been a dissident.

Saturday 18 January

As I wait at Heathrow for the plane back to Abu Dhabi, I hear the announcement for 'the flight to St Petersburg'. It strikes home for the first time – the actual reality of all the changes in Eastern Europe.

Monday 20 January

I am writing an obituary of Mohamed Omer Beshir for *The Guardian*. He was a wonderful man, but in many ways I feel critical of him. He was often slipshod and plagiarist in his published work and not always a good political judge. I remember him saying once that you could have a dialogue with the communists but not with Sadiq al-Mahdi.

Sunday 26 January

I call on the Minister of Education, Hamad al-Midfa'i. He would like there to be 30 or 40 teachers from Britain to offset the growing influence

---

48 Sudanese academic, diplomat and writer (1924–92).

of Islamist fundamentalists. In Iran, he says, fundamentalists exploited social divisions in the country.

He also tells a nice story about Sheikh Zayed.

A Libyan visitor was being abusive about Jews.

'They have a place in Arabia,' said Sheikh Zayed. 'They were in Madina at the time of the Prophet Muhammad, who told them to keep their religion. Are you denying this?'

Wednesday 29 January

I am invited to give a talk at the Islamia English School for the inauguration of a girls' English society. The Principal and his senior colleagues are all middle-class males. I am taken into a room where there are 50 nun-like girls aged between 12 and 17. Teachers wear gowns, and Islamic injunctions adorn the walls. The meeting starts with the *Fatiha*, the opening verse of the Koran, which is translated by one girl. I am introduced with excessive flattery. The theme of my talk is 'Minds and Imaginations'. I praise Islam and Sheikh Zayed, and in that context urge them all not to make prisons of their minds but to explore world literature – Dante, Tolstoy, Shakespeare. There are then some set speeches from sedate little girls. I look at their faces hoping to see a crack of mischief or merriment. In vain.

MOB has died. I fax my prepared obituary to *The Guardian*. I feel a sense of loss. He was such a bundle of energy and optimism. My obituary is a tribute.

Saturday 1 February

We must adjust to the here and now. But a total preoccupation is shallow consumerism. The there and then adds depth to perception.

Sunday 2 February

At the Embassy meeting, someone raises the idea of buying a walking and cycling machine for the Embassy Club.

'Why can't people just walk or cycle?' I ask innocently.

Conversation moves to jogging.

'When I see a fat man running along the Corniche in this hot weather,' observes the Consul, 'I hope to God that he's not British. An expatriate's death causes a lot of work.'

I call on Reem Metwalli at the Cultural Foundation. She has lost weight, and is depressed at the state of her country, Iraq. Because she is competent and well motivated she gets loaded with work. She is arranging, with Brian MacDermot of the Mathaf Gallery in London, an exhibition of orientalist paintings at the end of the month and asks me to say a few words at the opening.

Tuesday 4 February

I am in the anteroom of Sheikh Nahyan's majlis when Peter Hellyer comes in with David Steel, former leader of the Liberal Party, and Menzies Campbell, Lib Dem Member of Parliament. I help with interpreting as they are interviewed by a local journalist.

Sheikh Nahyan comes in, but I stay only for a few minutes. He has a host of academics, bankers and architects queuing up to see him.

I go to a party to meet the Chief Guide, Helen Barker, whose husband is an Ipswich solicitor. Other guests are mainly the UAE girl guides fraternity, or sorority, but I get into a conversation with someone about the quality of life.

Wednesday 5 February

Theresa returns after a fortnight's holiday in Malaysia, which she found cheap, beautiful, uncrowded and interesting.

We go to an exhibition of ancient and historic coins owned by Abdullah bin Jasim, a Dubai collector. They are insured for US$14 million and were brought to Abu Dhabi from Dubai under armed escort.

Sunday 9 February

I contribute to the teaching operation. I read one of my translations of *Dubai Tales* in English, while the students follow the story in Arabic. They are not accustomed to reading. 'No time,' they say. I observe some, as they read the Arabic, mouthing the words like a primary school pupil. With one class, not a lot is gained. It is better with a second class. There, a student argues that 'embrace' is too intimate; I should have written 'hug.' Another student says that 'those reading your translation will think people in the Emirates drink.'

Monday 10 February

I go to Al Ain and call at the Emirates Private School. I meet Adli Mustafa, who has set up schools in Fujairah (which he pronounces the Egyptian way, '*Fugaira*') and Sharjah (ditto, '*Shar'a*'). The schools are Arabic-medium and most of the pupils are Egyptian.

Tuesday 11 February

I call at the Women's Higher College of Technology. They have recently had their first 17 graduates.

I go on to the university and see Sudanese academic friends, Abbas Mohamed Ahmed and Sayyid Hamid Hurreiz. They suggest we go to the Book Fair.

'It's Islamic,' says Abbas, slightly defensively.

'Some of my best friends are Muslims,' I say.

We talk about MOB, feeling sad at the loss of a man who meant much to all of us. I tell them of a letter I have had from John Semple,[49] who is 'numb with grief'. When he phoned MOB a few days before he died, MOB sought to comfort John, saying, 'We'll all meet up at the Horse and Jockey'. It is nice to think of a Sudanese whose idea of the afterlife is a pub in rural Oxfordshire.

Thursday 13 February

Theresa's Iranian colleague is unwell. She is from a privileged background and went to a convent school in Kent. Her husband, Musaddiq, is Libyan, and owns three flats in central London – in St John's Wood, Knightsbridge and Mayfair.

Friday 14 February

We spend the day on Sadiyat Island. We stroll to the area behind the hotel and find a smallholding, with ducks, chickens and rabbits. A long, sandy, dusty track leads to some kind of oil-processing plant. It is beautifully relaxing to be on this island.

---

49 Friend and former British Council colleague in Sudan (1937–2016).

Monday 17 February

The (British-dominated) Thespians of Abu Dhabi Society is arranging for Frank Barrie to come with his one-man show about the Victorian actor, William Macready [*Macready!*]. The organiser has not managed a tour like this and is getting into a flap. I am resisting having to take over. Organising a tour is labour- and time-intensive. She is learning that and can barely cope, and suffers from high blood pressure. The Al Ain Drama Group is not offering any help, out of pique.

Tuesday 18 February

I am reading Rawlinson on Phoenicia,[50] written in 1889 when the author was 77. It is splendid: readable and authoritative without any condescension to a non-specialist reader. In those days, specialists could write for non-specialists. If you wanted to know about a subject, you could inform yourself about it. The book is like a good informative television programme.

Thursday 20 February

I talk with an Iraqi friend about the awfulness of Muslim fundamentalists, how their views are a travesty of Islam and its history. Islam has been at its best when it has been most liberal. 'There is no compulsion in religion.' And 'seek knowledge though it is in China'. These – the first from the Koran, the second a saying of the Prophet Muhammad – are watchwords of Islam and should be proclaimed from the rooftops.

Sunday 23 February

The other day the Ambassador was at a buffet with Abdul Rahman Abdullah, the Sudanese head of the United Nations here. The Ambassador said to Abdul Rahman, 'That's pork. You can't have that.'

50 George Rawlinson, *History of Phoenicia* (Longmans, Green & Co., London, 1889).

In a pure Gordon Memorial College[51] accent, Abdul Rahman replied, 'Looks tempting'.

What a lot of cultural and linguistic ironies are contained in those two words.

The Ambassador is touring next week with what I hear is Wan Seh Kai. Is this some Hong Kong businessman, I wonder? No, it is 1 Sec I – the First Secretary (Information).

Wednesday 26 February

At Al Ain I give a talk to the cloistered girls of the Higher College of Technology for Women. There are 15 women in the audience, two totally veiled. I have arranged to read Muhammad al-Murr's story 'Pepsi'. Copies of the Arabic, with some strong language Tipp-Exed out, have been distributed. I read my English translation as they read the Arabic. They seem spellbound. I then get them slowly to overcome their shyness and talk. One gives a line of her own poetry and asks me to translate it. Another gives me three lines of the medieval writer, Abu Firas. By the end of the hour we are great friends, and we carry on chatting outside.

Sunday 1 March

I give the same talk at the Higher College of Technology for Women in Dubai. I talk about how I got to know Muhammad al-Murr's writing. In the discussion a small girl compares, in excellent English, the humanising of the camel in 'Pepsi' to *Animal Farm*. Bright girl. I learn later that she is Azza, daughter of Sheikh Dr Sultan, Ruler of Sharjah. Discussion is about the language used and the bad behaviour of some characters. But there is a quiet pride in Dubai and the general accuracy of the portrayal of social life. I enjoy it all.

I go to Muhammad al-Murr's house and he shows me the treasure trove of purchases from Damascus, books published between 1840 and 1920, pamphlets, a guide in Arabic to Istanbul and so on. We go

---

51 Gordon Memorial College was the English-language secondary school after the foundation of the Anglo-Egyptian Condominium following the Battle of Omdurman in 1898. It served the elite of the Sudan, and graduates often had a distinctive ironic and clipped accent.

off to the Beach Club to a function of the French Cultural Centre. Amin Maalouf[52] gives a talk in Arabic. He is Lebanese but based in Paris and writes in French. He is defensive about not writing in Arabic, but when he is asked questions, he is more animated and very sensible. There should be no competition about languages. He is also positive about the Ottoman Empire.

Afterwards we have dinner at a restaurant and join Sultan Owais, who goes to Damascus three times a year.

'I first went to Damascus in 1962,' I say.

'So did I,' he says. 'How old are you?'

'Fifty-two.'

'I am sixty-seven.'

'We are a couple of youths.'

'No, we are two old men,' he says.

Muhammad tells me Sultan Owais gets VIP treatment when he goes to Damascus and is courted by ministers.

Monday 2 March

We have an American Muslim woman from Alabama working in the Dubai British Council library. She is having coffee and a fag with an Iranian colleague who is escaping from Islam. She will not shake hands with me and trills on about the beauty and discipline of Ramadan.

Friday 6 March

It is now Ramadan and we wake up at the Madina Zayed Rest House in the Liwa. We have our breakfast secretly in our room – tea from a flask and some cornflakes. We are solicitous about people who are fasting. But when we come downstairs we find that the rest house has prepared a breakfast for us, to eat in the privacy of our room. Now that is as it should be. We are both sensitive to the feelings of others. How much better than vying with a sense of smug superiority.

We go to Tarif, where David Heard started his career. When he graduated in Geology from Keele in 1963, he had three job offers. One

---

52 Lebanese writer (1949–), resident in France since 1976. Received Prix Goncourt, 1992 for *Le Rocher de Tanios*. Author of, among other books, *Les Croisades vues par les Arabes* and *Samarcande*.

was in the Antarctic Survey, which would have required him being away for two years. A second was in South Africa, where he would have been away from England for 18 months. The third was for a stint in Abu Dhabi, initially based here in Tarif – being away for nine months. He came here and, apart from leave periods, has been here ever since. We go on to another village. The landscape is bleak and featureless. The village is a collection of portable temporary structures. Nobody is around. It is as if the place has been struck by plague.

Saturday 7 March

Emirates News, edited by Peter Hellyer, publishes my memoir[53] of Mohamed Omer Beshir (MOB) – it is 40 days since he died.

Sunday 8 March

There is a possibility that Margaret Thatcher will come to Abu Dhabi next month.

I call at the majlis of Sheikh Nahyan at about 11 pm. I meet Samir Rizq of the university and a Palestinian/Jordanian, Riad, son of Burhan Kemal, whom I knew 23 years ago when I was working in Jordan and he was Under-Secretary at the Ministry of Education. Sheikh Nahyan invites me to stay for a meal. Which I do.

Monday 9 March

I call on the UAE Under-Secretary at the Ministry of Education. He is an unreconstructed Nasserite and is concerned about US global hegemony. I tell him it could be worse. An open society of 300 million people rightly has global responsibilities. We can try to persuade them.

I go on to the Ruler's diwan and call on Zaki Nusseibeh. We talk about literary freedom in the Arab world, and about the books we have been reading.

In the evening, David Heard telephones.

'Would you like to meet your landlord?' he asks.

---

53 Reprinted in Peter Clark, *Coffeehouse Footnotes* (Twopenny Press, Diss, 2010), pp. 111–3.

We do so. Muhammad Khadim Ghaith al-Qubaisi lives in a magnificent marble-inlaid palace with camels in the garden. We wait awhile, talking with Ali Sanad, who used to drive taxis years ago in Tarif, and an Adeni, Rashad al-Arifi, who is still bitter about the British. The landlord joins us and is very cordial. A Tunisian imam is also present.

David and I make a Ramadan call on Abdul Aziz al-Mubarak; an Austrian diplomat and a black American imam are also there.

Tuesday 10 March

I go to Al Ain, and at the Municipality learn that the zoo is closed. There is a crisis: an outbreak of foot-and-mouth disease. Half the oryx have died. There has been no mention of this in the papers. Vets are being summoned from all over the world. Can the British Council help urgently with a consultant who can advise on this disastrous situation?

Wednesday 11 March

I make some enquiries about the Al Ain oryx. Al Ain is one of the two major breeding grounds for the oryx – the other is in San Diego, California. There are perhaps only 500 in the world. The local breeding of the oryx is part of Sheikh Zayed's wish to recreate an imaginative Arabian past. Peter Hellyer tells me Sheikh Zayed has not been told about this crisis.

I send an 'immediate-urgent' fax to my headquarters, and phone my line manager and tell him 'This is important'. Richard Burge[54] at British Council London phones. They have identified a Dr Barclay Hastings, who can come out on Friday night. He is an American and will be bringing a working stock of drugs. His visit will cost £11,900. That needs to be paid up front. Peter Hellyer and David Heard give me good advice and at 11 pm David and I go to the majlis of Sheikh Nahyan. The place is crowded, forty or fifty people there. We sit with Sheikh Nahyan on the floor. He has a special contraption for his back as he plays cards. We outline the matter.

'Sheikh Zayed does not know yet,' he tells us. 'Nobody dares tell him.'

---

54 A zoologist and later Director, Zoological Society of London..

Somebody else calls and Sheikh Nahyan goes off with him to his private office. He joins us again after midnight. Trays of food have been brought in and the university Vice-Chancellor sits on Sheikh Nahyan's left. I have made the need for payment quite clear. Sheikh Nahyan tells the Vice-Chancellor to deal with it.

After dinner, the Vice-Chancellor asks me what it is all about. 'What's it got to do with the university?' he asks.

'Sheikh Nahyan is guaranteeing the payment and says you'll get it back from the Al Ain Municipality.'

The Vice-Chancellor is bemused, but it is agreed. I have to go to an office and see Hashim in the morning for some formalities and then see the Vice-Chancellor in Al Ain.

Thursday 12 March

David and I call on Hashim, a Palestinian who has been here for a long time. He studied English at Paignton in 1977. He is amazingly efficient, and types letters to the immigration office and to customs, saying Dr Hastings will bring in four medium-sized boxes with narcotics. Faxes are dispatched but there is a problem about licking envelopes in Ramadan. It leaves a nasty taste in the mouth, which he cannot wash out.

I then go to Al Ain and collect a cheque from the Vice-Chancellor, who had not heard of the crisis until last night.

Before sunset David joins me in Al Ain and we go to the vast, elaborate palace of Sheikh Tahnoun. In the majlis we join some nationals sitting on chairs drawn up in the shape of a horseshoe. Sheikh Tahnoun arrives and we follow him into a room where on the floor a vast spread for breaking the fast is awaiting us. Afterwards we drink coffee with Tahnoun. I sit and chat with his sons. Mansour is a medical student; Ahmad is in the Faculty of Business Administration. Sultan is studying Engineering and is one of the students we sent to Scotland last year. A man comes in and presents Sheikh Tahnoun with an elaborate gun and a dead bustard.

We go off and make a condolence call on Muhammad al-Butti. David is superb on the family genealogies.

Then to the majlis of Ahmad al-Suwaidi. His majlis is full of people from all over the Arab world. I talk to a Mauritanian, a couple of

Sudanese and a Libyan who used to be Ambassador here but has now obtained UAE nationality. Ahmad's majlis is more informal. We sit on the floor, on cushions. I also talk to Muhammad bin Sultan al-Dhahiri, head of the Abu Dhabi Civil Service.

Saturday 14 March

I go to the airport to meet Barclay Hastings, who is based at Whipsnade Zoo. A man from Sheikh Nahyan's private office is there, with a visa ready for him. We clear him into the country. One piece of luggage is missing – the gun for firing injections into sick beasts; but it turns up.

I drive Barclay to Al Ain and brief him. He is 34 and is a consultant all over the world – Chile, Czechoslovakia, Zaire, Turkey. He learns fast. At the Municipality, we meet the Acting Director of the zoo and the zoo's Egyptian vet, 'a scared rabbit', as Barclay describes him. He describes the course of the epidemic and tries to suggest that things are under control.

Barclay and I go to the zoo and meet other vets, Egyptian and German. There are five pens of oryx and half those in two pens have died; three more died last night. Animals are bred just to feed the oryx – pigeons, rabbits, mice, rats; those surplus to requirements go to the Al Ain sheikhs to feed their falcons. Barclay is ready to do a post-mortem on the latest victims. One vet wants to stay at home tomorrow. Another thinks 'it is all in Allah's hands'. There is an absence of both authority and morale. People are worried about their jobs. There is no system of veterinary reporting, policing or notification of diseases. Thousands of sheep and goats wander right up to the zoo's perimeter fence.

Sunday 15 March

I call on Dr Farida al-Badri at the Higher College of Technology for Women, and arrange for the Thesiger exhibition to be displayed there next month. I wonder if I could get Margaret Thatcher involved. She is the Chancellor of the University of Buckingham, of which Sheikh Nahyan is a graduate.

I go to the majlis of Sheikh Mubarak and Sheikh Nahyan before sunset. We are invited into a room for dinner and Sheikh Nahyan invites me to sit next to him.

Tuesday 17 March

I have to go to a British Council training session near Madras next month. I arrange to stay on in India and to go to Hyderabad – Pickthall's Hyderabad. In Dubai I book a return ticket from Madras, giving me three days in Hyderabad.

Ahmad Omar Khalafallah phones. He tells me how much he enjoyed my article on Mohamed Omer Beshir. He had been a friend of MOB since 1942 and welcomes an outsider writing about a courageous man who they all revered. I am greatly moved by this appreciation.

Wednesday 18 March

I collect Barclay from Al Ain and bring him to Abu Dhabi. He got on well with everybody; only the German resented him. Barclay describes him as old-fashioned, efficient, unimaginative and pedantic. I take him to the majlis of Sheikh Nahyan. David Heard and Peter Hellyer are both there. We are able to see Sheikh Nahyan privately and brief him. Barclay outlines proposed measures – mainly ensuring there is a space beyond the outside perimeter of the zoo to prevent sheep and goats, potential carriers of foot-and-mouth disease, from approaching the zoo animals too closely. Sheikh Nahyan will be seeing Sheikh Zayed later this evening.

Saturday 21 March

Sheikh Zayed would like Barclay to go to the island of Sir Bani Yas, where he has a sort of private zoo, tomorrow. It has become clear that Sheikh Zayed has been monitoring Barclay's progress.

Barclay and I go late at night to see Sheikh Nahyan. He is sitting on the floor, using his special backrest, playing rummy with friends. I have had no news about the flights to the island; nothing is certain until it actually happens. A group of ambassadors call – the Tunisian, the Jordanian, the Mauritanian and the Moroccan – the last looking splendid in his national dress, which includes a fez.

Sheikh Nahyan does bits of business throughout.

'You cannot go,' he tells me with a twinkle in his eye. 'You are a spy.'

I can, of course, but I am never sure. We join the ambassadors for a midnight feast. Arrangements are made and we are to see Sheikh Nahyan's zoo at 9.00 am tomorrow.

Sunday 22 March

Barclay and I call on Sheikh Nahyan, who looks a bit sleepy. His Palestinian aide accompanies us to Batin military airport, which looks like a British tropical airbase of 30 years ago. We are ushered through and go by bus to a small military plane. On the bus I observe a notice – 'Emergency Cosh.'

The seats line the fuselage walls and face into the plane; they are made of canvas. Views through the windows are restricted. The crew of three outnumbers us. With a roar and a shake, we are soon airborne over the east of the island of Abu Dhabi and then out to sea. I gaze out all the time – the dull, deserted islands, suddenly brightened by a palace. Abu Abyad, Jabal Dhanna and then round the island of Sir Bani Yas and down onto the runway, big enough for a jumbo jet. We are met off the plane by Jamal, a representative of the Ruler's Representative, and two vets, a Pakistani and a Palestinian. As I come down the steps of the plane I see emus fleeing, as if in alarm.

We spend a couple of hours on the island, which is full of animals, over which Sheikh Zayed keeps a firm control. He has three palaces and many belvederes. Emu, ostrich, rhea, llama, gazelle, oryx; some are in extensive pens, others roam wild. There is a precise record of the stock. Although the animals are healthy and happy, they are vulnerable to disease if animal import controls are relaxed. But it is an amazing place, a rich old man's dream. There is no pollution from hundreds of human visitors. We see peacocks in a palace garden and return by plane.

At about 11 pm we go back to see Sheikh Nahyan. I marvel at the way he conducts business, sitting on the floor, playing rummy, phoning around, listening to Barclay's debriefing and exchanging pertinent comments. The archaeologist Geoffrey King is there, as well as Mana Oteiba and Muhammad al-Fahim. We eat and are home by 1 am.

Monday 23 March

Sheikh Muhammad bin Zayed wants to see Barclay. He has to leave tonight, but we are able to see the Sheikh's representative, Muhammad al-Bowardi. Sheikh Muhammad has a project for the breeding of bustard. He wants a specialist urgently. Can we help?

In the last few days all sorts of possibilities for new courses of action have emerged. These cannot be anticipated in the 'business plans' we are required to devise in our annual procedures. You cannot anticipate the outbreak of foot-and-mouth among the oryx in Al Ain zoo. What we can do is too diffuse. It is not subject to simplistic analysis like selling sweets or furniture.

I see Barclay off onto the plane, with his tranquilliser gun and drugs.

Friday 27 March

I hear a story that General Norman Schwarzkopf, who led the Coalition forces in the liberation of Kuwait, visited the UAE and was taken to the desert on Sir Bani Yas to do some hunting. Schwarzkopf was actually a lousy shot. This astounded the sheikhs, who thought that the man who had organised the crushing of Iraq with all that precision bombing would be better at more basic military skills, like shooting straight.

Sunday 29 March

Margaret Thatcher is due out here on 27 April, when I will be in India. The Ambassador is not looking forward to the visit. He has witnessed her humiliating both Geoffrey Howe and Nigel Lawson in the presence of civil servants. She looks straight through you and does not let you finish the sentence. She constantly interrupts. On the other hand, she was the best-briefed prime minister in modern times.

I have been reading Barbara Castle's *Diaries*.[55] I am intrigued by the way she prepared the way for Margaret Thatcher. Firstly, she combined an ideological commitment with a consciousness of her own femininity. Secondly, she was tough on her civil servants. Thirdly, and oddly, both had Bernard Ingham as Press Secretary. As did Tony Benn. In some ways, Castle plus Benn equals Thatcher.

Tuesday 31 March

Geoffrey King has been doing some archaeological surveys on Sir Bani Yas. Sheikh Zayed came to the site and invited Geoffrey to dinner. Sheikh

---

55 Barbara Castle, *The Castle Diaries 1964–1976* (Macmillan, 1990). Castle (1910–2002) was a leading Labour politician.

Zayed was affable, interested, relaxed and full of useful information. Anything you want, he told Geoffrey, is yours.

I drive to Dubai and in the evening Ali Rashid Lootah takes me on a series of Ramadan calls. We go first to Saif al-Ghurair. The Minister of Electricity, Humaid Nasir al-Owaiss, is present, as well as the Kuwaiti and Egyptian Consuls-General. Jum'a al-Majid is there; he has plans to build a huge library. When I tell Saif about my successor, John Foley, the Egyptian Ambassador says he must be Egyptian – Fuli, a lover of *ful*, Egyptian beans. I wonder whether the British Council could have a role with the development of Jum'a al-Majid's library. Then to the home of Ibrahim Obeidallah, who must be 80-plus, for his son, Muhammad, looks an old man. I talk to a charming old man from Ras Al Khaimah, who tells me he used to smuggle and trade in East Africa: a surviving pirate.

The majlises of Dubai are far more relaxed and less formal than those of Abu Dhabi. We do not all stand when someone comes in. We loll around laughing more and discuss things in greater depth. Perhaps it is the commercial spirit of the city.

Wednesday 1 April

The British Club is arranging an election-night party next week, with special cocktails – Kinnock's Revenge and Major Surprise.

Thursday 2 April

I am woken up in the middle of the night by a mighty clap of thunder and heavy rain.

Roads are flooded. There have been 51 millimetres of rain. Cars are stranded. We go to collect Nat at the Al Khubairat British School. I drive through several inches of rain very slowly. At the school there is chaos. There is no relief from the downpour. Inside the roofs are leaking and the floors are wet. Bowls have been placed to collect the drips. Papers are scattered on the floor to mop up the moisture – a totally fruitless gesture.

In the afternoon, I sleep but wake up to our neighbour knocking at the door. Her husband is a Jordanian general. Half the electricity in the house is off. The microwave has to be filled for the Ramadan breakfast.

She wants me to phone the electricity authority on her behalf. An English male voice is more authoritative. Is her husband asleep? Is an Englishman more authoritative than a Jordanian general?

Friday 3 April
We are in Dubai, where Theresa has not been for some time. It has changed. Bits of buildings have gone up. It is a strangely attractive city, with an Indian appearance. The people, the noises, the smells are all redolent of a prosperous Bombay.

Saturday 4 April
It is damp, but no longer stormy. We take an abra across to Deira. A few days ago, there was a letter in *Gulf News* from a pompous Indian about how, after many years in Dubai, he ventured to take an abra and was upset at the lack of handrails, and how scruffy and dangerous it all was. That is precisely why I like them.

We have dinner with Christine and Leslie McLoughlin. One of the other guests is John Kirkbride, who taught at Brummana High School in Lebanon from 1964 to 1971. He studied Arabic at Durham University and knew Farida Akl, the old lady who, before the First World War, taught Arabic to T E Lawrence.

Tuesday 7 April
Back in Abu Dhabi after a few days' Eid holiday, I call on the Principal of the Higher College of Technology for Women about getting Margaret Thatcher to open the exhibition of photographs. I say that 'we could involve a distinguished British visitor whose identity I am not yet at liberty to disclose'.

Monday 13 April
I have a phone call from Geoffrey King. He has just discovered a prehistoric site, dating to 4000 BC or earlier. It immediately transforms our knowledge of the prehistory of the UAE.

I take Katie – all four of our children are now with us – to the Higher College of Technology for Women, where I give a talk, without notes, on translating Muhammad al-Murr. Again I distribute Arabic copies of his story, 'Pepsi', and read my translation. They are shy at first, but become more forthcoming. They ask questions – whether I am getting the cultural background, and about the dialect language. It is all very pleasant, relaxing and informal.

Tuesday 14 April

It has not yet been announced that Margaret Thatcher will be coming here on 27 April for a couple of days. We cannot talk about it. She will be the guest of the UAE government, who will be making all the arrangements. The Ambassador supports my bid for her to open the Thesiger exhibition at the Higher College for Technology for Women. This is part of an interesting experiment in women's technical education. Of the six such colleges in the country, only this has a British Principal, who previously taught at a college in Grantham, Margaret Thatcher's birthplace. The latter is currently the Chancellor of Sheikh Nahyan's alma mater, the University of Buckingham. Margaret Thatcher was also a great supporter of the British Council, which she saw as low-cost and high-profile. Alas, I shall be in India at the time. She will arrive in the morning and see Sheikh Zayed, and is due to go to the camel-racing in the afternoon. The Ambassador was asked how he would deal with her.

'I expect I shall grovel, like everybody else.'

Wednesday 15 April

I receive a fax from my headquarters confirming my appointment as Director of the British Council in Syria from September. Whoopee!

Friday 17 April

It is Good Friday.

Theresa brings to the house the Filipina girls who work at the Emirates Private School. They are appallingly paid and treated. Theresa has regularly got them out at Christmas and Easter, shedding a bit of light into their lives. Their only other treat is a weekly trip to the supermarket in a chauffeur-driven car. We take them in two cars to the beach at Ras Al Khadra. The beach is crowded with families shaded by sun umbrellas. Youths cruise, and some were offering money for time with one or more of the girls.

I hear that the Ajman University College of Science and Technology has classes in Abu Dhabi. To keep the sexes apart, they have built a wall up a staircase and along corridors. Even the classrooms have a screen down the middle. Both sexes can see the teacher and the blackboard, but cannot see each other.

Theresa takes the Filipina girls to the Catholic church.

Sunday 19 April

Beatrice de Cardi is here. I take her to the Ambassador's Residence for drinks on the patio, and ask her how she got involved in the archaeology of Ras Al Khaimah.

'I was working in Iranian Baluchistan at the time – in the 1960s. The Iranians were suspicious of me, and thought I was gun-running.'

I tell her that I am due to reopen the British Council in Syria.

'It's fun opening up. I opened up Trade Commission offices after Partition, in Karachi and then Lahore.'

Tuesday 21 April

Cecil Hourani[56] is in Abu Dhabi and I take him to the Queen's Birthday Party at the Embassy. He has spent time here with his Lebanese cousin, Amal Hourani, a constructor, who is building Officers' City, houses of amazing luxury for army officers.

'He has brought in a lot of people from the village,' he says.

'The village?' I ask.

'Yes, Marjayoun, the village in Lebanon where we come from. Thirty or so carpenters and other artisans have been recruited and flown in to help build this city.'

Wednesday 22 April

The embargo on the news of Margaret Thatcher's forthcoming visit is lifted.

I have a meeting of my staff.

'Guess who's going to open the Thesiger exhibition at the Women's

---

56 Anglo-Lebanese writer and cultural consultant (1917–). In December 2014 Peter was invited to have lunch with him at his Islington flat. Cecil cooked. He was busy writing a life of his father.

College?' I ask.

'Sheikha Fatima?' one colleague ventures.

'No, Margaret Thatcher,' I say.

'You're kidding.'

'If he can get Prince Charles to open the centre in Al Ain,' comments another colleague, 'why can't he get Margaret Thatcher to open this exhibition?'

A buzz of excitement and anticipation is built up; I encourage it.

'What do we call her?'

'Mrs Thatcher. And you do not curtsey. That's only for royalty. No, you cannot get the office to buy suits for the occasion. But we can buy some flowers for her.'

Thursday 23 April

Two senior Embassy colleagues and I are all leaving shortly. I start a rumour that it is all as a result of this month's General Election[57] – the Thatcherite hard core is being purged.

Peter went to India from 25 April to 5 May, attending a British Council training course at a luxury beach hotel south of Madras, not yet Chennai. He took some days' leave and went by train to Hyderabad. In the early 1980s he had written his book on Marmaduke Pickthall without knowing Hyderabad, where Pickthall spent the last ten years of his life.

Monday 27 April

Much of the day my thoughts are in Abu Dhabi, with Theresa and the opening of the Thesiger exhibition by Margaret Thatcher.

I am able to phone Theresa late at night. Sheikh Zayed did not get up until midday and Margaret Thatcher had to hang around until he was ready to see her. She was at the Higher College at 1.30 pm – the guests had been invited for 11.30 am. Margaret Thatcher was full of warm praise for the British Council and full of sentimentality about the photographs. Edward Henderson and Sheikh Nahyan took over explaining the pictures. 'That's my uncle. That's my father,' explained

---

57 John Major's Conservatives defeated the Labour Party under Neil Kinnock.

Theresa greets Margaret Thatcher in Abu Dhabi. Between them are Reem al-Metwalli and Edward Henderson.

Sheikh Nahyan. When she saw the picture of a depressed Sharjah souk, she said, 'I've always been enthusiastic about the market economy. People were so happy then.' Theresa says she was clearly trying to be gracious and charming, and raved at every picture. 'It was like taking a favourite but dotty aunt round an art gallery.' But she did say that the photos showed we were friends of the Emirates before the discovery of oil. My colleagues were gratified by her support.

I am happy that everything went well. All involved will remember the day for the rest of their lives. The event has brought the British Council once again to the heart of UK–UAE relations. And I am not indispensable. I can set it all up and slip away here to India. I feel Margaret Thatcher is a potential role model for Emirates women. Anything is possible.

Theresa also tells me about the reception for Margaret Thatcher at the Ambassador's Residence. Denis Thatcher was superb at small talk, a parody of himself. He was supportive of the British Council and asked Theresa how many people worked for the British Council.

'I'm not sure, really,' answered Theresa. 'I am just a spouse.'

There was a complicit twinkle in Denis's eyes.

Friday 1 May

The train from Madras to Hyderabad sets off on time at 6.15 am. It makes a din and the windows are filthy but I reflect that Marmaduke Pickthall must have taken this route after he gave his lectures in Madras in 1927.[58]

Saturday 2 May

I arrive in Hyderabad. The first ad I see is for the St David's Institute for English Conversation; another proclaims 'The famous Dr Jehan, specialist in skin diseases, VD and sex'. Fast food, I see, is Hurry Curry. I take a taxi to the Ritz Hotel, an attractive old building on a hill and only £8 a night. It was, I am pleased to learn, the house of Princess Nilűfer, from the Ottoman Imperial family, who was married to a son of the Nizam of Hyderabad. I have breakfast, using a tea-strainer, in a courtyard with Gothic tracery arcades.

At the British Library I meet a Mr Azm, who speaks of Pickthall as 'a multifaceted personality' who was interested in sport; there have been trophies in his name. I then meet Mustafa Sherwani, a delightful man of 71. His father was a historian, a contemporary of Jawaharlal Nehru and a close friend of Pickthall. Mustafa accompanied his father on a farewell call on Pickthall in 1935 – Mustafa would have been 14. He takes me to call on some old Hyderabadis. We go to the Banjara Hills, full of opulent, well-gardened villas.

The first we call on is Fazl-ur-Rahman, a former Vice-Chancellor of Aligarh University, born in 1901, physically frail but mentally alert. He first knew of Pickthall through the latter's writings in the *Bombay Chronicle* in the early 1920s, which he read when he was a student in Paris.

We come down from the Banjara Hills and call on Kamal Ullah, who was doctor to the Nizam's family; his wife is a cousin of Mustafa.

---

58 The lectures were reprinted as *The Cultural Side of Islam* (Committee of Muslim Lectures on Islam, Madras, 1927).

We try in vain to see Mufakhkham Jar, grandson of the Nizam and also, through his mother, Princess Durrushehvar, of the last Ottoman khalifa/caliph.

Sunday 3 May

I take a taxi for four hours – at £5 – for a tour of Pickthall's Hyderabad.[59] I see the outside of the Lake View Rest House, where Pickthall spent his last night in Hyderabad, and of the Administrative Staff College, which was the home of the Prince of Berar, husband of Princess Durrushehvar. I then go to the Women's College, which used to be the home and office of the British Resident – a huge classical building put up in 1810 on land presented to the British by the then Nizam. Behind it is a cemetery, overgrown with weeds, with heart-rending epitaphs of mainly young British. I get my driver, Krishna, to take me to the racecourse and to Barkas, a small Muslim outer suburb that housed the residential quarters of the Nizam's Arab guard. The name of the suburb is probably a corruption of 'barracks'. It is below the huge palace of Falaknuma, high on a hill and overlooking the city. And we also see the tomb of Raymond, a French officer, and nearby, the tomb of a young English girl who died in childbirth in 1809.

Krishna drops me off by Char Minar and I wander through the bazaar, buying a few presents. Then I come upon a bookshop. It is a treasure house, dusty and ill organised. The proprietor, I guess correctly, is a Hadrami. His grandfather came to Hyderabad to enlist in the Nizam's army. He has the volumes of the journal *Islamic Culture,* edited by Pickthall, from 1926 onwards. I find a copy of the two-volume translation by Pickthall of the Koran, published by the Government of Hyderabad Press. And *Islamic Poems* (in English) by Nawab Sir Nizamat Jung Bahadur, who was also the architect of Hill Fort, now the Ritz Hotel, where I am staying. The book dealer also offers me – I decline – some manuscript Korans. One is dated 780 AH (1378 AD) and is priced at £15,000. The cheapest is £600.

---

59 Marmaduke Pickthall wrote an affectionate account of Hyderabad: "Hyderabad: the Heart of India" (*Geographical,* no 6, 1936, pp. 400–21). The article was published one month before he died.

Monday 4 May

I am shown round the rooms of the hotel. Some are expansive suites. After breakfast I set off on foot for Golconda. I go through the well-maintained parks by the Legislative Assembly, one of the Nizam's last palaces, and through a poorer neighbourhood of the city. There are pro-Saddam Hussein slogans on walls and exhortations to read the Koran. Confessionally the area is mixed – Hindu temples, mosques and shrines all together.

I get lost in the marshlands between Hyderabad and Golconda, somewhere near a slaughterhouse. I take an *auto*, the three-wheeled open taxi, for the rest of the way. Golconda is a magnificent city-fort in walls that date back to between the 12th and 15th centuries. Though tired, I clamber up to the durbar at the top and gaze out, trying to feel my way into Indian history. Then down, back to the hotel for a meal, a beer and a sleep.

I get the night train back to Madras.

Tuesday 5 May

I have a quiet day in Madras. I start to translate a story by the Libyan writer, Ibrahim al-Kuni.[60] I go to the airport in the evening, and fly back to Dubai, where the British Council driver meets me. I am home at 2 am local time.

Back in Abu Dhabi.

Friday 8 May

David and Frauke Heard take us out in their boat. David is very much in charge and takes no risks, slowing down when the water gets choppy. We set off from sheikhland, past Sheikh Mubarak's residence and Sheikh Khalifa bin Zayed's palace ('Khally's Pally'). There are more boats and we see familiar buildings from unfamiliar angles. We reach one island and disembark. David erects some shades and we idle and chat for a few hours.

---

60 This was published: Ibrahim al Kouni, "The Maiden's Vow", tr. Peter Clark, in Mike Gerrard and Thomas McCarthy (eds), *Passport to Arabia* (Passport and Serpent's Tail, Huntingdon and London, 1993), pp. 233–56.

Saturday 9 May

I have a meeting with three visiting auditors. I talk to them generally, perhaps defensively. I am not a financial expert, I tell them, and you are here to advise me. I am conscious that my post is one of the most expensive in the British Council. The budgetary average is at £112,000 a year, the tenth- or eleventh-costliest in the British Council.

Sunday 10 May

I call on the Administration Officer at the British Embassy.

'What do I do with this?' he asks me, showing me a bill he has received from Dr Ron McCulloch, the community doctor: 'For house call on Mrs M Thatcher'. Has she slipped off without paying her bill? Was she expecting the doctor's services to be free? Or for the Embassy (the taxpayer) to pick it up?

I take two taxis during the day. The driver of the first is Syrian.

'You are from Dera'a,' I say.

He is. We talk about Syria, but I do not tell him I am going there this year.

'We have freedom there,' he says. 'Lovely food and drink. If you want to drink alcohol, you can. It's up to you. And women are treated the same as men.'

The second taxi driver is from Hyderabad.

'I was there last week,' I tell him, to his surprise.

Monday 11 May

Today's date, 110592, is 48 cubed. I wonder how many other people realise that.

I have been reading a book about the British in Tunisia and what a 19th-century consul, Richard Wood, said on his departure: 'We had a jolly time, and things ran smoothly more or less'. A nice sentiment; perhaps I can use it when I leave here. Wood served in both Tunis and Damascus.

Sunday 17 May

It is my 53rd birthday. In November I will have been in the British Council for 25 years. It has become an inseparable part of my identity.

Most happily, I can look back on years of life overseas, learning, observing, and being constantly aware of other people, other languages, other cultures. I regret that I have not taken the opportunity of learning Urdu while I have been here. The local English-language radio station wishes me a happy birthday and plays a record of Connie Francis singing 'Who's Sorry Now?'.

Monday 18 May

I go to Dubai and Muhammad al-Murr takes me to call on the poet and former pearl merchant, Sultan Ali. We go to his office and he shows me his private collection of pearls. They are wrapped up in two large red tablecloths. Sultan calls for a servant to bring two bowls and he pours some of the pearls into them: hundreds and thousands of pearls, of different sizes, some still sticking to the odd oyster shell. He caresses them fondly and casually. He shows me a necklace with pearls of equal size. 'This is worth 150,000 dirhams,' he says, adding with a snigger, 'more expensive than the girl who wears it'. We troop off with his nephew, the Minister of Electricity, to a nearby flat, and sit on the floor and eat fish and lentil soup.

Monday 25 May

My colleagues in Oman have organised an exhibition of Thesiger photographs in Salalah. It has been opened by Prince Philip.

From 7 to 12 June Peter went on a briefing visit to Damascus.[61]

Saturday 13 June

We go to Khor Fakkan, which is a detached part of the Emirate of Sharjah, the only Emirate that is dry. It is possible to take booze into the hotel for private consumption in one's room. So we have wine before and after, but not during, lunch. The hotel is splendid and caters largely for nationals and clean-living Arabs.

---

61 See Peter Clark, *Damascus Diaries: Life under the Assads* (Gilgamesh, London, 2015), pp. 2–12.

Sunday 14 June

On the way back we divert to Umm Al Quwain, past some boat-building in the creek, the fort and some round towers. Near the port is a garage called Al Ghob, opposite the Elite Restaurant. The chief characteristic of Umm Al Quwain seems to be topiary. We see all sorts of imaginative bits of green living sculpture – seats, elephants, falcons, a falling archway. We stop at the Beach Hotel for tea; it has the smell of stale beer, and seems to be not so much a hotel as a hard-drinking watering-hole; functional and boring.

In Ajman we call on Indian friends, Sultan and Fatima. Sultan's voice can be heard from a back room, melodiously chanting the Koran. Apparently, he is taking lessons on how to recite it correctly. Fatima tells us they will shortly be going to India for the month of Muharram. They are Shi'ites and she talks with sweet reasonableness about the commemoration of the 10 Muharram death of Hussein[62] and the awful cruelty of Yazid, the killer of babies – 'You know how cruel the Arabs are'. Sultan joins us and we giggle a lot. They were both at Catholic schools in Lahore.

Wednesday 17 June

I go to Ras Al Khaimah to make a farewell call on the Ruler, Sheikh Saqr bin Muhammad Al Qasimi. His beard is dyed black, though the hairs on his arms are white. A white beard may indicate wisdom, but it is also a reminder of the passing years, frailty and vulnerability. Mike Edwards, his British factotum, tells me of the Ruler's earlier life, when there were shootouts with tribesmen and when fish-heads added flavour to a meal.

Friday 19 June

Nat is getting disoriented about the move. It is the first move he will have been acutely conscious of. Abu Dhabi has been a good home for him. He is having no say in his future. His whole world is folding up. On Sunday we get rid of the cat, Jessica. On Monday the television goes. In

---

62 Grandson of the Prophet Muhammad. His death/martyrdom at the hands of the Umayyad Khalifa, Yazid, in 680 AD is commemorated throughout the Shi'ite world.

1988, when we left Tunisia, he was five years old. All decisions affecting him are made without consulting him.

Saturday 20 June

I have a visit from Hamad Ali of the Indian Islamia School. He is actually a Pakistani and can quote by heart long chunks of the works of Jawaharlal Nehru and Arnold J Toynbee. He tells me he has written in the *Khaleej Times* that my book on Pickthall should be widely available. I will tell my publishers, Quartet Books, that the UAE and Indian markets have been unexploited.

The Ambassador gives me a farewell dinner and makes a nice speech, saying I am 'a barrow-boy at heart, but active in many fields'.

Sunday 21 June

I attend my last Embassy weekly meeting. There is the report of a British couple who have been arrested and detained for three hours for snogging on the Corniche.

Theresa and I are guests of honour, with Sami Hajjar, my American opposite number, of the Minister of Education, Hamad al-Midfa'i. He talks of his three-storey house going back 50 years, and his pearl-merchant forebears with their links in Iran and India.

In the evening, another farewell party, hosted by Abdul Rahman Abdullah – a lot of Sudanese and United Nations staff. An Iraqi friend tells me that the UAE has severed telephone communications with Iraq, but Oman has not. So people drive to Al Ain, cross over to Buraimi and phone from there. With so many Iraqis in exile, bourgeois Baghdadi families arrange family weddings in Amman.

Monday 22 June

Buthaina and Tariq al-Metwalli give us a farewell dinner at the Marina Club. We say farewell to our Iraqi friends, including Najmuddim al-Hamouda, Qais al-Askari and Faisal al-Askari (was he named after King Faisal of Iraq?).

Tuesday 23 June

I take the cat, Jessica, to the Stables, where Karen and Abu Bakr al-Arifi will look after her. I collect a cage from the Stables. Jessica, all unawares, is in the study looking at a spider on the other side of the window. I seize her treacherously and bundle her into the cage. She screams, and I dump her on Abu Bakr's desk and drive off. The most painful farewell.

Wednesday 24 June

More farewells – the Embassy, Zaki Nusseibeh, my own staff. Marie-Reine, my PA, is in tears: I have never had that effect on anyone before.

Theresa, Nat and I transfer to a hotel. Frauke and David Heard join us and we have a drink together till late.

Thursday 25 June

David comes again to say goodbye at 9 in the morning.

A car from Emirates Airlines collects us and, with ten cases, we sweep off over the bridge and along the road to Dubai.

We have plenty of time at Dubai Airport and browse around the amazing eldorado of the duty-free shop in the basement. No wonder Dubai is so rich. It produces very little itself but imports and exports, constantly making a profit. Presentation and packaging are superb.

A plane is on the runway, surrounded by machines and vehicles, with pipes and leads extending into its body. I am reminded of the image of a patient about to have major surgery. It turns out that the plane I am gazing at is ours.

The plane sets off a quarter of an hour late, but we are soon airborne and flying over Iran. I order a glass of champagne and settle down to rereading *Our Mutual Friend*.

Family portrait.

INDEX

A

B

C